VIOLENCE AGAINST WOMEN:
PHILOSOPHICAL PERSPECTIVES

VIOLENCE AGAINST WOMEN

Philosophical Perspectives

EDITED BY

STANLEY G. FRENCH

WANDA TEAYS

LAURA M. PURDY

Cornell University Press | ITHACA AND LONDON

First published 1998 by Cornell University Press.
First printing, Cornell Paperbacks, 1998.

Printed in the United States of America.

Cornell University Press strives to use environmentally responsible suppliers and materials to the fullest extent possible in the publishing of its books. Such materials include vegetable-based, low-VOC inks and acid-free papers that are either recycled, totally chlorine-free, or partly composed of nonwood fibers.

Cloth printing   10   9   8   7   6   5   4   3   2   1
Paperback printing   10   9   8   7   6   5   4   3   2   1

Library of Congress Cataloging-in-Publication Data

Violence against women : philosophical perspectives / edited by
   Stanley G. French, Wanda Teays, Laura M. Purdy.
      p.   cm.
   Includes bibliographical references and index.
   ISBN 0-8014-3441-6 (cloth : alk. paper). — ISBN 0-8014-8452-9
   (pbk. : alk. paper)
   1. Women—Crimes against.   2. Sexual harassment of women.
3. Sexual abuse victims.   4. Family violence.   I. French, Stanley G.
II. Teays, Wanda.   III. Purdy, Laura Martha.
   HV6250.4.w65v565   1998
   362.88'082—dc21   97-46848

[iv]

We dedicate this anthology
to those women and girls who, in the face of violence
and overwhelming despair, found the inner strength to go on.

Contents

176259

Acknowledgments

We are grateful to the Society for Philosophy and Public Affairs for its support and encouragement.

We are thankful also to Sheryl Curtis, a doctoral candidate at Concordia University and a professional translator, who performed magic with her word processor in bringing order out of chaos.

We thank Willow Nardoni-Teays for all her help with reviewing the final manuscript, proofreading, and communications.

Finally, we wish to thank Alison Shonkwiler of Cornell University Press for her continuous encouragement and support.

S. F., W. T., *and* L. P.

VIOLENCE AGAINST WOMEN:
PHILOSOPHICAL PERSPECTIVES

Editors' Introduction

Women are the victims of widespread personal and systemic violence, the true scope and gender-specific nature of which emerge clearly when all types of violence are set in context in a collection such as this one. The sweep of violence—overt or subtle—is striking: common in North America and elsewhere are sexual assault and rape, wife battering, sexual harassment, prostitution, sadistic pornography, and sexual exploitation by medical personnel. Cultures beyond these shores add their own forms of violence such as dowry death and female genital mutilation as well as the disproportionate abortion of female fetuses and systematic neglect of girl children.

Only recently have philosophers begun to inquire into violence against women. Yet it is striking that such an important social phenomenon did not capture philosophical attention long ago. It cries out for conceptual analysis: what do we mean by "violence," and what can we conclude about the special forms of violence directed toward women? Moreover, such violence is precisely the sort of issue that ethics, political philosophy, and philosophy of law deal with; so how can there be an elaborate historical discourse on just war theory and no theory of rape or wife beating? Despite their impact on women's lives, such practices have simply been part of the backdrop, unnoticed and certainly not treated as fit subjects for serious theorizing.

According to former U.S. Surgeon General C. Everett Koop, domestic violence is the top problem for American women, causing more injuries than automobile accidents, muggings, and rapes combined. According to a U.S. Justice Department study, nearly 700,000 victims of violence or suspected violence treated in hospital emergency rooms in 1994 were hurt by someone they knew. Of these approximately 243,000 (or 34 percent) were injured by someone they knew intimately—a current or former spouse, boyfriend, or girlfriend. Of these, 203,000 (over 80 percent) were women.[1]

One of the distinctive characteristics of violence directed toward women is that it tends, unlike violence toward men, to come from those they know (Blodgett-Ford, 1993: 510). That it is rooted in asymmetrical assumptions about the nature of the two sexes is illustrated by the belated recognition of marital rape as a crime in most states. (Some, like Oklahoma and North Carolina, still fail to recognize it as such [Dowd, 1992: 569].) Sexist assumptions clearly play a role, too, in the massive exploitation of women as prostitutes. The consequences for these women may be dire, especially when, as in India, a majority are indentured slaves, many of whom are doomed to die of AIDS (Friedman, 1996: 12). The specifically sexual element in gender relations comes to the fore in pornography, especially sadistic pornography. Both the production of such materials and their disproportionate consumption by males reinforce and promote the attitudes toward women that fuel the practices discussed here. Such attitudes become especially apparent in war, when rape is used as a weapon against the enemy.[2]

VIOLENCE AS A SOCIAL INSTITUTION

Violence against women is a particularly insidious crime against humanity. It is pervasive, appearing as frequently in the houses of the rich as in those of the poor. It knows neither racial nor ethnic limitations—only cultural variations, such as female genital mutilation or dowry burnings. Furthermore, neither age nor physical attributes protect women from violations such as rape, battering, or prostitution.

The social failure to acknowledge, remedy, and prevent this violence speaks volumes. Police response has been lax. Courts have offered little recourse for women who have been raped, abused, stalked, or sexually harassed. Most domestic violence incidents are handled through mediation or in misdemeanor courts; only in the most serious cases, or with repeat offenders, are there felony charges.

Responsibility for violence against women is diminished by blaming women for their predicaments. Women are raped because they are in the wrong place, wearing the wrong clothes, or behaving the wrong way. Battered women should have left their partners, no matter what their circumstances. Prostitutes get what they deserve because they are selling sex and are seen as willing participants.

These perspectives are the result of a double standard. Both public opinion and the law hold that victims of sexual assault and spouse-battering should have foreseen the potential for harm and avoided it, in a way not expected of victims of robberies, fights, and carjackings. The striking coincidence is that those in the former group are far more likely to be female than male.[3]

That women are more likely to be victimized reflects the more general problem that they are not regarded by either courts or legislatures as having equal standing with men. How else can we interpret the reality that 90 percent of prostitution charges are leveled at female prostitutes, and only 10 percent at male customers? Adding insult to injury, in 1996 police in Costa Mesa, California, started, as an enforcement tool, to seize the clothes of suspected prostitutes after making an arrest; no other criminal suspects are treated in this manner.[4]

Such asymmetry in law enforcement extends to spousal murder: women who kill their husbands tend to get longer prison sentences than men who kill their wives. Perhaps this is because, as Victoria Mather observes, women who commit crimes are believed to be maladjusted.[5] Longer sentences are defensible on the grounds that more time is needed for rehabilitation. These attitudes reflect the bias that women endure. For example, in eighty-five cases where battered women argued that they killed in self-defense, testimony was offered in forty-four cases, but was admitted in only twenty-six. Seventeen of those twenty-six were still convicted.[6]

What is going on here? Perhaps, as Boccaccio explained, "in general Nature has given men proud and high spirits, while it has made women humble in character and submissive, more apt for delicate things than for ruling. Therefore, it should not be surprising if God's wrath is swifter and the sentence more severe against proud women whenever it happens that they surpass the boundaries of their weakness."[7] In short, sexism. As Laurence Thomas has put it, "sexism is deeply tied to the desire of men to assure that women affirm the gender identity of men" (1995: 161). Women are overtly and covertly pressured to accept this role and to trust that men will do their part. Thomas is right to emphasize that this situation assures systematic, reliable asymmetries of power, in contrast to capricious power differences such as those manifested in the Holocaust (1995: 154, 158). Such institutionalized power differences are obvious targets for moral analysis.

The need for systemic change is finally being recognized. For example, in 1994 Pamela Stuart, chair of the International Criminal Law Committee of the Criminal Justice Section of the American Bar Association, established a special task force on future war crimes tribunals. In the section on rape and sexual atrocities, the task force report suggested that acts of violence such as those recently committed in the former Yugoslavia and Rwanda could be prosecuted as violations of the genocide provisions of the Geneva Convention, or as violations of other war crimes statutes, not merely as rape (Koenig, 1994: 129).

A great deal of work lies ahead, however. As Michael Dowd asserts,

> there remains the problem of denial. Even the community of decent people finds society's inability to quell the tide of violence against women too horrific to accept. The reality of life for a battered woman is indeed beyond the knowledge of the average person, and while denying the truth of the battered woman's story can be easier than confronting it, the enlightened must aim to recognize the truth in order to foster society's acceptance of responsibility for the violence among us. (1992: 582)

No one can evade responsibility for ending this violence. Everyone has the responsibility to inform themselves about human rights issues, including this one. Everyone must speak up in opposition to abuses. Ending violence requires eradicating both what Paolo Freire describes as the piece of hate planted deep within us that encourages silence and complicity—and the systematic inequalities now evident in society at large.

UNDERTAKING A PHILOSOPHICAL ANALYSIS

What is the philosophical significance of violence against women? One important issue is whether Mill's dictum, that it is morally impermissible to sell ourselves into slavery because it negates the freedom that made our choice possible, applies to women's consent to activities that may not be in their best interest. Another is how different perspectives lead us to construct acts and relationships differently. For example, moral and legal questions about pornography are traditionally approached as a free speech issue, bringing to the fore questions relevant for purveyors and consumers of pornography rather than questions relating to specific risks for women.

Both kinds of issues arise with respect to prostitution. Shifting concern from alleged rights of consumers to spend as they see fit to concern about whether sexual services or goods should be rented or bought brings into view a number of riveting philosophical questions. Do we own our bodies? If not, what is our relationship to them? Which organisms have a right to control their bodies? Is contract pregnancy morally acceptable? May persons rent or sell bodily parts? (Church, 1997: 97). A range of positions on these questions is emerging, including extensions of Mill's view, such as Margaret Jane Radin's opinion that the body is inalienable property.[8]

Looking at pornography from the perspective of the consumed rather than that of the consumer raises new moral questions about the making of pornography as well as its effects on women as a class. The resulting debate may cause us to see "free speech" with new eyes. As Catharine MacKinnon notes in *Only Words*, "protecting pornography means protecting sexual abuse *as* speech, at the same time that both pornography and its protection have deprived women *of* speech, especially speech against sexual abuse" (1993a: 11). The courts have approached this state of affairs as if it were a matter of no consequence.

Why are such new issues and approaches emerging now? Feminism is largely responsible. Since the late 1960s, despite tremendous opposition, it has become an increasingly powerful social force. As a result, many hitherto unquestioned practices, rules, and institutions have been examined anew. Philosophy, as the discipline that questions everything, might have been in the forefront of this movement. Unfortunately philosophers have often taken for granted many of society's basic premises, just like ordinary mortals living the unexamined life. Only slowly have feminists (some already sensitive to gender bias, others radicalized by their graduate studies) worked their way up through the professional ranks and dragged the field, kicking and screaming, into the contemporary world.

Isolated feminist philosophical works, such as Mary Wollstonecraft's *A Vindication of the Rights of Woman*, Harriet Taylor's *Enfranchisement of Women*, and Virginia Woolf's *Three Guineas*, appeared long before the advent of second-wave feminism. Much more work began to appear after it, however, encouraged in part by the formation of the Society for Women in Philosophy. Recent feminist philosophy and law journals have provided a forum for feminist philosophizing, but there has been no concentrated philosophical focus on violence. A feminist approach to the topic, as we see in this book, emphasizes the need for systematic analysis of apparently purely personal experience, bringing home the implications of philosophical investigation.

Recently there has also been a move in feminist philosophy to integrate issues of gender, race, and class. Progress has been slow, in part because of the difficulty of the theoretical task, in part because of entrenched sexist, racist, and elitist attitudes, even among those who recognize the importance of eradicating them. As Angela Davis observes in a discussion of the connections between race and gender, "myth of the Black rapist renders people oblivious to the realities of rape and to the fact, for example, that over 90 percent of all rapes are intraracial rather than interracial" (1990: 43). Such distorted attitudes are, as Davis charges, racist by their nature, and create a serious obstacle to eradicating violence against women.

These new perspectives demand that we rethink many moral and metaphysical concepts: "race," "gender," "equality," "justice," "freedom," "power," "consent," "reasonable man," "privacy," "ownership," "bodily integrity," "rape," "harassment," and "pornography/erotica." One example of such rethinking is Linda Bell's argument that the prevailing view of power (citing bell hooks's definition, "domination and control over people or things") is unnecessarily narrow and hierarchical. This inadequate conception of power seems to channel people into harmful relationships of superiority and inferiority, rather than opening up possibilities of more egalitarian empowerment (Bell, 1993: 75). In short, feminism argues that apparently abstract conceptual analysis can have significant moral consequences.

None of this is to say that there is only one "correct" feminism. On the contrary, to be a feminist is to believe both that justice requires equal consideration of women's interests and that justice is often violated. Beyond this core notion, feminism is still growing and developing, speculating and revising. "That feminism is many and not one is to be expected," Rosemarie Tong contends, "because women are many and not one. The more feminist thoughts we have, the better. By refusing to center, congeal, and cement their separate thoughts into a unified truth too inflexible to change, feminists resist patriarchal dogma" (1989: 7).

This volume was conceived in the spirit of social transformation. It attempts to convey the breadth of the topic, as well as treating some areas in depth.

Section I includes articles by Susan J. Brison, Patricia Kazan, and Catharine A. MacKinnon. Brison's experience of sexual assault provides her with a jumping-off point for considering a range of philosophical issues raised by sexual violence, including its effects on personal identity, survivors' assumptions about the external world, notions of "harm," the role of denial, and victim-blaming and its political implications for gender equality. Patricia Kazan analyzes the concept of sexual assault in relation to the idea of consent. She considers two contrasting models: (1) the attitudinal model, where consent is identified with subjective mental states; and (2) the performative model, which identifies consent with language or behavior. She argues that neither suffices, as the attitudinal model has trouble with the normative character of consent and the performative model has trouble detecting coercion; she offers a third model, integrating elements from both, that she believes will avoid these difficulties. Catharine MacKinnon turns her attention to institutionalized sexual assault, specifically genocidal rape in Bosnia-Herzegovina and Croatia. She argues that this episode shows that human rights have not been women's rights, and calls for change.

Section II focuses on domestic violence—violence against women in the privacy of their own homes. Here we find articles by Wanda Teays on battered women, Roksana Nazneen on dowry deaths, and Semra Asefa on female genital mutilation. Teays argues that self-defense can be a justifiable defense for battered women who kill their abusers. She suggests that we reject both the battered woman syndrome defense (because it offers an excuse rather than a justification), and the imperfect self-defense argument (since this pictures the woman as *unreasonably* fearing imminent threat to her life). Teays argues that a case can be made for perfect self-defense, at least under certain conditions. Next, Roksana Nazneen focuses on dowry deaths and other domestic violence in Bangladesh. She argues that conflicts over dowry payments are common, with the bride's death a frequent result. Often, too, violence is directed at young wives for infertility or for producing only girls. In Bangladesh such violence is often justified by reference to Islam. Semra Asefa, examining female genital mutilation, contends that existing studies have focused on the socio-anthropological roots or physical consequences of the practice, ignoring the psychological scars it leaves. She rejects the argument that it is a cultural practice that should be protected from interference by outsiders, and asserts that international organizations must help eradicate it, given that it is a human rights violation.

Section III contains two perspectives on sexual harassment. Debra A. DeBruin argues that we ought to adopt the "reasonable woman" standard for determining what constitutes sexual harassment, rather than either the "reasonable man" or "reasonable person" standard. Such a gender-specific conception is not a violation of justice, she contends, but is, on the contrary, necessary for justice. In the second article in this section, Abby Wilkerson analyzes the medical treatment of domestic violence and rape, arguing that mainstream medicine often treats the symptoms of violence while ignoring or obscuring the causes. Furthermore, traditional medical approaches take for granted a demeaning notion of "women's place." Situating her critique in terms of feminist epistemology, Wilkerson argues that we need to recognize the social nature of the problem in order to facilitate prevention and treatment. She lays out a model of knowledge that incorporates subjectivity and examines the links between epistemological and moral questions.

Section IV takes on pornography and prostitution. The first article, by Edith L. Pacillo, considers public policy dimensions of current thinking about pornography, as illustrated in several recent judicial decisions involving sexual violence and pornography. She argues that the First Amendment should not shield pornographers from liability when their publications cause bodily harm, and recommends a "negligent publication" standard that would balance the potential for such harm against free speech interests. In the second article, Clelia Smyth Anderson and Yolanda Estes contend that prostitution violates the individual dignity of both prostitute and client in treating the participants as mere means. In their view, sex without mutual concern and desire constitutes violent objectification that prevents the participants from recognizing themselves and each other as subjects. Money cannot provide adequate compensation for such dehumanization.

Section V looks at a variety of policies and perspectives on violence against women. Arnold R. Eiser uses the example of female genital mutilation to explore different cultures' attitudes toward violence. He concludes that the neo-Kantian approach outlined in Lawrence Kohlberg's stages of moral development cannot be sustained across cultural boundaries but that health qualifies as a transcultural value both on empirical and pragmatic grounds. Hence female genital mutilation can be rejected without requiring the rejection of notions of individual autonomy. In the second article, Natalie Dandekar provides a feminist analysis of policies governing the last forty years of international development. She argues that misconceptions about women inherent in industrialization of developing countries are a form of violence against women. Nadya Burton wraps up the volume by examining the conceptualizing of violence by such figures as Susan Brownmiller, Andrea Dworkin, Diana Russell, and Susan Griffin in classic feminist texts published between 1971 and 1985. She sees these writers as having constructed a rhetoric of violence (emphasizing fear, victimhood, and lack of resistance) intended to free women from violence but which in fact undermined women's agency and capacity for acting strongly in their own defense.

SECTION 1

SEXUAL ASSAULT

Surviving Sexual Violence: A Philosophical Perspective

SUSAN J. BRISON

This is an unorthodox philosophy article, in both style and subject matter. Its primary aim is not to defend a thesis by means of argumentation, but rather to give the reader an imaginative access to what is, for some, an unimaginable experience, that of a survivor of rape. The fact that there is so little philosophical writing about violence against women results not only from a lack of understanding of its prevalence and of the severity of its effects, but also from the mistaken view that it is not a properly philosophical subject. I hope in this essay to illuminate the nature and extent of the harm done by sexual violence and to show why philosophers should start taking this problem more seriously.

On July 4, 1990, at 10:30 in the morning, I went for a walk along a peaceful-looking country road in a village outside Grenoble, France. It was a gorgeous day, and I didn't envy my husband, Tom, who had to stay inside and work on a manuscript with a French colleague of his. I sang to myself as I set out, stopping to pet a goat and pick a few wild strawberries along

This chapter is reprinted (with minor changes) by permission of the *Journal of Social Philosophy*, where it appeared in vol. 24, no. 1, Spring 1993 (pp. 5–22).

I would like to thank the North American Society for Social Philosophy for inviting me to give the substance of it as a plenary address at the Eighth International Social Philosophy Conference, Davidson College, August 1, 1992. I am also grateful to the Franklin J. Matchette Foundation for sponsoring the talk. This essay was written just two years after I had been raped and it would be different in many ways were I to write it now, in 1997. But I have left it in its original form (except for a few minor stylistic revisions) in order to convey my perspective soon after the event.

the way. About an hour and a half later, I was lying face down in a muddy creek bed at the bottom of a dark ravine, struggling to stay alive. I had been grabbed from behind, pulled into the bushes, beaten and sexually assaulted. Feeling absolutely helpless and entirely at my assailant's mercy, I talked to him, calling him "sir." I tried to appeal to his humanity, and, when that failed, I addressed myself to his self-interest. He called me a whore and told me to shut up. Although I had said I'd do whatever he wanted, as the sexual assault began I instinctively fought back, which so enraged my attacker that he strangled me until I lost consciousness. When I awoke, I was being dragged by my feet down into the ravine. I had often, while dreaming, thought I was awake, but now I was awake and convinced I was having a nightmare. But it was no dream. After ordering me, in a gruff Gestapo-like voice, to get on my hands and knees, my assailant strangled me again. I wish I could convey the horror of losing consciousness while my animal instincts desperately fought the effects of strangulation. This time I was sure I was dying. But I revived, just in time to see him lunging toward me with a rock. He smashed it into my forehead, knocking me out, and eventually, after another strangulation attempt, he left me for dead.

After my assailant left, I managed to climb out of the ravine, and I was rescued by a farmer who called the police, a doctor, and an ambulance. I was taken to emergency at the Grenoble hospital where I underwent neurological tests, x-rays, blood tests, and a gynecological exam. Leaves and twigs were taken from my hair for evidence, my fingernails were scraped, and my mouth was swabbed for samples. I had multiple head injuries, my eyes were swollen shut, and I had a fractured trachea which made breathing difficult. I was not permitted to drink or eat anything for the first thirty hours, though Tom, who never left my side, was allowed to dab my blood-encrusted lips with a wet towel. The next day, I was transferred out of emergency and into my own room. But I could not be left alone even for a few minutes. I was terrified my assailant would find me and finish the job. When someone later brought in the local paper with a story about my attack, I was greatly relieved that it referred to me as *Mlle. M. R.* and didn't even mention that I was an American. Even by the time I left the hospital, eleven days later, I was so concerned about my assailant tracking me down that I put only my lawyer's address on the hospital records.

Although fears for my safety may have initially explained why I wanted to remain anonymous, by that time my assailant had been apprehended, indicted for rape and attempted murder, and incarcerated without possibility of bail. Still, I didn't want people to know that I had been sexually assaulted. I don't know whether this was because I could still hardly believe it myself, because keeping this information confidential was one of the few ways I could feel in control of my life, or because, in spite of my conviction that I had done nothing wrong, I felt ashamed.

When I started telling people about the attack, I said, simply, that I was the victim of an attempted murder. People typically asked, in horror, "What was the motivation? Were you mugged?" and when I replied "No, it started as a sexual assault," most inquirers were satisfied with that as an explanation of why some man wanted to murder me. I would have thought that a murder attempt *plus* a sexual assault would require more, not less, of an explanation than a murder attempt by itself. (After all, there are *two* criminal acts to explain here.)

One reason sexual violence is taken for granted by many is because it is so very prevalent. The FBI, notorious for underestimating the frequency of sex crimes, notes that, in the United States, a rape occurs on an average every six minutes.[1] But this figure covers only the reported cases of rape, and some researchers claim that only about 10 percent of all rapes get reported.[2] Every fifteen seconds, a woman is beaten.[3] The every-dayness of sexual violence, as evidenced by these mind-numbing statistics, leads many to think that male violence against women is natural, a given, something not in need of explanation, and not amenable to change. And yet, through some extraordinary mental gymnastics, while most people take sexual violence for granted, they simultaneously manage to deny that it really exists—or, rather, that it could happen to them. We continue to think that we—and the women we love—are immune to it, provided, that is, that we don't do anything "foolish." How many of us have swallowed the potentially lethal lie that "if you don't do anything wrong, if you're just careful enough, you'll be safe"? How many of us have believed its damaging, victim-blaming corollary: "if you are attacked, it's because *you* did something wrong"? These are lies, and in telling my story I hope to expose them, as well as to help bridge the gap between those of us who have been victimized and those who have not.

But what, you may be thinking, does this have to do with philosophy? Why tell my story in this academic forum? Judging from the virtual lack of philosophical writing on sexual violence, one might well conclude there is nothing here of interest to philosophers. Certainly, I came across nothing in my search for philosophical help with explaining what had happened to me and putting my shattered world back together.[4] Yet sexual violence and its aftermath raise numerous philosophical issues in a variety of areas in our discipline. The disintegration of the self experienced by victims of violence challenges our notions of personal identity over time, a major preoccupation of metaphysics. A victim's seemingly justified skepticism about everyone and everything is pertinent to epistemology, especially if the goal of epistemology is, as Wilfrid Sellars put it, that of feeling at home in the world. In aesthetics—as well as in philosophy of law—the discussion of sexual violence in—or as—art could use the illumination provided by a victim's perspective. Perhaps the most important issues posed by sexual violence are in the areas of social, political, and legal philosophy, and insight into these, as well, requires an understanding of what it's like to be a victim of such violence.

One of the few articles written by philosophers on violence against women is Ross Harrison's (1986) "Rape: A Case Study in Political Philosophy."[5] In this article Harrison argues that not only do utilitarians need to assess the harmfulness of rape in order to decide whether the harm to the victim outweighs the benefit to the rapist, but even on a rights-based approach to criminal justice we need to be able to assess the benefits and harms involved in criminalizing and punishing violent acts such as rape. In his view, it is not always the case, contra Ronald Dworkin, that rights trump considerations of utility, so, even on a rights-based account of justice, we need to give an account of why, in the case of rape, the pleasure gained by the perpetrator (or by multiple perpetrators, in the case of gang-rape) is always outweighted by the harm done to the victim. He points out the peculiar difficulty most of us have in imagining the pleasure a rapist gets out of an assault, but, he asserts confidently, "There is no problem imagining what it is like to be a victim" (51). To his credit, he acknowledges the importance, to political philosophy, of trying to imagine others' experience, for otherwise we could not compare harms and benefits, which he argues must be done even in cases of conflicts of rights in order to decide which of competing rights should take priority. But imagining what it is like to be a rape victim is no simple matter, since much of what a victim goes through is unimaginable. Still, it's essential to try to convey it.

In my efforts to tell the victim's story—my story, our story—I've been inspired and instructed not only by feminist philosophers who have refused to accept the dichotomy between the personal and the political, but also by critical race theorists such as Patricia Williams, Mari Matsuda, and Charles Lawrence, who have incorporated first-person narrative accounts into their discussions of the law. In writing about hate speech, they have argued persuasively that one cannot do justice to the issues involved in debates about restrictions on speech without listening to the victims' stories.[6] In describing the effects of racial harassment on victims, they have departed from the academic convention of speaking in the impersonal, "universal" voice and related incidents they themselves experienced. In her groundbreaking book *The Alchemy of Race and Rights*, Williams (1991) describes how it felt to learn about her great-great-grandmother who was purchased at age eleven by a slave owner who raped and impregnated her the following year. And in describing instances of everyday racism she herself has lived through, she gives us imaginative access to what it's like to be the victim of racial discrimination. Some may consider such first-person accounts in academic writing to be self-indulgent, but I consider them a welcome antidote to the arrogance of those who write in a magisterial voice that in the guise of "universality" silences those who most need to be heard.

Philosophers are far behind legal theorists in acknowledging the need for a diversity of voices. We are trained to write in an abstract, universal voice and to shun first-person narratives as biased and inappropriate for academic discourse. Some topics, however, such as the impact of racial and sexual violence on victims, cannot even be broached unless those affected by such crimes can tell of their experiences in their own words. Unwittingly further illustrating the need for the victim's perspective, Harrison writes, elsewhere in his article on rape, "What principally distinguishes rape from normal sexual activity is the consent of the raped women" (1986: 52). There is no parallel to this in the case of other crimes, such as theft or murder. Try "What principally distinguishes theft from normal gift-giving is the consent of the person stolen from." We don't think of theft as "gift-giving minus consent." We don't think of murder as "assisted suicide minus consent." Why not? In the latter case, it could be because assisted suicide is relatively rare (even compared with murder) and so it's odd to use it as the more familiar thing to which we are analogizing. But in the former case, gift-giving is presumably more prevalent than theft (at least in academic circles) and yet it still sounds odd to explicate theft in terms of gift-giving minus consent. In the cases of both theft and murder, the notion of violation seems built into our conceptions of the physical acts constituting the crimes, so it is inconceivable that one could consent to the act in question. Why is it so easy for a philosopher such as Harrison to think of rape, however, as normal sexual activity minus consent? This may be because the nature of the violation in the case of rape hasn't been all that obvious. Witness the phenomenon of rape jokes, the prevalence of pornography glorifying rape, the common attitude that, in the case of women, "no" means "yes," that women really want it.[7]

Since I was assaulted by a stranger, in a "safe" place, and was so visibly injured when I encountered the police and medical personnel, I was, throughout my hospitalization and my dealings with the police, spared the insult, suffered by so many rape victims, of not being believed or of being said to have asked for the attack. However, it became clear to me as I gave my deposition from my hospital bed that this would still be an issue in my assailant's trial. During my deposition, I recalled being on the verge of giving up my struggle to live when I was galvanized by a sudden, piercing image of Tom's future pain on finding my corpse in that ravine. At this point in my deposition, I paused, glanced over at the police officer who was typing the transcript, and asked whether it was appropriate to include this image of my husband in my recounting of the facts. The *gendarme* replied that it definitely was and that it was a very good thing I mentioned my husband, since my assailant, who had confessed to the sexual assault, was claiming I had provoked it. As serious as the occasion was, and as much as it hurt to laugh, I couldn't help it—the suggestion was so ludicrous. Could it have been those baggy Gap jeans I was wearing that morning? Or was it the heavy sweatshirt? My maddeningly seductive jogging shoes? Or was it simply my walking along minding my own business that had provoked his murderous rage?

After I completed my deposition, which lasted eight hours, the police officer asked me to read and sign the transcript he'd typed to certify that it was accurate. I was surprised to see that it began with the words, "Comme je suis sportive . . ."—"Since I am athletic . . ."—added by the police to explain to the court just what possessed me to go for a walk by myself that fine morning. I was too exhausted by this point to protest "no, I'm not an athlete, I'm a philosophy professor," and I figured the officer knew what he was doing, so I let it stand. That evening, my assailant confessed to the assault. I retained a lawyer, and met him along with the investigating magistrate, when I gave my second deposition toward the end of my hospitalization. Although what occurred was officially a crime against the state, not against me, I was advised to pursue a civil suit in order to recover the unreimbursed medical expenses, and, in any case, I needed an advocate to explain the French legal system to me. I was told that since this was an "easy" case, the trial would occur within a year. In fact, the trial took place two and a half years after the assault, due to the delaying tactics of my assailant's lawyer who was trying to get him off on an insanity defense. According to Article 64 of the French criminal code, if the defendant is determined to have been insane at the time, then, legally, there was "ni crime, ni délit"—neither crime nor offense. The jury, however, did not accept the insanity plea and found my assailant guilty of rape and attempted murder, sentencing him to ten years in prison.

As things turned out, my experience with the criminal justice system was better than that of most sexual assault victims. I did, however, occasionally get glimpses of the humiliating insensitivity victims routinely endure. Before I could be released from the hospital, for example, I had to undergo a second forensic examination at a different hospital. I was taken in a wheelchair out to a hospital van, driven to another hospital, taken to an office where there were no receptionists and where I was greeted by two male doctors I had never seen before. When they told me to take off my clothes and stand in the middle of the room, I refused. I had to ask for a hospital gown to put on. For about an hour the two of them went over me like a piece of meat, calling out measurements of bruises and other assessments of damage, as if they were performing an autopsy. This was just the first of many incidents in which I felt as if I was experiencing things posthumously. When the inconceivable happens, one starts to doubt even the most mundane, realistic perceptions. Perhaps I'm not really here, I thought, perhaps I did die in that ravine. The line between life and death, once so clear and sustaining, now seemed carelessly drawn and easily erased.

For the first several months after my attack, I led a spectral existence, not quite sure whether I had died and the world went on without me, or whether I was alive but in a totally alien world. Tom and I returned to the States, and I continued to convalesce, but I felt as though I'd somehow outlived myself. I sat in our apartment and stared outside for hours, through the blur of a detached vitreous, feeling like Robert Lowell's newly widowed mother, described in one of his poems as mooning in a window "as if she had stayed on a train / one stop past her destination" (1977: 82).

My sense of unreality was fed by the massive denial of those around me—a reaction I learned is an almost universal response to rape. Where the facts would appear to be incontrovertible, denial takes the shape of attempts to explain the assault in ways that leave the observers' world view unscathed. Even those who are able to acknowledge the existence of violence try to protect themselves from the realization that the world in which it occurs is their world and so they find it hard to identify with the victim. They cannot allow themselves to imagine the victim's shattered life, or else their illusions about their own safety and control over their lives might begin to crumble. The most well-meaning individuals, caught up in the myth of their own immunity, can inadvertently add to the victim's suffering by suggesting that the attack was avoidable or somehow her fault. One victims' assistance coordinator, whom I had phoned for legal advice, stressed that she herself had never been a victim and said I would benefit from the experience by learning not to be so trusting of people and to take basic safety precautions like not going out alone late at night. She didn't pause long enough during her lecture for me to point out that I was attacked suddenly, from behind, in broad daylight.

We are not taught to empathize with victims. In crime novels and detective films, it is the villain, or the one who solves the murder mystery, who

attracts our attention; the victim, a merely passive pretext for our enter-
tainment, is conveniently disposed of—and forgotten—early on. We identify with the agents' strength and skill, for good or evil, and join the victim,
if at all, only in our nightmares. Though one might say, as did Clarence
Thomas, looking at convicted criminals on their way to jail, "but for the
grace of God, there go I,"[8] a victim's fate prompts an almost instinctive "It
could never happen to me." This may explain why there is, in our criminal system, so little concern for justice for victims—especially rape victims.
They have no constitutionally protected rights *qua* victims. They have no
right to a speedy trial or to compensation for damages (though states have
been changing this in recent years), or to privacy vis-à-vis the press. As a
result of their victimization, they often lose their jobs, their homes, their
spouses—in addition to losing a great deal of money, time, sleep, self-
esteem, and peace of mind. The rights to "life, liberty, and the pursuit of
happiness," possessed, in the abstract, by all of us, are of little use to victims who can lose years of their lives, their freedom to move about in the
world without debilitating fear, and any hope of returning to the pleasures
of life as they once knew it.

People also fail to recognize that if a victim could not have anticipated
an attack, she can have no assurance that she will be able to avoid one in
the future. More to reassure themselves than to comfort the victim, some
deny that such a thing could happen again. One friend, succumbing to the
gambler's fallacy, pointed out that my having had such extraordinary bad
luck meant that the odds of my being attacked again were now quite slim
(as if fate, though not completely benign, would surely give me a break
now, perhaps in the interest of fairness). Others thought it would be most
comforting to pretend nothing had happened. The first card I received
from my mother, while I was still in the hospital, made no mention of the
attack or of my pain and featured the "bluebird of happiness," sent to keep
me ever cheerful. The second had an illustration of a bright summery
scene with the greeting: "Isn't the sun nice? Isn't the wind nice? Isn't everything nice?" Weeks passed before I learned, what I should have been able
to guess, that after she and my father received Tom's first call from the
hospital they held each other and sobbed. They didn't want to burden me
with their pain—a pain which I now realize must have been greater than
my own.

Some devout relatives were quick to give God all the credit for my survival but none of the blame for what I had to endure. Others acknowledged the suffering that had been inflicted on me, but as no more than a
blip on the graph of God's benevolence—a necessary, fleeting evil, there
to make possible an even greater show of good. One relative with whom I

have been close since childhood did not write or call at all until three months after the attack, and then sent a belated birthday card with a note saying that she was sorry to hear about my "horrible experience" but pleased to think that as a result I "will become stronger and will be able to help so many people. A real blessing from above for sure." Such attempts at theodicy discounted the horror I had to endure. But I learned that everyone needs to try and make sense, in however inadequate a way, of such senseless violence. I watched my own see-sawing attempts to find something for which to be grateful, something to redeem the unmitigated awfulness: I was glad I didn't have to reproach myself (or endure others' reproaches) for having done something careless, but I wished I had done something I could consider reckless so that I could simply refrain from doing it in the future. I was glad I did not yet have a child, who would have to grow up with the knowledge that even the protector could not be protected, but I felt an inexpressible loss when I recalled how much Tom and I had wanted a baby and how joyful were our attempts to conceive. It is difficult, even now, to imagine getting pregnant, because it is so hard to let even my husband near me, and because it would be harder still to let a child leave my side.

It might be gathered from this litany of complaints that I was the recipient of constant, if misguided, attempts at consolation during the first few months of my recovery. This was not the case. It seemed to me that the half-life of most people's concern was less than that of the sleeping pills I took to ward off flashbacks and nightmares—just long enough to allow the construction of a comforting illusion that lulls the shock to sleep. During the first few months after my assault, most of the relatives and friends of the family notified by my parents almost immediately after the attack didn't phone, write, or even send a get well card, in spite of my extended hospital stay. These are all caring, decent people who would have sent wishes for a speedy recovery if I'd had, say, an appendectomy. Their early lack of response was so striking that I wondered whether it was the result of self-protective denial, a reluctance to mention something so unspeakable, or a symptom of our society's widespread emotional illiteracy that prevents most people from conveying any feeling that can't be expressed in a Hallmark card.

In the case of rape, the intersection of multiple taboos—against talking openly about trauma, about violence, about sex—causes conversational gridlock, paralyzing the would-be supporter. We lack the vocabulary for expressing appropriate concern, and we have no social conventions to ease the awkwardness. Ronald de Sousa (1987) has written persuasively about the importance of grasping paradigm scenarios in early childhood in order to learn appropriate emotional responses to situations. We do not learn—early or later in life—how to react to a rape. What typically results from this ignorance is bewilderment on the part of victims and silence on the part of others, often the result of misguided caution. When, a few months after the assault, I railed at my parents, "Why haven't my relatives called or written?" they replied, "They all expressed their concern to us, but they didn't want to remind you of what happened." Didn't they realize I thought about the attack every minute of every day and that their inability to respond made me feel as though I had, in fact, died and no one had bothered to come to the funeral?

For the next several months, I felt angry, scared, and helpless, and I wished I could blame myself for what had happened so that I would feel less vulnerable, more in control of my life. Those who haven't been sexually violated may have difficulty understanding why women who survive assault often blame themselves, and may wrongly attribute it to a sex-linked trait of masochism or lack of self-esteem. They don't know that it can be less painful to believe that you did something blameworthy than it is to think that you live in a world where you can be attacked at any time, in any place, simply because you are a woman. It is hard to go on after an attack that is both random—and thus completely unpredictable—and not random, that is, a crime of hatred toward the group to which you happen to belong. If I hadn't been the one who was attacked on that road in France, it would have been the next woman to come along. But had my husband walked down that road instead, he would have been safe.

Although I didn't blame myself for the attack, neither could I blame my attacker. Tom wanted to kill him, but I, like other rape victims I came to know, found it almost impossible to get angry with my assailant. I think the terror I still felt precluded the appropriate angry response. It may be that experiencing anger toward an attacker requires imagining oneself in proximity to him, a prospect too frightening for a victim in the early stages of recovery to conjure up. As Aristotle observed in the Rhetoric, Book I, "no one grows angry with a person on whom there is no prospect of taking vengeance, and we feel comparatively little anger, or none at all, with those who are much our superiors in power."[9] The anger was still there, however, but it got directed toward safer targets: my family and closest friends. My anger spread, giving me painful shooting signs that I was coming back to life. I could not accept what had happened to me. What was I supposed to do? How could everyone else carry on with their lives when women were dying? How could Tom go on teaching his classes, seeing students, chatting with colleagues . . . and why should he be able to walk down the street when I couldn't?

The incompatibility of fear of my assailant and appropriate anger toward him became most apparent after I began taking a women's self-defense class. It became clear that the way to break out of the double bind of self-blame versus powerlessness was through empowerment—physical as well as political. Learning to fight back is a crucial part of this process, not only because it enables us to experience justified, healing rage, but also because, as Iris Young has observed in her essay "Throwing Like a Girl," "women in sexist society are physically handicapped," moving about hesitantly, fearfully, in a constricted lived space, routinely underestimating what strength we actually have (1990b: 153). We have to learn to feel entitled to occupy space, to defend ourselves. The hardest thing for most of the women in my self-defense class to do was simply to yell "No!" Women have been taught not to fight back when being attacked, to rely instead on placating or pleading with one's assailant—strategies that researchers have found to be least effective in resisting rape (Bart and O'Brien, 1984).

The instructor of the class, a survivor herself, helped me through the difficult first lessons, through the flashbacks and the fear, and showed me I could be tougher than ever. As I was leaving after one session, I saw a student arrive for the next class—with a guide dog. I was furious that, in addition to everything else this woman had to struggle with, she had to worry about being raped. I thought I understood something of her fear since I felt, for the first time in my life, like I had a perceptual deficit—not the blurred vision from the detached vitreous, but, rather, the more hazardous lack of eyes in the back of my head. I tried to compensate for this on my walks by looking over my shoulder a lot and punctuating my purposeful, straight-ahead stride with an occasional pirouette, which must have made me look more whimsical than terrified.

The confidence I gained from learning how to fight back effectively not only enabled me to walk down the street again, it gave me back my life. But it was a changed life. A paradoxical life. I began to feel stronger than ever before, and more vulnerable, more determined to fight to change the world, but in need of several naps a day. News that friends found distressing in a less visceral way—the trials of the defendants in the Central Park jogger case, the controversy over *American Psycho*, the Gulf War, the Kennedy rape case, the Tyson trial, the fatal stabbing of law professor Mary Jo Frug near Harvard Square, the ax murders of two women graduate students at Dartmouth College—triggered debilitating flashbacks in me. Unlike survivors of wars or earthquakes, who inhabit a common shattered world, rape victims face the cataclysmic destruction of their world alone, surrounded by people who find it hard to understand what's so distressing. I realized that I exhibited every symptom of post-traumatic stress disorder—dissociation, flashbacks, hypervigilance, exaggerated startle response, sleep disorders, inability to concentrate, diminished interest in significant activities, and a sense of a foreshortened future.[10] I could understand why children exposed to urban violence have such trouble envisioning their futures. Although I had always been career-oriented, always planning for my future, I could no longer imagine how I would get through each day, let alone what I might be doing in a year's time. I didn't think I would ever write or teach philosophy again.

The American Psychiatric Association's *Diagnostic and Statistical Manual* defines post-traumatic stress disorder, in part, as the result of "an event that is outside the range of usual human experience."[11] Because the trauma is, to most people, inconceivable, it's also unspeakable. Even when I managed to find the words—and the strength—to describe my ordeal, it was hard for others to hear about it. They would have preferred me to just "buck up," as one friend urged me to do. But it's essential to talk about it, again and again. It's a way of remastering the trauma, although it can be retraumatizing when people refuse to listen. In my case, each time someone failed to respond it felt as though I were alone again in the ravine, dying, screaming. And still no one could hear me. Or, worse, they heard me, but refused to help.

I now know they were trying to help, but that recovering from trauma takes time, patience and, most of all, determination on the part of the survivor. After about six months, I began to be able to take more responsibility for my own recovery, and stopped expecting others to pull me through. I entered the final stage of my recovery, a period of gradual acceptance and integration of what had happened. I joined a rape survivors' support group, I got a great deal of therapy, and I became involved in political activities, such as promoting the Violence against Women Act (which was eventually passed by Congress in 1994).[12] Gradually, I was able to return to work.

When I resumed teaching at Dartmouth in the fall of 1991, the first student who came to see me in my office during freshman orientation week told me that she had been raped. The following spring four Dartmouth students reported sexual assaults to the local police. In the aftermath of these recent reports, the women students on my campus were told to use their heads, lock their doors, not to go out after dark without a male escort. They were advised: just don't do anything stupid.

Although colleges are eager to "protect" women by limiting their freedom of movement or providing them with male escorts, they continue to be reluctant to teach women to protect themselves. After months of lobbying the administration at my college, we were able to convince them to offer a women's self-defense and rape prevention course. It was offered the next year as a Physical Education course, and nearly a hundred students and employees signed up for it. Shortly after the course began, I was informed that the women students were not going to be allowed to get P.E. credit for it, since the administration had determined that it discriminated against men. I was initially told that granting credit for the course was in violation of Title IX, which prohibits sex discrimination in education programs receiving federal funding—even though Title IX law makes an explicit exception for P.E. classes involving substantial bodily contact, and even though every term the college offers several martial arts courses, for credit, that are open to men. I was then informed by an administrator that, even if Title IX permitted it, offering a women's self-defense course for credit violated "the College's non-discrimination clause—a clause which, I hope, all reasonable men and women support as good policy." The implication that I was not a "reasonable woman" didn't sit well with me as a philosopher, so I wrote a letter to the appropriate administrative committee criticizing my college's position that single-sex sports, male-only fraternities, female-only sororities, and pregnancy leave policies are not discriminatory, in an invidious sense, while a women's self-defense class is. The administration finally agreed to grant P.E. credit for the course, but shortly after that battle was over, I read in the *New York Times* that "a rape prevention ride service offered to women in the city of Madison and on the University of Wisconsin campus may lose its university financing because it discriminates against men."[13] The dean of students at Wisconsin said that this group—the Women's Transit Authority, which had been providing free nighttime rides to women students for nineteen years—must change its policy to allow male drivers and passengers. These are, in my view, examples of the application of what Catharine MacKinnon refers to as "the stupid theory of equality."[14] To argue that rape prevention polices for women discriminate against men is like arguing that money spent making university buildings more accessible to disabled persons discriminates against those able-bodied persons who do not benefit from these improvements.[15]

Sexual violence victimizes not only those women who are directly attacked, but *all* women. The fear of rape has long functioned to keep women in their place. Whether or not one agrees with the claims of those, such as Susan Brownmiller (1975), who argue that rape is a means by which *all* men keep *all* women subordinate, the fact that all women's lives are restricted by sexual violence is indisputable. The authors of *The Female Fear*, Margaret Gordon and Stephanie Riger, cite studies substantiating what every woman already knows—that the fear of rape prevents women from enjoying what men consider to be their birthright. Fifty percent of women never use public transportation after dark because of fear of rape. Women are eight times more likely than men to avoid walking in their own neighborhoods after dark, for the same reason (Gordon and Riger, 1991). In a seminar I taught at Dartmouth on Violence Against Women, the men in the class were stunned by the extent to which women in the class took precautions against assault every day—locking doors and windows, checking the back seat of the car, not walking alone at night, looking in closets on returning home. And this is at a "safe" rural New England campus.

Although women still have their work and leisure opportunities unfairly restricted by their relative lack of safety, paternalistic legislation excluding women from some of the "riskier" forms of employment (for example, bartending[16]) has, thankfully, disappeared, except, that is, in the military. We are still debating whether women should be permitted to engage in combat, and the latest rationale for keeping women out of battle is that they are more vulnerable than men to sexual violence. Those wanting to limit women's role in the military have used the reported indecent assaults on the two female American prisoners of war in Iraq as evidence for women's unsuitability for combat.[17] One might as well argue that the fact that women are much more likely than men to be sexually assaulted on college campuses is evidence that women are not suited to post-secondary education. No one, to my knowledge, has proposed returning Ivy League colleges to their former all-male status as a solution to the problem of campus rape. Some have, however, seriously proposed enacting after-dark curfews for women, in spite of the fact that men are the perpetrators of the assaults. This is yet another indication of how natural it still seems to many people to address the problem of sexual violence by curtailing women's lives. The absurdity of this approach becomes apparent once one realizes that a woman can be sexually assaulted, at any time—in "safe" places, in broad daylight, even in her own home.

For months after my assault, I was afraid of people finding out about it— afraid of their reactions and their inability to respond. I was afraid that my professional work would be discredited, that I would be viewed as "biased," or, even worse, not properly "philosophical." Now I am no longer afraid of what might happen if I speak out about sexual violence. I'm much more afraid of what *will* continue to happen if I don't. Sexual violence is a problem of catastrophic proportions—a fact obscured by its mundanity, by its relentless occurrence, by the fact that so many of us have been victims of it. Imagine the moral outrage, the emergency response we would surely mobilize, if all of these everyday assaults occurred at the same time or were restricted to one geographic region? But why should the spatio-temporal coordinates of the vast numbers of sexual assaults be considered to be morally relevant? From the victim's point of view, the fact that she is isolated in her rape and her recovery, combined with the ordinariness of the crime that leads to its trivialization, makes the assault and its aftermath even more traumatic.

As devastating as sexual violence is, however, I want to stress that it is possible to survive it, and even to flourish after it, although it doesn't seem that way at the time. Whenever I see a survivor struggling with the overwhelming anger and sadness, I'm reminded of a sweet motherly woman in my rape survivors' support group who sat silently throughout the group's first meeting. At the end of the hour she finally asked, softly, through tears: "Can anyone tell me if it ever stops hurting?" At the time I had the same question, and wasn't satisfied with any answer. Now I can say, yes, it does stop hurting, at least for longer periods of time. A year after the assault, I was pleased to discover that I could go for fifteen minutes without thinking about my attack. Now I can go for hours at a stretch without a flashback. That's on a good day. On a bad day, I may still take to my bed with lead in my veins, unable to find one good reason to go on.

Our group facilitator told us the first meeting: "You will never be the same. But you can be better." I protested that I had lost too much: my security, my self-esteem, my love, and my work. I had been happy with the way things were. How could they ever be better now? As a survivor, she knew how I felt, but she also knew that, as she put it, "When your life is so shattered, you're forced to pick up the pieces, and you have a chance to stop and examine them. You can say, 'I don't want this one anymore' or 'I think I'll work on that one.'" I have had to give up more than I would ever have chosen to. But I have gained important skills and insights, and I no longer feel tainted by my victimization. Granted, those of us who live through sexual assault aren't given ticker tape parades or the keys to our cities, but it's an honor to be a survivor. Although it's not exactly the sort of thing I can put on my résumé, it's the accomplishment of which I'm most proud.

Now, more than two years after the assault, I can acknowledge the good things that have come from the recovery process—the clarity, the confidence, the determination, the many supporters and survivors who have brought meaning back into my world. This is not to say that the attack and its aftermath were, on balance, a good thing, or, as one relative put it, "a real blessing from above." I would rather not have gone down that road. It's been hard for me, as a philosopher, to learn the lesson that knowledge isn't always desirable, that the truth doesn't always set you free. Sometimes, it fills you with incapacitating terror, and then, uncontrollable rage. But I suppose you should embrace it anyway, for the reason Nietzsche exhorts you to love your enemies: if it doesn't kill you, it makes you stronger.

People ask me if I'm recovered now, and I reply that it depends on what that means. If they mean, "am I back to where I was before the attack"? I have to say, no, and I never will be. I am not the same person who set off, singing, on that sunny Fourth of July in the French countryside. I left her— and her trust, her innocence, her joie de vivre—in a rocky creek bed at the bottom of a ravine. I had to in order to survive. I now have my own understanding of what a friend described to me as a Jewish custom of giving those who have outlived a brush with death new names. The trauma has changed me forever, and if I insist too often that my friends and family acknowledge it, that's because I'm afraid they don't know who I am.

But if recovery means being able to incorporate this awful knowledge into my life and carry on, then, yes, I'm recovered. I don't wake each day with a start, thinking: "this can't have happened to me!" It happened. I have no guarantee that it won't happen again, although my self-defense classes have given me the confidence to move about in the world and to go for longer and longer walks—with my two big dogs. Sometimes I even manage to enjoy myself. And I no longer cringe when I see a woman jogging alone on the country road where I live, though I may still have a slight urge to rush out and protect her, to tell her to come inside where she'll be safe. But I catch myself, like a mother learning to let go, and cheer her on, thinking, may she always be so carefree, so at home in her world. She has every right to be.

Sexual Assault and the Problem of Consent

PATRICIA KAZAN

Sexual assault is frequently defined as sexual relations without consent.[1] Thus, lack of consent is an important part of the crime of sexual assault. But what is it to consent to sex? The 1992 amendments to the Canadian Criminal Code, section 273.1, define consent as "voluntary agreement." This definition is followed by a nonexhaustive list of circumstances that may vitiate consent: no consent is obtained where agreement is expressed by a person other than the complainant; where the complainant is unconscious; where the complainant is induced by the accused to consent through an abuse of a position of trust, power, or authority; or where the complainant expresses, by words or conduct, a lack of agreement to engage in or to continue a sexual activity.[2]

Although some countries, such as Australia, supplement this list of vitiating circumstances with a positive account of consent,[3] Canadian law does not. Given the absence of statutory guidelines on how to interpret the phrase "voluntary agreement," the widespread debate among Canadian legal scholars as to what constitutes consent is not surprising. Two ap-

Some of the ideas expressed in this essay were first presented in my commentary on Brett 1994, delivered at the Annual Congress of the Canadian Philosophical Association, June 1994. Versions of this paper were presented at the Forum Speakers' series, the University of Toronto, March 1995; the Canadian Law and Society Association, Annual Meeting at Université du Québec à Montréal, June 1995; and the Canadian Section of the International Association for Philosophy of Law and Social Philosophy (CS-IVR), Annual Meeting at UQAM, June 1995. I thank the members of the Philosophy Department at the University of Toronto, and members of CS-IVR for their helpful comments. Special thanks to Brian Baigrie for discussion and editorial advice.

proaches predominate in contemporary legal scholarship: an *attitudinal* account, which identifies consent with the agent's mental states; and a *performative* account, which identifies consent with the agent's behavior or utterances. Both accounts are problematic. By shedding light on the difficulties inherent in these two accounts, I will argue that an adequate account of consent must not only address the sexist stereotypes that surround the issue of consent, but also distinguish genuine from coerced consent, particularly where coercion takes the form of subtle and implicit threats. A meaningful consent standard, which respects the consenting agent's sexual autonomy, goes beyond the attitudinal and performative accounts, while extracting the best features of both.

THE ATTITUDINAL MODEL OF CONSENT

The courts and legal theorists traditionally have adopted an attitudinal approach to consent, treating it as a subjective question about the attitude of the agent(s) in question.[4] Nearly a half century ago, the editors of the *Yale Law Journal* concluded that if a woman is legally capable of granting consent, her subjective attitude towards the sexual act determines whether or not it is rape (Editorial Board, 1952). More recently, the English Court of Appeal in the 1982 case of *Olugboya* directed the jury to determine consent by considering "the state of mind of the victim immediately before the act of sexual intercourse."[5] Canadian criminal law also appears to endorse an attitudinal account of consent—theorists have remarked that "since consent is a state of mind, any test designed to determine a purely subjective matter should also be subjective" (Bryant, 1989: 108).

On the attitudinal account, consent consists in any one of a range of mental states, from desire to grudging acquiescence, held by the consenting agent. It is a subjective matter whose determination involves the state of mind of the agent. The agent's behavior is regarded merely as an indication of consent—her actions are the objective evidence or tokens from which consent is inferred. As such, it is questionable whether one can be mistaken about one's own consent. Indeed, in this account, consent has an incorrigible character: "one consents when he himself thinks he consents" (Editorial Board, 1952: 65).

Feminist legal theorists have charged the attitudinal account with putting the complainant on trial. To determine the complainant's attitude toward sexual relations, courts have delved into the complainant's sexual history. Evidence that the woman was promiscuous or wore revealing clothes has often been interpreted as proof that she held a positive attitude toward sex. Feminists therefore have pressed for an account of consent that shows a positive affirmation of consent. For instance, the feminist slogan "'no' means 'no'" attaches significance to any actions or words indicating nonconsent. By focusing on behavior or utterances, instead of attitudes, feminists sought to replace a subjective (and often sexist) determination of the courts with an objective (sex-neutral) determination of consent.

THE PERFORMATIVE MODEL OF CONSENT

Though a performative account of consent, which emphasizes the agent's behavior or utterances, is implicit in the writings of many feminist legal scholars, Nathan Brett has been the most vocal proponent.[6] Brett's argument stems from his contention that the attitudinal account fails to capture the normative significance of the activity of consenting. In his view, consent is a permission-giving activity which changes the prevailing patterns of rights and obligations between individuals. The act of consenting is then comparable to the act of promising. As J. L. Austin has pointed out, the words "I promise" have a performative character in the sense that the uttering of these words is a part of doing an action, namely, promising.[7] Applying Austin's analysis to consent, Brett maintains that consent has a similar performative character in the sense that to consent is just to behave or speak in a manner that conventionally signifies consent.

From a normative perspective, consenting differs from promising insofar as promising pertains to one's own activities and involves taking on a previously nonexistent obligation, whereas consent is directly concerned with the acts of another and "involves releasing that other person from an obligation to refrain from acting within a certain area otherwise prohibited" (Brett, 1994: 7). Thus consent constitutes "a limited withdrawal of a right not to be interfered with," requiring communication between the parties involved in the form of external acts that have conventional significance—through words or conduct that signify consent (Brett, 1994: 1). Simply changing one's attitudes or mental states will not suffice.

In the performative account, consent is characterized as an objective question concerning the external acts of the agent, not her mental states, subjective feelings, and attitudes; it is not to be identified with subjective willingness or approval.

The performative account, in shifting the focus in a sexual assault trial away from the complainant's supposed mental states to the behavior of the respective parties, attempts to set a new legal standard for consent. For instance, a person who has indicated consent through her free and uncoerced behavior, perhaps by signing a medical consent form, cannot claim after the fact that she never really consented because she held a negative attitude or aversion to the acts in question. Similarly, persons wishing to engage in sexual relations cannot presume their partner's consent based solely on an assumption of subjective desire or willingness; they must attend to their partner's behavior and utterances.[8] Brett maintains that it is no longer possible for rapists to claim "to 'see through' the protests of their victims, to find 'consent' where it was clearly denied" (1994: 14).

DIFFICULTIES WITH THE PERFORMATIVE MODEL

The performative account loses some of its appeal when we examine it with respect to our commonsense notions of consent and to the problem of coercion. The performative model does not sit well with our everyday notion of consent. We cannot dissociate consent from our attitudes, desires, and intentions without losing its normative significance. And second, the performative model of consent is unable to identify some situations which our commonsense intuitions readily identify as coercive. Behavior is often normatively ambiguous—not only do individuals often find it difficult to recognize the significance of each other's behavior, but some subtle forms of coercion cannot be identified if we focus exclusively on behavioral cues. Contrary to the performative account, determining consent requires more than attending to an agent's behavior or utterances.

Lack of Fit with Commonsense Notions of Consent

The performative account denies an essential connection between a person's mental states and the act of consenting. Consent may well be accompanied by feelings of willingness or approval, but in this view such attitudes or mental states are not necessary for the performance of consent. As Brett suggests, a person can genuinely consent to a root canal while harboring a negative attitude or an aversion to dental surgery. By the same token, a person may desire sexual relations, but withhold consent for reasons of principle. A negative attitude toward dental surgery does not negate consent any more than a positive attitude or desire for sex disproves nonconsent. As long as the consent was informed and uncoerced, the performative account judges the agent's behavior to be consensual, irrespective of her particular attitudes concerning the subject of consent. We may well be conflicted or even ambivalent in our attitudes toward the object of consent, but this fact by itself does not undermine the legitimacy of our consent.

By dissociating consent from our attitudes and desires, the performative model seems to clash with our commonsense understanding of a connection between the act of consenting and our attitudes or desires. The model seems right to stipulate that public communication is necessary for consent to have the normative, permission-granting character we associate it with; that a person might grant consent in disregard of or direct opposition to her desires or intentions contradicts our everyday experience. If the evidence indicates that attitudes or intentions are not in accord with consensual behavior, we tend to suspect that the performance of consent was coerced or disingenuous.

Brett rightly points out that it is indeed possible to speak intelligibly about a person granting or withholding consent despite a contrary desire. Even so, he makes it seem as though the actor has consented against her will, portraying consent in narrow behavioral terms, as a public token, rather than as an act in which attitudes, desires, and deliberation play a crucial role. True consent is more than just a behavior or utterance imbued with conventional significance; it is an expression of the will reflecting our considered judgment.

Brett is right to hold that consent expresses our willingness to grant access to that area of our autonomy normally protected by the law from intrusion, but he neglects to add that our will is not exercised in a dispositional vacuum. It is directed (or perhaps inclined) by our reasons, desires, attitudes and intentions. To say that the will is directed is not, of course, to imply that it is somehow compelled. We might say that our will is free when it is exercised in sympathy with our reasons, desires or intentions, and that it is coerced or constrained when we are prevented from acting according to these inclinations. To consent, then, is not just to behave in an assenting manner, but to be affected in a sympathetic way. We cannot make sense of consent as a permission-giving activity, I submit, unless we regard consent as something that is in sympathy with our attitudes, desires, and intentions. To suggest that consent can be dissociated from these attitudinal states is tantamount to the claim that we can grant permission to others against our will.

If the above argument is sound, how do we make sense of cases where the agent's consensual behavior is accompanied by a negative attitude towards consent? In my view, we can draw a distinction between our attitudes toward the act of consenting and our attitudes toward the object of consent. The reluctant dental patient may well have a negative attitude toward the object of consent—dental surgery—but her consent would not be genuine unless she also held a positive attitude toward the act of consenting. Insofar as consent is an intentional act, reflecting the agent's desires and motivations, it must be willingly granted. We might conclude that the agent consented to dental work, despite her aversion, because her desire to get her teeth fixed outweighed her desire to avoid surgery and thus motivated her consent.

We can apply this distinction in a similar manner to the case of the person who intentionally withholds consent in the face of strong sexual desires. Such behavior is rendered intelligible as an expression of nonconsent, only if we infer that the agent's desire for sex (the object of consent) was overridden by another more compelling aversion to the act of consenting, such as the desire to remain faithful to her partner. Although this individual desired the object of consent, namely, to engage in sexual relations, her negative attitude motivated her to withhold consent.

Cases that might seem to undermine the claim that genuine consent requires that the agent's internal motivations be in sympathy with her behavior are those in which the agent is said to be uncertain or ambivalent. Can a person who expresses uncertainty genuinely consent? This question is really about whether consent is genuine if it is not fully informed as to the nature and quality of the object of her consent. For example, when a doctor hasn't properly informed a patient as to what will happen to her in the operating room, her consent to surgery is negated. But not all cases of insufficient information regarding the object of consent are cases of nonconsent. Sometimes we are not fully informed as to our own feelings towards the object of consent. An unfamiliar activity or a new partner may make it difficult for a person to predict whether she will enjoy the activity or if it will live up to her expectations. The lack of information about our own feelings does not, however, negate the act of consent.

Lack of information as to the nature and quality of the object of consent negates consent, whereas lack of information regarding one's feelings toward the object of consent does not. Thus, I might consent to go skydiving (expressing a positive attitude by signing a consent form), even though I do not know whether I will enjoy the activity. As long as I know what is involved in skydiving, namely, jumping out of a plane at a high altitude, knowing that I may not land safely, I am satisfactorily informed despite my uncertain feelings. My consent to surgery is genuine if I sign the consent form in full knowledge of the details of the operation, regardless of whether I know how I will feel afterward. And, as far as consent to sex is concerned, as long as the agent knows that what she is consenting to is in fact sexual intercourse, she cannot claim after the fact that she never really consented because the activity didn't live up to her expectations.[9] Thus, the fact that we may lack information about ourselves and how we will react to participation in a particular activity does not negate our consent. What counts is whether we know exactly what we are consenting to. As long as our internal motivations are in sympathy with the act of consenting, the lack of information about our own feelings does not negate consent.

Thus far I have argued that what counts for consent is not merely that the agent give the right outward signs, but rather that her outward behavior conform to her innermost feelings and desires regarding the act of consenting. Some might argue, that sex is the kind of activity that requires a sympathetic attitude toward both the act of consenting and the object of consent. In other words, one should engage in sex only if one actually desires the activity itself. Opponents of legalized prostitution, for example, have argued that prostitution is wrong because the prostitute consents only for financial gain and not because she truly desires sex. In a medical context, by contrast, we do not normally think it important for the patient to desire the treatment she has consented to. Even if the patient looks upon the treatment with great displeasure and apprehension, we consider her consent to be genuine if she signs the medical release form through her own volition.

It is difficult to say why we place sexual relations in this special category of activities that we think people should consent to only if they honestly desire to engage in the activity. One must concede that, in some cases, people do genuinely consent to sex they don't want. There is much debate, particularly among feminists, over whether such cases are instances of genuine consent. The focus of the debate generally centers on the context in which these persons might have granted their consent. Feminists ask questions about whether prostitutes or subjugated wives are in a position to withhold consent to sex when the consequences of not consenting may range from withdrawal of emotional and economic support to verbal and physical abuse. Evidence that a woman had consented to sex to avoid such consequences would indeed give us cause to question the validity of her consent. But there is no reason to believe that consent to unwanted sex is always invalid. In some cases, a person may genuinely consent to the sexual demands of his or her partner out of love and affection. It is also possible that some women and men may freely choose to use their bodies for the purposes of prostitution. As far as determining the validity of consent is concerned, what we need to know is whether the agent's consensual behavior is voluntary. And, to make this determination, we need to examine the agent's desires and intentions. Even if the agent does not actually desire the object of her consent, namely, sexual relations, as long as she voluntarily granted her consent, the law must treat her consent as genuine.

Distinguishing between our attitudes towards the act and the object of consent reveals that there is a much more complex relationship between our attitudes and behavior regarding consent than the performative account allows. From the fact that a person's attitudes toward the object of consent conflict with the act of consent, it doesn't follow that consent is dissociated from her attitudes and desires. If anything, the opposite would seem to be true: we can make sense of consenting as an intentional act only if we suppose that it is backed by a sympathetic attitude. While a positive attitude may not be sufficient for consent (since consent must be publicly communicated in order for it to impact on the prevailing pattern of rights and obligations), it is nonetheless necessary in order for consent to have the normative permission-granting character that we ordinarily attach to it. I submit that it is the failure to distinguish between our attitudes toward the act of consenting and the object of consent which leads to the erroneous conclusion that a positive attitude is not an essential component of consent.

The Ambiguity of Performances

Consideration of the agent's attitudes or mental states not only plays a key role in our commonsense notion of consent, but it is also important in helping us to distinguish genuine consent from nonconsent, feigned consent, or coerced consent. The second difficulty with the performative account is that performances are often normatively ambiguous. There are two ways in which a performance of consent can be ambiguous: when they mean different things to different people, making it hard for individuals to recognize the significance of each other's behavior; and when coerced consent looks identical to genuine consent. I will address each of these ambiguities separately.

The first ambiguity arises from the lack of consensus about what sort of behavior constitutes consent in sexual relations. Conventions governing sexual consent are not always clear, and two people may have conflicting or incompatible understandings of what behavior constitutes consent.[10] For instance, one person may give what she believed to be an explicit indication of nonconsent, while another person may interpret her behavior as a sign of consent.[11] Given that consenting is a normatively significant act, a failure to clearly communicate consent through behavior has implications for how the parties regard the legitimacy of each other's conduct: person B regards his own conduct as legitimate, and person A regards it as assaultive. Depending on whose perspective we adopt, we will get a different picture of the normative significance of the event. Attending solely to behavioral cues and verbalizations may fail to resolve the question of consent where two persons disagree on what counts as an indication of consent. In this sense, attending to performances is no better than attending solely to attitudes because both approaches are open to subjective interpretation.

The lack of standardized conventions delineating the behavior or utterances that communicate consent presents a practical problem. We will need to supplement our attention to verbal and behavioral cues in order to resolve instances of miscommunication. To determine the significance of the consenting party's behavior, we need to assess what the consenting agent meant to express by her particular conduct. This may necessitate an inquiry into her attitudes and intentions toward the act of consent. If we find that her behavior reflected a sympathetic attitude towards the act of consent, then we have good reason to conclude that her behavioral was consensual. It is a separate question whether the defendant in a sexual assault trial can be held responsible for knowing the true nature of the complainant's attitudes. And, unfortunately, the courts have shown a marked tendency for setting the standard of responsibility for consent to sex quite low, often accepting the defendant's standard of consent without much debate. In Canadian courts this may soon change with the recent introduction of a standard of responsibility that requires that the defendant demonstrate that "reasonable steps" were taken to ascertain the complainant's attitude toward the act of consent.[12]

The second ambiguity arises from the fact that feigned or coerced consent may be behaviorally indistinguishable from genuine consent. Such cases emphasize the need to appeal to an agent's attitudes in order to determine the matter of consent. The 1985 Supreme Court case of *R. v. Sansregret* demonstrates the difficulty of distinguishing feigned consent from genuine consent.[13] In *Sansregret*, the complainant Terry Wood feigned consent to sex in order to appease her dangerously irate ex-boyfriend. The accused, John Henry Sansregret, had broken into Ms. Wood's apartment in the middle of the night. While brandishing a knife, he threatened her. Ms. Wood feigned consent to sex in order to avoid being killed. Following sexual intercourse with the accused, she escaped and contacted the police.

If we were to attend only to Ms. Wood's behavior and utterances, we would have to conclude the consent was genuine. But the coercive nature of the situation suggests that her consent was not genuine. In the performative account, we need not confine our considerations solely to the behavior and utterances of the consenting agent. We may also take into consideration the context of the situation by looking for evidence of physical force or threats. However, Brett cautions against taking into consideration subjective mental states, claiming that we should confine our attention to the "objective facts" of the matter, focusing only on external behavior and facts about the situation. Brett thinks that we can then distinguish cases of feigned consent, as in the *Sansregret* case, from cases of genuine consent. One merit of the performative account, according to Brett, is that it shows why force eliminates consent. In his words, "since consent brings about a shift in the rights and obligations of individuals—a normative change—this is not something that can be achieved by force" (1994: 10). Compliant cooperative behavior in response to force or coercion does not constitute evidence of consent.

To grant permission is to grant liberty or license to someone or something. An agent's behavior has the property of licensing or liberating another if this is in fact what the agent intended to communicate by her behavior. What the agent intended to communicate depends on whether she was favorably disposed to the act of consenting: if so, her actions are justly interpreted as consensual. Coerced behavior, in contrast, does not have this permission-granting character because it does not reflect the agent's true desires or intentions. Thus, to say that force cannot be used to obtain permission is another way of saying that you can't make someone consent if they don't want to. Coerced consent is a mere performance, that is, it consists of behavior lacking the requisite mental state to transform it into an act of normative significance. We may be coerced through threats of violence to behave or perform as though we consent, but because we do so unwillingly our attitudes put the lie to our performance (except for those who are willfully blind to the fact that our sympathies are not in accord with our performance).

Evidence of force or threats can be useful indicators of coercion, because we think it likely that such behavior would incline the will of the average person. But we cannot decide the question of consent by "looking at the situation itself, [and] not simply examining the mind and attitudes of [the] person," as Brett suggests (1994: 11). A great deal depends on our interpretation of the defendant's behavior and whether we find it sufficiently coercive to invalidate consent. This determination depends to a large extent on whose perspective one adopts. Arguably, waving a knife and uttering threats, as the defendant did in *Sansregret*, would be intimidating to most people.

Coercion does not always take the form of overt threats and physical force, but may involve implicit threats. For instance, imagine you are alone on a city street, confronted by four individuals, each of whom is twice your size.[14] One of them asks for your wallet, politely, without uttering or gesturing in a threatening manner. We would not normally consider cooperation with this request an indication that the individual had willingly consented to hand over his wallet. But in the absence of any verbal or physical performances which might be construed as threatening, it is difficult to see how the performative model could classify this situation as nonconsensual.

If we cannot appeal to any threatening external behavior that suggests coercion, how can we identify it as coercive on the performative account? Proponents of the performative account might suggest that we attend to the "objective facts" of the situation. But which facts count as "objective" in this context? An answer to this question depends on what we mean by the term "objective." On the performative account, "objective" refers to the external features of the agent's behavior—facts that are independent of the agent's attitude or mental state. One might be tempted to argue that any situation in which there are four against one is in fact objectively threatening. We might say that the size and number of the persons asking for the wallet is an external fact, but is it sufficient to pose an objective threat? If we say yes, then anyone who consented in the presence of four big people was coerced. But surely this question also depends on such facts as whether the victim believed that the persons asking for her wallet were members of a violent gang or whether they knew that their presence was threatening enough in itself to ensure compliance.

The threat in this situation, at least in part, is a reflection of the agent's perception of the situation. If you are a martial arts expert, you may not find a confrontation with four men remotely threatening. But if you are not trained in self-defense, lack physical strength, or have been previously mugged or raped, such a confrontation could be threatening. A rapist can exploit his victim's fear and her belief that she cannot defend herself to coerce her consent without using force or explicit threats.

It is doubtful that these differences in perspective can be classified as "objective facts," at least in the way that Brett uses the term. Facts about perspective can be internal in the sense that they have to do with the agent's psychological makeup (for instance, whether she is easily frightened or has been previously mugged), but they can also be contextual. Contextual facts include facts about the history between the parties, such as whether the consenting agent believed the person who confronted her to be violent, whether she felt she could defend herself against possible retaliation if she did not submit, and whether the person confronting her knew that he could capitalize on her fear.[15] Assuming the impact of such contextual facts on a person's perception of coercion in a given situation, we cannot rely on so-called objective facts of the situation to determine consent. To understand the *context* in which the agent acted, we need to inquire into her perceptions and attitude toward her (apparently) consensual behavior.

While most cases of coerced consent are distinguishable from genuine consent by the lack of a positive attitude toward the act of consenting, there are notable exceptions, such as the "Stockholm Syndrome," which victims of kidnapping, confinement, and abuse allegedly suffer when they begin to take on the beliefs and attitudes of their captors. This transference is thought to be a consequence of acute psychological stress and/or physical abuse; in such a situation we might reason that the agent's consent was not genuine because of psychological duress.[16] Psychological duress differs from coercion in the following way. In cases of coercion, the aggressor constrains the victim's choices so that she can no longer choose a course of action that accords with her sympathies. The victim is still capable of intentional action and makes a choice, but it is not a choice she would entertain without the presence of coercion. In psychological duress, by contrast, the traumatic situation created by the aggressor undermines the victim's thought processes, making it impossible for her to act or reason in a self-preserving manner. In cases involving the "Stockholm Syndrome," evidence of a sympathetic attitude toward the act of consent may give a false indication of consent. In such cases we must appeal to the broader context of the situation, what we know about human psychology, and perhaps even the particular characteristics and dispositions of the agent(s) in question, in order to determine the matter of consent.[17] We must ask whether the agent's sympathetic attitude might have been otherwise had it not been for the presence of psychological duress. Thus the problem of psychological duress does not undermine the key role that attitudes play in determining the matter of consent.

THE SOCIAL CHARACTER OF CONSENT AND COERCION

The performative account places far too much confidence in our ability to determine the "objective facts" of the matter. The so-called objective facts may depend on the individual's perspective as well as on the social and cultural context which shape and color these facts.[18] Coercion and consent have an inescapable social character, and the defining conventions are not universally shared. What's more, the conventions are colored by sexist stereotypes[19] that characterize women as wanting sex, regardless of what they say or do to indicate the contrary, and these continue to shape what society and the courts view as consensual behavior. Many men continue to interpret behavior such as accepting a drink or a ride home as an expression of sexual consent. Courts and commentators reflect these stereotypes by reading consent into a woman's behavior and attitudes based on her past sexual conduct.

Susan Estrich claims in her surveys of appellate decisions (1986, 1987) that the legal definition of prohibitive force is based on the archetype of a "schoolboy" fight. In this model, force is recognized only when an attacker comes at you with fists clenched or legs kicking. The law consistently refuses to acknowledge nonviolent forms of coercion which vary from this model of force, dismissing them as mere seduction.[20] Cases recognizing threats short of force as sufficient for rape convictions are virtually nonexistent. In Estrich's view, this definition of force "protects male access to women where guns and beatings are not needed to secure it" (1987: 62).[21] Against this model Estrich advances a gender-sensitive conception of force which would include nonviolent coercive behavior ranging from the abuse of trust, power, and authority, to economic and psychological pressure, fraud, misrepresentation, and the failure to disclose critical information.[22]

Classifying nonviolent coercion as criminal behavior challenges the law's traditional practice of treating it as a harmless form of seduction.[23] The courts may recognize nonviolent coercion as reprehensible behavior, but they do not consider it to be proscribed by law. This treatment of nonviolent sexual coercion is at odds with how it is regarded in other areas of the law. For instance, common law protects parties to commercial transactions whose choices are coerced by violent threats, economic extortion, fraud, or even the failure to disclose facts relevant to a transaction.[24] In view of such protections, it is hypocritical to permit a much broader range of coercive practices to manipulate and deceive a woman into granting consent where sexual relations are concerned.[25] This double standard reflects sexist stereotypes that characterize coercion as an everyday, inescapable, and perhaps even desirable feature of sexual relations.[26]

While Estrich sees the solution to the problem of implicit or nonviolent forms of coercion in an expanded conception of force, Stephen Schulhofer abandons this force requirement, arguing for a conception of sexual assault as an offense against personal autonomy, centering on "meaningful consent" (1992: 41). In Schulhofer's view, there is a limit to how far we can stretch the conception of force before we face inevitable boundary questions: if a disparity in social and economic power (like a disparity in physical strength) is sufficient to support a finding of force, then many seemingly consensual relationships become suspect (ibid.: 51). Once the conception of force extends beyond bodily injury, we need to be able to say what it protects. What we should be protecting, he submits, is sexual autonomy and the freedom to choose our sexual interactions. The issue for Schulhofer, then, is not what counts as forceful behavior but which factors constrain meaningful consent. In his view, a concept of meaningful consent can be constructed from conceptions of human dignity and equality, and from a respect for each individual's conception of bodily freedom and sexual intimacy (ibid.: 70). This approach need not imply a naive, laissez-faire liberalism that is insensitive to inequalities in power and authority. On the contrary, the objective is to protect individuals from real-world conditions that constrain freedom of choice, but without dictating how that freedom should be used.

OBJECTIVE STANDARDS AND SEXUAL ASSAULT LAW

Given the wealth of case evidence detailing sexist interpretations of consent, it seems ill-advised to rely on so-called objective facts to determine consent. By directing us to attend to such "facts" as behavior and utterances, and ignoring the social character of these so-called facts, the performative account of consent falls prey to the same concerns that bedevil objective standards of reasonableness in the law generally. When determining whether the accused's conduct is reasonable, one must ask whose standard is being applied (Bronitt, 1994: 252). The suggestion that there are objective standards presupposes a community consensus on what constitutes reasonable and unreasonable conduct. However, the standard of judgment typically employed is far from objective; rather it is constructed according to social and cultural values in a decidedly discretionary manner. Recently, both Canadian and American courts have responded to the discovery of sex bias in standards of reasonableness in self-defense law.[27] This sex bias has unjustly ignored the different perspectives of reasonableness among battered women who have been forced to kill their abusive husbands in self-defense. To address this problem, legal theorists have attempted to reconceive standards of reasonableness according to a gender-sensitive perspective.[28] A similar effort would have to be made by anyone seeking to use performances, such as behavior or utterances, as indicators of consent. Sexist standards of what counts as consensual behavior must be replaced by more appropriate standards.

The suggestion that the performative account of consent is not immune to the influence of sexist attitudes will come as a great disappointment to its proponents. One of the putative merits of such an account was that it moved consent from the realm of the subjective, where it was a matter of either the complainant's or the defendant's perspective, to the realm of the objective, where it could be observed as an object in the world. The problem is that the public realm is just as susceptible to bias as the personal realm. How we interpret the so-called objective facts about behavior and situations, as we have seen, is often a matter of personal perspectives and cultural stereotypes.

A MEANINGFUL CONCEPTION OF CONSENT

A "meaningful consent" standard requires that we combine features of both the performative and the attitudinal accounts of consent. The performative account is right to hold that consent must be communicated in a publicly recognizable fashion: since attitudes by themselves cannot change the prevailing pattern of rights and obligations, it seems clear that a positive attitude is not sufficient proof of consent. Even so, attending solely to behavior and utterances does not always settle the matter of consent—genuine consent requires that the agent's outward behavior be in sympathy with her internal motivations. Moreover, we have seen that performances can be normatively ambiguous: not only do we often disagree on the significance of behavior and utterances, but sometimes feigned or coerced consent is behaviorally indistinguishable from genuine consent. In many cases, we will have to appeal to the consenting agent's attitude toward the act of consent to determine the matter.

In summary, to determine the matter of consent to sex we must first attend to the consenting agent's behavior and utterances; anything less than an affirmative expression of willingness to participate in sexual relations should be regarded as nonconsent. Second, we must be cognizant of the critical role that attitudes play in consent—while a negative attitude towards the object of consent will not invalidate consent, a negative attitude towards the act of consent will. Third, and most important, a meaningful consent standard requires that we examine the context in which consent was granted. Even if a woman says "yes," there remains the difficulty of determining whether the circumstances in which she expressed consent invalidated the consent. Coercion can take many forms. By focusing only on external behavior, such as force and threats, the performative model cannot account for the many subtle ways in which a woman's will may be overcome. Consent is more than just a matter of what one says or does, but is intimately connected to the range of choices available to us. These constraints on sexual autonomy can only be fully appreciated by attending to the context of the situation—we must examine the relationship between the parties, and consider the woman's perspective on the range and kinds of options available to her.

Finally, consent should be treated as the defining feature of the crime of sexual assault. The determination of factors that vitiate consent requires that we make some difficult decisions about which constraints on sexual autonomy should be viewed as illegitimate (that is, we will have to decide what forms of extortion, abuse of power or authority, fraud, misrepresentation, or deception should count as illegitimate). Indeed, our determination may be that not all constraints on sexual autonomy should fall into the category of sexual assault—some constraints might be more suitably treated under a separate category of offense, such as "nonviolent sexual misconduct." And, in cases where we determine that illegitimate infringements vitiate consent to sex, we still must decide whether the question of culpability should take into account whether the defendant was (or should have been) aware of the presence of such infringements. These and other considerations must be addressed if we hope to articulate a "meaningful consent" standard that respects individual sexual autonomy.

Rape, Genocide, and Women's Human Rights

CATHARINE A. MACKINNON

Human rights have not been women's rights—not in theory or in reality, not legally or socially, not domestically or internationally. Rights that human beings have by virtue of being human have not been rights to which women have had access, nor have violations of women as such been part of the definition of the violation of the human as such on which human rights law has traditionally been predicated.

This is not because women's human rights have not been violated. The eliding of women in the human rights setting happens in two ways. When women are violated like men who are otherwise like them—when women's arms and legs are cut and bleed like the arms and legs of men; when women, with men, are shot in pits and gassed in vans; when women's bodies are hidden with men's at the bottom of abandoned mines; when women's and men's skulls are sent from Auschwitz to Strasbourg for experiments—these atrocities are not marked in the history of violations of women's human rights. The women are counted as Argentinean or Honduran or Jewish—which, of course, they are. When what happens to women also happens to men, like being beaten and disappearing and being tortured to death, the fact that those it happened to are *women* is not registered in the record of human atrocity.

Reprinted from *Harvard Women's Law Journal* 17 (1994), copyright © 1994 by the President and Fellows of Harvard College. Earlier versions of this article were delivered at the UN World Conference on Human Rights, Vienna, on June 17, 1993, and at the Zagreb Law School on June 25, 1993. The intellectual and research collaboration of Natalie Nenadic and Asja Armanda, all the women of Kareta Feminist Group, and the survivors made this work possible.

The other way violations of women are obscured is this: when no war has been declared, and life goes on in a state of everyday hostilities, women are beaten by men to whom we are close. Wives disappear from supermarket parking lots. Prostitutes float up in rivers or turn up under piles of rags in abandoned buildings. These atrocities are not counted as human rights violations, their victims as the *desaparecidos* of everyday life. In the record of human rights violations they are overlooked entirely, because the victims are women and what was done to them smells of sex. When a woman is tortured in an Argentine prison cell, even as it is forgotten that she is a woman, it is seen that her human rights are violated because what is done to her is also done to men. Her suffering has the dignity, and her death the honor, of a crime against humanity. But when a woman is tortured by her husband in her home, humanity is not violated. Here she is a woman—but *only* a woman. Her violation outrages the conscience of few beyond her friends.

What is done to women is either too specific to women to be seen as human or too generic to human beings to be seen as specific to women. Atrocities committed against women are either too human to fit the notion of female or too female to fit the notion of human. "Human" and "female" are mutually exclusive by definition; you cannot be a woman and a human being at the same time.

Women are violated in many ways in which men are violated. But women are also violated in ways men are not, or that are exceptional for men. Many of these sex-specific violations are sexual and reproductive.

Women are violated sexually and reproductively every day in every country in the world. The notion that these acts violate women's human rights has been created by women, not states or governments. Women have created the idea that women have human rights out of a refusal to believe that the reality of violation we live with is what it means for us to be human— as our governments seem largely to believe.

Women have created the idea of women's human rights by refusing to abandon ourselves and each other, out of attachment to a principle of our own humanity—one defined against nearly everything around us, against nearly everything we have lived through, certainly not by transcending the reality of our violations, but by refusing to deny their reality as violations. In this project, women have learned that one day of real experience is worth volumes of all of their theories. If we believed the existing approaches to human rights, we would not believe we had any. We have learned to look at the reality of women's lives first and to hold human rights law accountable to what we need, rather than to look at human rights law to see how much of what happens to women can be fit into it, as we are taught to do as lawyers.

In pursuit of this reality-based approach, consider one situation of the mass violation of women's human rights now occurring in the heart of Europe. In this campaign of extermination, which began with the Serbian invasion of Croatia in 1991 and exploded in the Serbian aggression against Bosnia and Herzegovina in 1992, evidence documents that women are being sexually and reproductively violated on a mass scale, as a matter of conscious policy, in pursuit of a genocide through war.

In October 1992 I received a communication from an American researcher of Croatian and Bosnian descent working with refugees and gathering information on this war. She said that Serbian forces had exterminated Croatians and Muslims in the hundreds of thousands "in an operation they've coined 'ethnic cleansing'"; that in this genocide thousands of Muslim and Croatian girls and women were raped and made forcibly pregnant in settings including Serbian-run concentration camps, of which "about twenty are solely rape/death camps for Muslim and Croatian women and children."[1] She had received reports of the making and use of pornography as part of the genocide. "One Croatian woman described being tortured by electric shocks and gang-raped in a camp by Serbian men dressed in Croatian uniforms who filmed the rapes and forced her to 'confess' on film that Croatians had raped her."[2] She also reported that some United Nations troops were targeting women:

> In the streets of Zagreb, UN troops often ask local women how much they cost. There are reports of refugee women being forced to sexually service the UN troops to receive aid. Tomorrow I talk to two survivors of mass rape—thirty men per day for over three months. We've heard the UN passed a resolution to collect evidence as the first step for a war crime trial, but it is said here that there is no precedent for trying sexual atrocities.[3]

Whether or not these practices are formally illegal—and it is easy to say with complacency that rape, prostitution, pornography, and sexual murder are illegal—they are widely permitted under both domestic and international law. They are allowed, whether understood, one man to another, as an excess of passion in peace or the spoils of victory in war, or as the liberties, civil or otherwise, of their perpetrators. They are legally rationalized, officially winked at, and in some instances formally condoned. Whether or not they are regarded as crimes, in no country in the world are they recognized as violations of the human rights of their victims.

This war exemplifies how existing approaches to violations of women's rights can serve to confuse who is doing what to whom and thus can cover up and work to condone atrocities. These atrocities also give an urgency, if any was needed, to the project of reenvisioning human rights so that violations of humanity include what happens to women.

The war against Croatia and Bosnia-Herzegovina, and their partial occupation, is being carried out by Serbian forces in collaboration with the Serbian regime in Belgrade, governing what remains of Yugoslavia. This is an international war. All the state parties have adopted relevant laws of nations that prohibit these acts; they are covered in any case by customary international law and *jus cogens* (in codified form).[4] Yet so far nothing has been invoked to stop these abuses or to hold their perpetrators accountable. The excuses offered for this lack of action are illuminating.

In this war, the fact of Serbian aggression is beyond question, just as the fact of male aggression against women is beyond question, both here and in everyday life. "Ethnic cleansing" is a euphemism for genocide. It is a policy of ethnic extermination of non-Serbs with the aim of "all Serbs in one nation," a clearly announced goal of "Greater Serbia," of territorial conquest and aggrandizement. That this is a war against non-Serbian civilians, not between advancing and retreating armies, is also beyond question. Yet this war of aggression—once admitted to exist at all—has repeatedly been construed as bilateral, as a civil war or an ethnic conflict, to the accompaniment of much international head-scratching about why people cannot seem to get along and a lot of pious clucking about the human rights violations of "all sides" as if they were comparable. This three-pronged maneuver is familiar to those who work with the issue of rape: blame women for getting ourselves raped by men we know, chastise us for not liking them very well afterward, and then criticize our lack of neutrality in not considering rapes of men to be a comparable emergency.

One result of this approach is that the rapes in this war are not grasped as either a strategy in genocide or a practice of misogyny, far less both at once. They are not understood as continuous both with this particular ethnic war of aggression and with the gendered war or aggression of everyday life. Genocide does not come from nowhere, nor does rape as a ready and convenient tool of it. Nor is a continuity an equation. These rapes are to everyday rape what the Holocaust was to everyday anti-Semitism. Without everyday anti-Semitism a Holocaust is impossible, but anyone who has lived through a pogrom knows the difference.

What is happening here is first a genocide, in which ethnicity is a tool for political hegemony; the war is an instrument of the genocide; the rapes are an instrument of the war. The Bosnian Serbs under the command of Radovan Karadžic do not control the state; their war is against the people and the democratically elected government of Bosnia-Herzegovina. If you control the state and want to commit genocide, as the Nazis did under the

Third Reich, you do not need a war. You do it with the state mechanisms at hand. This is being done now, quietly, to Hungarians and Croatians in occupied eastern Croatia and in Vojvodina, formerly an autonomous region now annexed to Serbia.[5] This is virtually invisible to the world.

Now consider the situation of the Albanians in Kosova. They are surrounded; they are within a state. When Serbia moves on them militarily, going beyond the segregation and oppression they suffer now, it may not look like a war to anyone else. It will not cross international borders, the way much international law wants to see before it feels violated. But it will be another facet of the campaign to eliminate non-Serbs from areas targeted for "cleansing," a genocide.

To call such campaigns to exterminate non-Serbs "civil war" is like calling the Holocaust a civil war between German Aryans and German Jews. If and when the reality in Vojvodina comes out, or Albanians are "cleansed," perhaps that too will be packaged for Western consumption as ancient ethnic hatreds, a bog like Vietnam, or some other formulation to justify doing nothing about it.

In this genocide through war, mass rape is a tool, a tactic, a policy, a plan, a strategy, as well as a practice. Muslim and Croatian women and girls are raped, then often killed, by Serbian military men, regulars and irregulars, in a variety of formations, in their homes, on hillsides, in camps—camps that used to be factories, schools, farms, mines, sports arenas, post offices, restaurants, hotels, or houses of prostitution. The camps can be outdoor enclosures of barbed wire or buildings where people are held, beaten, and killed and where women, and sometimes men, are raped. Sometimes the women are also raped after they are killed. Some of these camps are rape/death camps exclusively for women, organized like the brothels of what is called peacetime, sometimes in locations that were brothels before the war.

In the West, the sexual atrocities have been discussed largely as rape *or* as genocide, not as what they are, which is rape as genocide, rape directed toward women because they are Muslim or Croatian. It is as if people cannot think more than one thought at once. The mass rape is either part of a campaign by Serbia against non-Serbia, or an onslaught by combatants against civilians, or an attack by men against women, but never all at the same time. Or—this is the feminist version of the whitewash—these atrocities are presented as just another instance of aggression by all men against all women all the time. If this were the opening volley in a counter-offensive against rape as a war against all women, it would be one thing. But the way it works here is the opposite: to make sure that no one who cares about rape takes a side in *this* war against *these* particular rapes. It does not so much galvanize opposition to rape whenever and wherever it occurs, but rather obscures the fact that these rapes are being done by *some* men against *certain* women for specific reasons, here and now. The point seems to be to obscure, by any means available, exactly who is doing what to whom and why.

The result is that these rapes are grasped in either their ethnic or religious particularity, as attacks on a culture, meaning men, or in their sex specificity, meaning as attacks on women. But not as both at once. Attacks on women, it seems, cannot define attacks on people. If they are gendered attacks, they are not ethnic; if they are ethnic attacks, they are not gendered. One cancels the other. But when a rape is a genocidal act, as it is here, it is an act to destroy a people. What is done to women defines that destruction. Also, aren't women a people?

These rapes have also been widely treated as an inevitable by-product of armed conflict. Every time there is a war, there is rape. Of course, rape does occur in all wars, both within and between all sides. As to rape on one's own side, aggression elsewhere is always sustained by corresponding levels of suppression and manipulation at home. Then, when the army comes back, it visits on the women at home the escalated level of assault the men were taught and practiced on women in the war zone. The United States knows this well from the war in Vietnam. Men's domestic violence against women of the same ethnicity escalated—including their skill at inflicting torture without leaving visible marks. But sexual aggression against Asian women through prostitution and pornography exploded in the United States: American men got a particular taste for violating them over there. This must be happening to Serbian women now.

Rape *is* a daily act by men against women; it is always an act of domination by men over women. But the role of these rapes in this genocidal war of aggression is a matter of fact, not of ideological spin. It means that Muslim and Croatian women are facing two layers of men on top of them rather than one, one layer engaged in exterminating the other, and two layers of justification—"just war" and "just life." Add the representation of this war as a civil war among equal aggressors, and these women are facing three times the usual number of reasons for the world to do nothing about it.

All the cover-ups ignore the fact that this is a genocide. The "civil war" cover-up obscures the role of Belgrade in invading first Croatia, then Bosnia-Herzegovina, and now in occupying parts of both. A civil war is not an invasion by another country. If this is a civil war, neither Croatia nor Bosnia-Herzegovina is a nation, but they are both recognized as such. In a civil war, aggression is mutual. This is not a reciprocal genocide. Muslims and Croatians are not advancing and retreating into and out of Serbia. They are not carrying out genocide against Serbs on their own territories. There are no concentration camps for Serbs in Sarajevo or Zagreb. The term "civil war" translates, in all languages, as "not my problem." In construing this situation as a civil war at bottom, the international community has defined it in terms of what it has been willing to do about it.

It is not that there are no elements of common culture here, at least as imposed through decades of Communist rule, meaning Serbian hegemony. It is not that there are no conflicts between or within sides, or shifting of sides in complex ways. It is not that the men on one side rape and the men on the other side do not. It is, rather, that none of these factors defines this emergency, none of them created it, none of them is driving it, and none of them explains it. Defining it in these terms is a smoke screen, a propaganda tool, whether sincere or cynical, behind which Serbia continues to expand its territory by exterminating people and raping women en masse.

The feminist version of the cover-up is particularly useful to the perpetrators because it seems to acknowledge the atrocities—which are hard to deny (although they do that too)—and appears to occupy the ground on which women have effectively aroused outrage against them. But its function is to exonerate the rapists and to deflect intervention. If all men do this all the time, especially in war, how can one pick a side in this one? And since all men do this all the time, war or no war, why do anything special about this now? This war becomes just a form of business as usual (Brownmiller, 1994: 180). But genocide is not business as usual—not even for men.

This is often accompanied by a blanket critique of "nationalism" as if identification with the will to exterminate can be equated with identification with the will to survive extermination; as if an ethnic concept of nation (like the Serbian fascist one) is the same as a multiethnic concept of nation (like the Bosnian one); and as if those who are being killed because of the nation they belong to should find some loftier justification for staying alive than a national survival.

Like all rape, genocidal rape is particular as well as part of the generic, and its particularity matters. This is ethnic rape as an official policy of war in a genocidal campaign for political control. That means not only a policy of the pleasure of male power unleashed, which happens all the time in so-called peace; not only a policy to defile, torture, humiliate, degrade, and demoralize the other side, which happens all the time in war; and not only a policy of men posturing to gain advantage and ground over other men. It is specifically rape under orders. This is not rape out of control. It is rape under control. It is also rape unto death, rape as massacre, rape to kill and to make the victims wish they were dead. It is rape as an instrument of forced exile, rape to make you leave your home and never want to go back. It is rape to be seen and heard and watched and told to others: rape as spectacle. It is rape to drive a wedge through a community, to shatter a society, to destroy a people. It is rape as genocide.

It is also rape made sexy for the perpetrators by the power of the rapist, which is absolute, to select the victims at will. They walk into rooms of captive women and point, "you, you, and you," and take you out. Many never return. It is rape made more arousing by the ethnic hostility against the designated "enemy," made to feel justified by the notion that it is "for Serbia," which they say as they thrust into the women and make them sing patriotic songs.[6] It is rape made to seem right by decades of lies about the supposed behavior of that enemy—years and years of propaganda campaigns, including in schools, full of historical lies and falsified data. In this effort, rapes and murders carried out by Serbs against non-Serbs are presented to the Serbian population on television as rapes and murders of Serbs by Muslims and Croats. The way in which pornography is believed in the men's bodies as well as in their minds gives this war propaganda a special potency.

This is also rape made especially exciting for the perpetrators by knowing that there are no limits on what they can do, by knowing that these women can and will be raped to death. Although the orders provide motivation enough, the rapes are made sexually enjoyable, irresistible even, by the fact that the women are about to be sacrificed, by the powerlessness of the women and children in the face of their imminent murder at the hands of their rapists. This is murder as the ultimate sexual act.

It will not help to say that this is violence, not sex, for the men involved. When the men are told to take the women away and not bring them back, first they rape them, then they kill them, and then sometimes rape them again and cut off their breasts and tear out their wombs (Džombic, 1992). One woman was allowed to live only as long as she kept her Serbian captor hard all night orally, night after night after night, from midnight to 5:00 A.M. What he got was sex for him. The aggression was the sex.

This is rape as torture as well as rape as extermination. In the camps, it is at once mass rape and serial rape in a way that is indistinguishable from prostitution. Prostitution is that part of everyday non-war life that is closest to what we see done to women in this war. The daily life of prostituted women consists of serial rape, war or no war. The brothel-like arrangement of the rape/death camps parallels the brothels of so-called peacetime: captive women impounded to be passed from man to man in order to be raped.

This is also rape as a policy of ethnic uniformity and ethnic conquest, of annexation and expansion, of acquisition by one nation of other nations. It is rape because a Serb wants your apartment. Most distinctively, this is rape as ethnic expansion through forced reproduction. African-American women were forcibly impregnated through rape under slavery. The Nazis required Eastern European women to get special permission for abortions if impregnated by German men.[7] In genocide, it is more usual for the babies on the other side to be killed. Croatian and Muslim women are being raped, and then denied abortions, to help make a Serbian state by making Serbian babies (Džombic, 1992).

If this were a racial rape, as Americans are familiar with it, the children would be regarded as polluted, dirty, and contaminated even as they are sometimes given comparative privileges based on "white" blood. But because this is ethnic rape, lacking racial markers, the children are regarded by the aggressors as somehow clean and purified, as "cleansed" ethnically. The babies made with Muslim and Croatian women are regarded as Serbian babies. The idea seems to be to create a fifth column within Muslim and Croatian society of children—all sons?—who will rise up and join their fathers. Much Serbian fascist ideology simply adopts and adapts Nazi views. This one is the ultimate achievement of the Nazi ideology that culture is genetic.

The spectacle of the United Nations troops violating those they are there to protect adds a touch of the perverse. My correspondent added that some United Nations troops are participating in raping Muslim and Croatian women taken from Serb-run rape/death camps. She reports that "the UN presence has apparently increased the trafficking in women and girls through the opening of brothels, brothel-massage parlours, peep shows, and the local production of pornographic films."[8] There are also reports that a former United Nations Protection Force (UNPROFOR) commander accepted offers from a Serbian commander to bring him Muslim girls for sexual use.[9] All this is an example of the male bond across official lines. It pointedly poses a problem women have always had with male protection: who is going to watch the men who are watching the men who are supposedly watching out for us? Each layer of male protection adds a layer to violence against women. Perhaps intervention by a force of armed women should be considered.

Now, the use of media technology is highly developed. Before, the Nazis took pictures of women in camps, forced women into brothels in camps, and took pictures of naked women running to their deaths. They also created events that did not happen through media manipulation. In this war the aggressors have at hand the new cheap, mobile, accessible, and self-contained moving-picture technology. The saturation of what was Yugoslavia with pornography upon the dissolution of communism—pornography that was largely controlled by Serbs, who had the power—has created a population of men prepared to experience sexual pleasure in torturing and killing women. It also paved the way for the use on television of footage of actual rapes, with the ethnicity of the victims and perpetrators switched, to inflame Serbs against Muslims and Croatians (MacKinnon, 1993b: 24–30). In the conscious and open use of pornography, in making pornography of atrocities, in the sophisticated use of pornography as war propaganda, this is perhaps the first truly modern war.

Although these facts flagrantly violate provision after provision of international law, virtually nothing has been done about them for well over two years. Now the international machinery seems finally to be lumbering into action, even as more men, women, and children are being liquidated daily. To explain this slow response, it is important to consider that most human rights instruments empower states to act against states, not individuals or groups to act for themselves. This is particularly odd given that international human rights law recognizes only violations of human rights by state actors. In other words, only entities like those who do the harm are empowered to act to stop them. It would have seemed clear after 1945 that states often violate the rights of those who are not states and who have no state to act for them. The existing structure of international law was substantially created in response to this. Yet its architects could not bring themselves to empower individuals and groups to act against individuals, groups, or states when their human rights were violated.[10]

This problem is particularly severe for women's human rights because women are typically raped not by governments but by what are called individual men. The government just does nothing about it. This may be tantamount to being raped by the state, but it is legally seen as "private," therefore as not a human rights violation. In an international world order in which only states can violate human rights, most rape is left out. The role of the state in permitting women to be raped with impunity can be exposed, but the structural problem in addressing it remains.

There is a convergence here between ways of thinking about women and ways of thinking about international law and politics. The more a conflict can be framed as within a state—as a civil war, as domestic, as private—the less effective the human rights model becomes. The closer a fight comes to home, the more "feminized" the victims become, no matter what their gender, and the less likely it is that international human rights will be found violated, no matter what was done.[11] Croatia and Bosnia-Herzegovina are being treated like women,[12] women gang-raped on a mass scale. This is not an analogy; far less is it a suggestion that this rape is wrong only because the women belong to a man's state. It identifies the treatment of a whole polity by the treatment of the women there.[13]

In the structure of international human rights, based as it is on the interest of states in their sovereignty as such, no state has an incentive to break rank by going after another state for how it treats women—thus setting a standard of human rights treatment for women that no state is prepared to meet within its own borders or is willing to be held to internationally. When men sit in rooms, being states, they are largely being men. They protect each other; they identify with each other; they try not to limit each other in ways they themselves do not want to be limited. In other words, they do not represent women. There is no state we can point to and say, "This state effectively guarantees women's human rights. There we are free and equal."

In this statist structure, each state's lack of protection of women's human rights is internationally protected, and that is called protecting state sovereignty. A similar structure of insulation between women and accountability for their violations exists domestically. Raped women are compelled to go to the state; men make the laws and decide if they will enforce them. When women are discriminated against, they have to go to a human rights commission and try to get it to move. This is called protecting the community. It is the same with international human rights, only more so: only the state can hurt you, but to redress it you have to get the state to act for you. In international law there are a few exceptions to this, but in the current emergency in Bosnia-Herzegovina and Croatia they are of no use. Each state finds its reasons to do nothing, which can be read as not wanting to set a higher standard of accountability for atrocities to women than those they are prepared to be held to themselves.

Formally, wartime is an exception to the part of this picture that exempts most rape, because atrocities by soldiers against civilians are always considered state acts. The trouble has been that men do in war what they do in peace, only more so, so when it comes to women, the complacency that surrounds peacetime extends to wartime, no matter what the law says. Every country in this world has a legal obligation to stop the Serbian aggressors from doing what they are doing, but until Bosnia-Herzegovina went to the International Court of Justice and sued Serbia for genocide, including rape, no one did a thing.[14] In so doing, Bosnia-Herzegovina is standing up for women in a way that no state ever has. The survivors I work with also filed their own civil suit in New York against Karadžic for an injunction against genocide, rape, torture, forced pregnancy, forced prostitution, and other sex and ethnic discrimination that violates women's international human rights.[15]

A war crimes tribunal to enforce accountability for mass genocidal rape is being prepared by the United Nations.[16] There are precedents in the Tokyo trials after World War II for command responsibility for mass rape. Beyond precedent, the voices of the victims have been heard in the structuring of the new tribunal. To my knowledge, no one asked Jewish survivors how the trials at Nuremberg should be conducted, nor do I think the women raped in Nanking were asked what they needed in order to be able to testify about their rapes. The issue of accountability to victims has been raised here formally for the first time: how can we create a war crimes tribunal that is accessible to victims of mass sexual atrocity? What will make it possible for victims of genocidal rape to speak about their violations?

The genocidal rapes of this war present the world with an historic opportunity: that this becomes the time and place, and these the women, when the world recognizes that violence against women violates human rights. That when a women is raped, the humanity of a human being is recognized to be violated. When the world says never again—not in war, not in peace—and this time means it.

SECTION 2

DOMESTIC VIOLENCE

Standards of Perfection and Battered Women's Self-defense

WANDA TEAYS

> The privilege, ancient though it may be, to beat her with a stick, to pull her hair, choke her, spit in her face, or kick her about the floor, or to inflict upon her like indignities is not now acknowledged by our law.
>
> —*Fulgham v. State*, 46 Ala. 143, 146–47 (1871)

In this country a woman is "more likely to be assaulted, injured, raped, or killed by a male partner than by any other type of assailant" (Madden, 1993: 45). It is estimated that a woman is battered every fifteen seconds and that 23 percent of pregnant women suffer battering (Hanson, 1993: 53). These personal assaults are the number one cause of injury to women—more than rapes, muggings, and auto accidents combined. The current estimate is that 42 percent of women who are murdered are killed by husbands or boyfriends—approximately 1,500 women each year.

In the majority of cases where women were murdered by partners, there had been some warning. For example, "a review of homicide records in two American cities found that, in 85–90% of the cases of homicide between domestic partners the police had been called to a home in response to a domestic disturbance at least once during the two years that preceded the homicide; in 54% of the cases, the police had been called five times or more" (*Harvard Law Review*, 1993: 1581). Battered women often seek a stronger police response than they receive. Sayoko Blodgett-Ford cites a study that "eighty-two percent of battered women requested that their batterer be arrested but police arrested only fourteen percent of these batterers" (1993: 533).

Battered women have reason to fear their batterers: "over two-thirds of battered women have been told by their attackers that they would kill them" (Hanson, 1993: 36). They often endure a catch-22 situation: they can live with violence or they can attempt to leave and, potentially at least, face even greater violence or death. The greatest danger battered women face is when they attempt to separate from their abuser (Blodgett-Ford, 1993: 259; Hanson, 1993: 33).

The social context offers little encouragement. The FBI and other law enforcement experts contend that wife abuse is the most unreported crime in the United States (Schneider, 1992: 230). Battered women are often seen as mentally impaired. Or masochistic. We see this suggested in *People v. Powell*, where the court states: "a battered woman does not like the beatings but likes the loving behavior which occurs after the beating and she becomes submissive and passive" (Schneider, 1992: 218). Presumably the "loving behavior" rather than the battering is the reason the woman becomes "submissive and passive."

Such views ignore the broader social context, with its complex messages about gender bias and role expectations. The implication that women tolerate battering so they can receive "loving behavior" afterward grossly oversimplifies the abusive relationship and the way violence gradually escalates. It also overlooks the ways women are encouraged to take responsibility for the man's violent behavior, and the obstacles that block escape. Battered women are discouraged from leaving or become too terrified by threats to leave.

Such threats are often aimed at those close to the woman (such as children and parents), forcing her to weigh risks to herself against risks to them. Even when she does leave, often she returns because of the paucity of resources. An estimated 70 percent of women are turned away from shelters because of overcrowding (Hanson, 1993: 37).

Legislation directly addressing protection from battering has been left totally to the states: "The absence of federal guidelines in the realm of enforcement creates a situation in which the states have been left to establish their own" (Lengyel, 1990: 60). As of 1990 Arkansas, Delaware, New Mexico, and Puerto Rico had no legislation addressing domestic violence.

Courts and legislators have been lax in their treatment of batterers. We see this reflected in the statement of the New Jersey legislature: "The Legislature finds that battered adults presently experience substantial difficulty in gaining access to protection from the judicial system, particularly due to that system's inability to generate a prompt response in an emergency situation" (Lengyel, 1990: 61). Of 19,350 defendants who appeared in Cook County (Chicago) Domestic Violence Court in 1989, only 1,331 were convicted and only eighty-seven of these were given jail terms (Burleigh, 1990: 1).

Michael Dowd notes the disturbing historical blindness to the problem of battering: "In many parts of Europe, a man could kill his wife without penalty well into the 1600's. By contrast, a wife who killed her husband was penalized as if she had committed treason because her act of homicide was considered analogous to murdering the king. . . . English common law sanctioned wife-beating under the infamous 'rule of thumb' which decreed that a man might use a 'rod not thicker than his thumb' with which to chastise his wife" (1992: 568). By 1910 only thirty-five states had passed reform legislation classifying wife-beating as an assault (Dowd, 1992: 568). Furthermore, throughout most of the nineteenth century, state courts provided few avenues for addressing domestic violence, and judges gave husbands dominion over wives and children (Minow, 1990: 270). As Martha Minow observes, the result of a policy of "nonintervention" by the state bolstered the authority of the man (Ibid.: 276); thus the battered woman has had limited options. Not until the 1970s and 1980s did courts and legislatures change the view that family disputes were off limits for the state (Ibid.: 272).

The police have a poor record of handling domestic violence calls. The *Harvard Law Review* reports that the police "often fail to respond to domestic disturbance calls, are unlikely to make an arrest when they do respond and emphasize mediation of disputes" (1993: 1581). Don Kates observes that the traditional function of the police has been to deter crime or apprehend criminals after the crime has been committed; the police do not function as bodyguards and "courts have frequently held that the police have no duty to protect individual citizens" (as quoted in Blodgett-Ford, 1993: 532). As a result, women have been ill-equipped to stop escalating violence.

Dowd hypothesizes that recent changes in arresting wife beaters comes "less out of concern for the individual woman than as a result of lawsuits based on equal protection claims for a failure to protect" (1992: 569). However, the importance of police response in affecting behavior needs to be acknowledged: "Data from a National Crime Survey shows that only 15% of victims who called the police following a domestic violence attack were attacked again within an average of six months, while 41% who did not call the police were attacked again" (Murphy, 1992: 399).

Perhaps the fundamental problem is that "battered women have known that they could expect little protection from a society made up of individuals who resembled, at least in thought, the men who beat them" (Dowd,

1992: 569). Wife battering and murder take place in a social context that has considered the wife subservient to and, in terms of social status, derivative of the husband.

For example, it wasn't until the 1970s that testimony about the battered wife syndrome was introduced in criminal trials. Previously, the topic was neither studied nor seriously discussed in academic circles (Andersen and Read-Andersen, 1992: 374). Such concepts as marital rape are still not recognized across the board, though one element of wife battering is sexual assault. "Some states," Dowd notes, "require physical injury to accompany the rape, while North Carolina and Oklahoma still view marital rape as no crime at all" (1992: 569).

One reason domestic violence, incest, and marital rape have been so badly handled legally and socially is that we have erected walls around the arena where it generally takes place—the home. That is, the premium placed on rights of privacy means certain actions have fallen outside the public eye. And we have been very reluctant to change that; for to do so has been seen as a violation of privacy and of the perceived need to keep the government "off our backs."

We need to look at our predisposition to separate the public and private in such definitive ways—ways that result in deeply held policies about the sanctity of the home. As a society, we are reluctant to interfere with "private" behavior, short of murder, that goes on behind the closed doors of citizens' homes. This situation may be illustrated by looking at the Supreme Court ruling in the *DeShaney* child abuse case. Here the state was not held responsible or liable for failing to act on a case of child abuse, even though it had been brought to the state's attention long before the beating that resulted in brain damage and paralysis for Joshua DeShaney. Dissenting Justices Brennan and Blackmun decried the Court's "sterile formalism" and, as Justice Blackmun noted, the resulting failure to see a duty on the part of the state to actively intervene and "aid the boy once the State learned of the severe danger to which he was exposed" (*DeShaney v. Winnebago County Department of Social Services*, 1012).

Justice Blackmun remarked that "the Fourteenth Amendment precedent may be read more broadly or narrowly depending upon how one chooses to read it. Faced with the choice, I would adopt a 'sympathetic' reading, one which comports with dictates of fundamental justice and recognizes that compassion need not be exiled from the province of judging" (*DeShaney v. Winnebago County Department of Social Services*, 1012). Justice dictates that human rights considerations not be forsaken for the right of privacy. Compassion calls for us to reexamine our assumptions and our approach to the forms of cruelty that take place in the privacy of the home, whether the issue is child abuse or spousal abuse.

A home may be a "castle" for the man, but it is potentially a torture chamber for his victims. Sharon Angella Allard notes:

> The Anglo-American legal tradition initially viewed women as property. This view was based on the patriarchal gender stereotypes of active, masculine, powerful, and authoritative men and passive, feminine, powerless, and deferential women . . . . British jurist William Blackstone held that men were responsible for the actions of their wives and therefore authorized to control them. Included within men's responsibility was a duty to protect their wives. Therefore, "good" women were not expected to have to defend themselves in any fashion. Women were certainly not permitted to kill their protectors for any reason. (1991: 198)

(Allard contends that the stereotypes and assumptions underlying this critique render black women, perceived as "bad" or immoral and not deserving of any male protection, an exception. Exploitation and abuse of women of color is tied to stereotypical thinking that made them more vulnerable to violence, as well as to societal prohibitions that gave a degree of protection for white women [1991: 196].)

Battered women have very few resources when violence occurs. Some women are driven to kill. Elizabeth Bochnak remarks that "lack of adequate police protection creates a situation in which a woman may feel it necessary to respond in self-defense to a potentially lethal battery or sexual assault. Ironically, the same court and law enforcement system will prosecute her for responding in the only manner left open to her" (1981: 12).

When all the avenues of response are exhausted, it is no wonder some women will respond with a fatal counterattack. In the sections that follow, I examine the ways in which the legal system has reacted to women who killed their abusers. I look at the question of justifying, in contrast to excusing, the murder, followed by an examination of the imperfect self-defense. Finally I ask whether the traditional concept of self-defense can be applied to the battered woman who kills an abusive mate.

JUSTIFICATION AND EXCUSE

Our notions of justification and excuse are caught up with our concept of moral agency. We consider someone to be a moral agent if he or she is a competent adult—that is, one who can comprehend the difference between right and wrong, be held responsible for decisions freely made, and thereby be held accountable for actions taken under noncoercive circumstances. Only moral agents can make justifiable decisions or actions. A dog that chases the postal worker up the street would not be thought to be justified in its behavior, since we do not ordinarily consider a dog to be capable of rational thought and moral reasoning. On the other hand, we could excuse the dog's behavior, since we might understand how it happened (say, the postal worker taunted the dog).

We typically say that an action is excusable if it can be understood in light of the circumstances, but otherwise falls outside of the realm of rational thought. We might excuse a battered woman who kills her abuser if we could say she was overcome by rage or passion, causing her to be temporarily insane or mentally incapacitated. Or we might excuse her if she had something like an irresistible impulse (as in the case of Lorena Bobbitt) which overcame her ability to control her behavior.

Elizabeth Schneider puts the distinction this way: "Self-defense as justification focuses on the act of defending oneself; it rests on a determination that the act was right because of its circumstances. In contrast, a finding of excuse, like insanity or heat of passion, focuses on the actor; it is a finding that the act, although wrong, should be tolerated because of the actor's characteristics or state of mind" (1992: 233).

The excuse, then, may take two different forms: cognitive deficiency and volitional deficiency. We can excuse someone if she did not realize she violated the law (defective cognition) or cannot prevent herself from breaking it (defective volition). Defective cognition is often defended with an insanity plea, where someone argues she didn't know her conduct was wrong. Defective volition often involves an act committed under duress, as with death threats, where the normal ability to control one's conduct would be disrupted (Coughlin, 1994: 15). Either one of these defenses might be employed in excusing a battered woman who kills.

The courts have often seen the battered woman as mentally impaired or having some other diminished capacity. In *State v. Hundley*, for example, battered women were judged to be "terror-stricken people whose mental state is distorted and bears a marked resemblance to that of a hostage or prisoner of war" (*Harvard Law Review*, 1993: 1592). In *People v. Torres* the court concluded: "Numbed by a dread of imminent aggression, these [battered] women are unable to think clearly about the means of escape from this abusive family existence; and [overcome by] emotional paralysis" (Schneider, 1992: 217). The expert in *People v. Emick* described the battered wife syndrome as a "multistage form of a family 'disease'" (Ibid.).

The court in *State v. Kelly* described the condition as "psychological torpor" (Anderson and Read-Anderson, 1992; 371).

All these decisions rest on the premise that the woman either momentarily or for some prolonged period lacks the mental capacity to judge the nature and character of her actions. In effect this denies the status of the woman as a moral agent. She would, therefore, not be subject to the judgment of the criminal law.

In order to assess her culpability, the defense frequently brings in experts on the "battered woman syndrome." The stages of this syndrome are "tension building," which involves relatively minor incidents of abuse, "acute battering incidents," and the "loving-contrite" stage, when the abuse ceases and pleas for forgiveness and promises of "never again" are made (Crocker, 1985: 128).

How much allowance, if any, should be made for victims of the battered woman syndrome is central. Dowd argues that "battered women sometimes suffer from some form of malady, like post-traumatic stress disorder, as a result of the continual violence" (1992: 577). Hon. Sheila Murphy speaks of the abusive home as a battlefield and notes that "the battered woman syndrome is comparable to the post-traumatic stress syndrome evidenced by veterans returning from Vietnam" (1992: 404). Anne Coughlin considers the brainwashing defense to be part of the anatomy of the battered woman syndrome, particularly if the syndrome is precipitated by "psychological abuse" (1994: 21).

Some argue that the battered woman syndrome sets the stage for "learned helplessness," brainwashing, or a similar loss of control over the victim's ability to think and act clearly. This explains the use of analogies comparing battered women to hostages, veterans, psychologically disabled people, prisoners of war, or concentration camp prisoners who learn to identify with guards to prolong survival. Irving Sloan claims that "legal writers dealing with this subject have been urged that menopause or Pre-Menstrual Syndrome may also have affected her emotional stability and state of mind" (1987: 32). The victim's excuse, then, becomes one based on a diminished capacity or duress (loss of control).

When behavior is excused, as opposed to justified, a problem is that the legal and moral consequences may be undesirable. If we consider the battered woman to be insane when she kills her abuser, than we perceive her to be a potentially dangerous, not reasonable, person. Schneider asserts that a battered woman syndrome defense "sounds like passivity or incapacity, it does not address the basic fact of the woman's action and contradicts a presentation of reasonableness" (1992: 218). Paul Robinson points out that "unlike most defendants who successfully offer a criminal defense, a defendant found not guilty by reason of insanity is rarely released after acquittal. It is more likely that he will be committed to a mental institution" (1984: 304). Thus resorting to an excuse as a defense may not benefit the defendant. If a woman is thought to be "maladjusted" when she strikes back at her abuser, the court may impose a prison sentence in order to attempt to "cure" or "rehabilitate" her.

We need to re-examine the wisdom of using such excuses as mental or emotional defects. Even if it gets the woman out of one predicament, such as a homicide charge, it may be at the cost of another serious predicament.

Our legal system puts considerable significance on individuals being held accountable for their behavior. Richard Boldt asserts that criminal law generally "regards the great bulk of human activity as having been produced through the agency of an individual's free will" (1992: 2245). As a result, individuals can be blamed only when they could have acted otherwise (Hart, 1968: 173). Conduct may be wrong, but an excuse represents a legal conclusion that criminal liability is inappropriate.

IMPERFECT SELF-DEFENSE

A great deal depends on whether the court considers self-defense to be "perfect" or "imperfect." A perfect self-defense entitles the defendant to an acquittal, whereas an imperfect self-defense merely reduces the grade of the offense to manslaughter.

When a battered woman who kills pursues an imperfect self-defense, this route carries a high probability of prison time (Creach, 1982: 615). Acquittal is clearly preferable. We therefore need to look closely at both imperfect self-defense and perfect self-defense in order to see which is the better path to recommend. If evidence can be presented about the context of the battering that led up to the woman killing the abuser, it would then seem that a perfect self-defense could be upheld. First, though, we need to understand what an imperfect self-defense entails and why it is not to be recommended.

An imperfect self-defense rests on an unreasonable belief in the imminence of a threat to life or great bodily harm, leading to the decision to defend oneself with lethal force. This defense mitigates murder to voluntary manslaughter. The California Supreme Court has asserted that this doctrine differs significantly from the doctrine of diminished capacity (*People v. Christian S.*, 6607).

"Murder is the unlawful killing of a human being, or a fetus, *with* malice aforethought" (California Penal Code, sect. 187). One of the key elements in the imperfect self-defense in *People v. Christian S.* is that the doctrine negated the malice requirement of a murder charge because of the defendant's honest belief that he was in danger. The issue in *Christian S.* was not that the defendant was unaware of his obligations to society, but that he (however unreasonably) perceived an imminent threat to his life after being harassed and threatened for a year by a skinhead. Feeling threatened enough to respond with deadly force need not be in any way related to a person's mental capacity. As the court ruled:

> The two doctrines [of diminished capacity and imperfect self-defense] relate to the concept of malice, but the similarity ends there. Unlike diminished capacity, imperfect self-defense is not rooted in any notion of mental capacity or awareness of the need to act lawfully. To the contrary, a person may be entirely free of any mental disease, defect, or intoxication and may be fully aware of the need to act lawfully—and thus not have a diminished capacity—but actually although unreasonably believe in the need for self-defense. Put simply, an awareness of the need to act lawfully does not—in fact or logic—depend on whether the putative victim's belief in the need for self-defense is correct. . . . The diminished capacity defense could be—and often has been—asserted when self-defense was not an issue; and, conversely, imperfect self-defense could be raised when there was no claim of diminished capacity. (*People v. Christian S.*, 6610)

In this case, then, the court draws a clear distinction between diminished capacity and imperfect self-defense and asserts that the one in no way entails the other. For those seeking to defend battered women who kill an abusive partner without turning to a diminished capacity defense, one option is to turn to an imperfect self-defense. This is problematic in two respects.

First, the court in *People v. Christian S.* makes it clear that the concept of imminence is still a central issue. We see this in the court's claim that "fear of future harm—no matter how great the fear and no matter how great the likelihood of the harm—will not suffice. The defendant's fear must be of *imminent* danger to life or great bodily injury. . . . *An imminent peril is one that, from appearance, must be instantly dealt with*" (*People v. Christian S.*, 6612).

Second, an imperfect self-defense only mitigates the murder charge to voluntary manslaughter. It does not absolve the defendant of responsibility in the way that a perfect self-defense would. Thus anyone who employs an imperfect self-defense argument has offered an excuse rather than a justification. Even though the person is not considered mentally deficient or incapacitated, the claim is that the defendant was, nevertheless, unreasonable in the belief that harm was imminent.

The case of Christian S. is not analogous to the situation of a battered woman. Christian S. was being harassed and threatened by the skinhead and may have unreasonably concluded (without sufficient evidence) that the threat was an imminent one. This situation seems inherently different from the case of a battered woman who has repeatedly been beaten, threatened, and terrorized and might reasonably infer that the threat to her life would be greatest if she tried to escape.

Christian S. had not been brutalized and beaten by the skinhead, which would constitute actual physical evidence that the violence was real and not simply a threat. Verbal harassment, however frightening, is not the same as a pattern of escalating physical violence. Christian S. did not live with the perpetrator and, thus, had access to resources that the typical battered woman does not. Christian S. may have unreasonably inferred that the threat of danger was imminent, whereas repeated beatings, life threats, police calls, and so on give the battered woman reasonable cause to believe that the threat is real and, depending on the particular circumstance, may be imminent.

Donald Creach argues that applying an imperfect self-defense to battered women who kill should be treated as a kind of partial determinism. His argument is that being strongly influenced by external forces yet retaining some choice in how to respond constitutes partially determined conduct. Partial determinism, he contends, can be seen in cases where a person, through no fault of her own, is attacked and chooses the best outcome available and the law does not blame her for so acting (1982: 615).

Creach observes that intentionality is central to criminal law; it is assumed that people can choose how to respond to an apparent attack. If the battered woman argues that she was partially determined by external conditions, however, the judge or jury is put in the position of having to use an intentionalist model that doesn't leave room for her explanations. Creach goes on to argue that she may fail to show a reasonable belief in imminent danger because of the external factors of her situation. What was an unreasonable-looking fear may have seemed reasonable, given the context of the abusive relationship.

The question here really turns on our definitions of "reasonable," "imminent," and "immediate," rather than what determinism entails. The trouble with a partial determinism defense is that, as with diminished capacity, the woman could not have acted otherwise (at least in that particular situation, being "partially" determined by external conditions). However well intended Creach is to suggest partial determinism as the grounds for an imperfect self-defense, I would not recommend this route.

To suggest that battered women are partially determined raises many more problems than it solves. For example, why not say batterers also are partially determined by their external conditions or an earlier environment (family, work, collegial relations gone sour)? If we allow her to be excused by her partially determined life, we ought also to allow his actions to be excused (or at least be seen as understandable) in light of his partially determined life. No one is then culpable—or at least not completely. Far better to hold the man responsible for his actions and try to understand her actions within the overall context of the batterer's behavior, the evidence of harm and potential for greater harm, the failure of outside resources to help, and the social context that tolerates domestic violence.

I endorse neither a diminished capacity defense nor an imperfect self-defense for battered women who kill their abusers. Assuming a woman has sufficient evidence (such as the beatings, the patterns of escalating violence, the increased threats or violence when she seeks help from police or community resources, and death threats to her parents, children, or other loved ones), the best defense seems to be a perfect self-defense. Let us see if it makes sense to argue that there are cases when perfect self-defense can apply to battered women who strike back.

PERFECT SELF-DEFENSE

The two key elements in establishing a perfect or justifiable self-defense are these: (1) reasonably apparent imminent danger of death or great bodily harm, and (2) a reasonable belief that the danger was real, whether it was or not. (Sloan, 1987: 1). The two key words here are "imminent" and "reasonable." Both are questioned by prosecutors of battered women who kill.

Barriers to a fair application of these conditions, however, become clear in Elizabeth Bochnak's comments about the traditional double standard:

Standards of justifiable homicide have been based on male models and expectations. Familiar images of self-defense are a soldier, a man protecting his home, family, or the chastity of his wife, or a man fighting off an assailant. . . . The acts of men and women are subject to a different set of legal expectations and standards. The man's act, while not always legally condoned, is viewed sympathetically . . . since his conduct conforms to the expectation that a real man would fight to the death to protect his pride and property. . . . The law, however, has never protected a wife who killed her husband after finding him with another woman. A woman's husband simply does not belong to her in the same way that she belongs to him. (1981: 14)

Such gender bias creates a fundamental asymmetry. Take, for example, the FBI statistics that "women are more likely to be charged with first- or second-degree murder for killing men than are men who kill women" (as noted in Madden, 1993: 35, fn. 171). Two studies of women who killed their abusers found that 72–80 percent resulted in convictions or plea bargains—an extraordinarily high number (ibid.: 52, fn. 174).

Legal history reveals societal values. In the nineteenth-century case of *Maher v. People*, for instance, it was found that an ordinary man would be provoked to murder a man known to have committed adultery with his wife (*Maher v. People*, 212, as noted in Crocker, 1985: 124). Alison Madden also observes that paramour laws in the nineteenth and early twentieth century permitted a man to kill a man caught *in flagrante delicto* with his wife, or who had committed a rape upon his daughter; whereas modern law allows adultery as a justification only to reduce the offense from homicide to manslaughter (1993: 23).

It is unimaginable that a court would rule that it was reasonable for an ordinary woman to kill a woman known to have committed adultery with her husband. That is not to say society is not sympathetic to female victims of an adulterous mate, but the sympathy falls far short of condoning murder because of it.

As noted by W. Prosser, in discussing the law of torts, the concept of what is "reasonable" has to be understood relative to the perceived norm: "This reasonably prudent man is not infallible or perfect. In foresight, caution, courage, judgment, self-control, altruism and the like he represents, and does not excel, the general average of the community. He is capable of making mistakes and errors of judgment, of being selfish, or being afraid—but only to the extent that any such shortcoming embodies the normal standard of community behavior" (Prosser, 1971: 150–51, as quoted in Crocker, 1985: 124).

The "normal standard of community behavior" may vary dramatically between men and women, members of the dominant culture and members of a historically oppressed group, members of the upper class and members of the lower class, and so on. Norms and standards are rooted in a social context, and that weighs on the interpretation and application of the law. As Minow warns, "impartiality is the guise that partiality takes to seal bias against exposure" (1990: 376). Anger or violence in a man wronged by his wife is often explained away as pride, protection, or healthy possessiveness. But the woman who is angry or violent elicits pity, irritation, or fear rather than sympathy.

We see this bias in the different kinds of prison sentences for men who kill their wives in contrast to women who kill their husbands (with or without the battering defense). Bochnak's observations offer further evidence of asymmetry in pointing to the differing response to rape victims. She notes that "case law, for example, allows the use of deadly force to prevent forcible sodomy between males, but has not yet sanctioned a woman's right to use deadly force to repel a rape. Underlying this distinction is the belief that the invasion of a man's body is a more egregious offense than the invasion of a woman's body" (1981: 14).

The concept of justifiable homicide should not be examined in the abstract, then, for our understanding is colored by issues of race, class, and gender. Self-defense requirements are steeped in prejudicial attitudes based on gender stereotypes. Schneider asserts that because of such bias, "a woman who kills her husband is viewed as inherently unreasonable because she is violating the norm of appropriate behavior for women" (1992: 219).

As Crocker explains, justification would compel a legal recognition that a woman's capacity for reasonable judgment comparable to a man's can be the basis for engaging in the "correct behavior" of self-defense (1985: 131). Rethinking the concept of justification would not only free the woman from such unsavory consequences as being committed to a mental institution or being thought unfit to care for her children, but it would recognize that she, as much as a man, is capable of rationally determining when her life is at stake and when self-defense is required. This recognition is at the heart of establishing the claim that she has acted rightly in resorting to lethal self-defense.

An allowable "perfect" self-defense has two key requirements: first, that force is necessary to prevent an imminent threat of unlawful physical force—qualified in some jurisdictions to include the criterion that retreat is impossible; and second, that the woman reasonably believes her attacker is using or is about to use deadly force (*Harvard Law Review*, 1993: 1576). Madden asserts that, whereas the duty to retreat varies according to jurisdiction, "the majority rule is that a person need not retreat when attacked; a person may stand his or her ground and use deadly force to defend against impending danger of death or serious bodily harm" (1993: 72).

One of the central issues, which we will examine further, arises when the woman uses deadly force when the abuser is asleep or otherwise incapacitated. Such nonconfrontational cases, rarer than confrontational cases, seem to be the most troubling to courts. These cases raise the ire of prosecutors because they can't understand why the woman didn't leave rather than kill, and because they fear that, if women can get away with killing a sleeping man (batterer or not), then "we're going to get a lot of women claiming to be battered. In our view, it is not a proper defense to murder" (Madden, 1993: 35).

The three conditions that might justify a battered woman killing her abuser are: first, after or during a beating, her abuser attacked her with a deadly weapon or in a manner that she reasonably interpreted to pose an imminent or immediate threat of deadly force; second, she did not provoke the attack; and third, she was under no duty to retreat or was unable to retreat (*Harvard Law Review*, 1993: 1577). These conditions may appear to be straightforward, but each poses difficulties. The notions of provocation and retreat are understood within a social context bounded by norms about human behavior and morality. And the concepts of "imminent," "immediate," and "reasonable" have much to do with how our values shape our use of language. Courts seem reluctant to acknowledge this, often treating concepts as if they were abstract entities outside of space and time.

It is often assumed that a woman provokes the abuser to batter her (even when there is insufficient evidence to prove provocation), and the idea that she has a duty to retreat overlooks the social reality of the hazardous and volatile relationship she has with her partner. The assumption of a duty to retreat also ignores or downplays the unresponsiveness of police, courts, and community to which she has to turn in order to attempt an escape.

Given the statistical evidence that women are at their greatest risk when attempting to separate from the abuser, the assumption that a woman is free to leave should not necessarily be taken for granted. In fact, leaving may put her and her children in the most dangerous situation. Thus the woman faces an extraordinary dilemma, having to weigh the threats to herself and others against the cost of staying in a situation where the batterer may continue or escalate the violence. By leaving she faces the risk of his killing her. By staying she risks further beatings and being thought either a masochist or partially responsible for provoking them.

Popular misconceptions about battered women were discussed in *State v. Kelly*, such as masochism, purposely provoking husbands into violent behavior, and "most critically . . . that women who remain in battering relationships are free to leave their abusers at any time" (*State v. Kelly*, 370).

However, the argument that "a battered woman would appear to always have the alternative of leaving the violent relationship instead of killing"

(Cutler, 1989: 275) assumes certain latitudes not necessarily available to battered women: the ability to leave, the freedom and money to come and go, the resources in the community to help her escape an abusive relationship, and the willingness of the abusive partner to let her leave without causing her greater harm or death. It follows that we need to look more closely at the basis for expectations of safe retreat than has been done, particularly since in some states retreat is still a requirement. And even when it is not a legal expectation, it is often a social expectation that may affect the receptivity of a jury to the woman's defense.

Given the social context, the woman is isolated, with support not easily available. In zeroing in on the woman, the traditional approach looks through the wrong end of the telescope, isolating the woman. She *is* isolated, but we don't need to lose perspective. The problem is not "learned helplessness"—it's that she learns there is no help.

Heinrich, Jordan, and Hemza-Placek remark on the feeling of imprisonment: "Those with the syndrome subjectively perceive that they are 'imprisoned' with no escape alternative. While repetitive or chronic physical abuse is often associated with pervasive low self-esteem, it does not necessarily follow that the battered victim has a 'mental illness'" (quoted in Cutler, 1989: 274).

The battered woman is not losing her mind when she feels trapped on all sides. The social support is for the captor, not the hostage; and so she learns there is no help and she must rescue herself. This political dimension has not been given its due. Such support was evident, for example, in the cheering thousands who waved at O. J. Simpson as he attempted to escape the police, and in the signs outside the jail in which Simpson awaited trial: "Go O. J.: Guilty or Not, We Love You."

In addition to problems of the social context, there are conceptual difficulties in the "perfect" self-defense criteria. Specifically, what is a "reasonable" interpretation of (or "reasonable belief" about) the threat, what is an "imminent" threat, and would accepting the concept of an "immediate" threat in place of an "imminent" one open the door for female vigilantes murdering their abusers?

How the terms "imminent," "immediate," and "reasonable" are understood has a lot to do with the way a person's actions are interpreted and how the courts respond to those actions. This is more complex than may appear on the surface. The court ruled in *People v. Odum* that "threats do not justify using [a] gun in self-defense" (*People v. Odum*, 279). One of the issues here is how seriously the threats are to be taken. Furthermore, such a ruling assumes the attacker and the victim are of more or less equal size and strength (otherwise the gun serves to "equalize" the situation), which is of questionable application to the case of a woman battered by a presumably larger and stronger husband or boyfriend.

If a person is threatened by an unarmed stranger on the street, pulling out a gun could be viewed as hasty, if not unjustified. However, if the unarmed stranger was stalking the potential victim and the threats began to escalate, it may not be unjustified to believe that the threat was serious enough to warrant carrying a weapon.

The concern over size should not be dismissed in trying to understand how a reasonable women might justifiably fear the battering mate. The discrepancy in size and weight of abuser and abused may be a reason that a battered woman would not kill the abuser during a violent confrontation, but only afterward. Given that a jury might question why she didn't leave then instead of killing him, the greatest difficulty for an allowable self-defense justification occurs in the nonconfrontational cases.

This difficulty is compounded by the fact that women are frequently viewed with suspicion from the outset. Deborah Kochan contends that there are "long held views of women as *inherently* unreasonable" (1989: 99). *Harvard Law Review* points out that "trial courts often refuse to apply, or are incapable of applying, existing self-defense standards to a battered woman's claims because judges assume these women act in revenge or as vigilantes, rather than as reasonable people" (1993: 1576). They are masochists if they stay and either demented or vigilantes if they strike back. What is a reasonable woman to do?

The conceptual is not always as abstract as it is made to seem. What is understood through the perspective of the norm (by which laws are developed) may blur when viewed through competing perspectives. Kochan remarks that "it has been said that female homicide is so different from male homicide that women and men may be said to live in two different cultures, each with its own 'subculture of violence.' If this is true then it should come as no surprise that laws created to address male homicide, and applied within the framework of an ethic of principles, do not adequately address circumstances under which women kill" (1989: 96).

Difference of perspective may especially affect what is meant by "imminent" and whether it entails the sense of "immediate." *People v. Aris* is a case where the two were thought to be synonymous: there the court defined "imminent peril" as "immediate and present and not prospective or even in the near future" (*People v. Aris*, 172). But Andersen and Read-Andersen contend that what appears "imminent" to a battered woman may not be so to a judge with "cool hindsight" (1992: 404–406).

Given that she has seen a pattern of escalating violence aimed at her, the victim is in a position to appraise signs that the violence is about to escalate further. From her knowledge of his moods and violent behavior, she may detect even slight changes and, consequently, have a basis for evaluating how seriously to take the threats or the behavior. Violence need only symbolize the threat of future abuse in order to keep the victim in fear and to control her behavior (Fischer, Vidmar, and Ellis, 1993: 2126). Courts seem to be oblivious to the fact that a battered woman may have a highly developed self-defense mechanism born of the years of abuse, and consequently be able to evaluate whether a threat is truly imminent or not.

We need to remember that the notion of an "imminent threat" relates to something happening under extreme circumstances, often with limited time to make decisions. Even when the batterer has passed out or is asleep, the victim may have no assurance that he won't wake up at any time. Thus the threat may still be experienced as "imminent."

Suppose someone bursts into your house, breaks your jaw, and kicks you so hard you can only crawl. After putting out his cigarette on your arm, he then has a few of your beers. Before he stretches out on your couch for a snooze, he tells you that, when he wakes up, he will slit your throat and cut out your heart. He then nods off. You cannot be sure how long he will sleep. Would you be justified in killing him?

Perhaps you think the danger is not imminent enough, so you crawl to the phone to call the police. Perhaps the line is busy, or you are put on hold. Or perhaps your attacker starts to stir. Or perhaps you get through, but the police don't respond. Or perhaps you called before, when the last attacker came into your house, and the police don't take you seriously. These are not implausible scenarios.

The question is, what would a *reasonable* person do in these circumstances, and does the battered woman's response fit those standards? Part of the problem is that the battered woman's situation is so different from the traditional view of a self-defense case. Kochan points out that the traditional model, which anticipates a one-time attack/defense, "does not accommodate a scenario that includes repeated attacks over time (battering), nor does it need to because men are not, in significant numbers, subjected to repeated and vicious physical abuse during the course of their *everyday* lives" (1989: 576). Since we have a hard time picturing a reasonable man allowing another man to beat him regularly (outside of a prison), it seems incomprehensible that the battered woman doesn't just leave.

It is unthinkable to say of the victims of robberies or muggings, however, that they should have run from the scene and are to blame (or are masochistic) because they did not. We do not expect victims of carjackings to try to escape, and they are not thought to be mentally deficient or pathological or responsible for the violence that befell them. But because of certain deeply held beliefs about men and women in our culture, we look upon victims of domestic violence differently: "Her failure to leave raises the question of whether the woman was really battered (for if she was, why did she stay?), as well as the question of whether, by staying, she had in a sense 'assumed the risk' of death. . . . The second issue (and the more pressing one in many cases) is the reasonableness of the battered woman's belief that she was in particular jeopardy at the time that she responded in self-defense" (Schneider, 1992: 229).

There are ways judges and juries can better understand the woman's actions as reasonable. For instance, the defense could bring in expert testimony that "the battered woman's response to the danger . . . cannot be understood in a vacuum . . . [but] was molded by the passivity in which women have been trained. A battered woman who does not leave her husband, seek help, or fight back is behaving according to societal expectations" (Crocker, 1985: 135). Perhaps such expert testimony would clarify for judges and juries how the societal context influences our behavior and our expectations. (We must be very careful, however, not to allow such testimony to be perceived as an excuse, which encourages courts to see the situation as one of diminished capacity or loss of control due to duress.)

We need to rethink "imminence" and what it means to be "reasonable," in light of the evidence. All of the following are relevant: the woman has endured a history of battering, with a pattern of escalating violence, and has sought to remedy the situation by calling the police or, when possible without a greater threat to her life or those close to her, attempted to get help from others, or pursued resources in the community. Since we are not dealing with a one-time attack or combat, a reasonable woman has to weigh her options in light of the threat.

(This is not simply a subjective matter, either, for the threat is not a product of her imagination. And even if it were, the subjective test is not an avenue most women have open to them. Sloan notes that "while many states have adopted the Model Penal Code which sanctions the subjective test in self-defense situations, only the most 'enlightened' courts are actually applying it in the battered spouse cases where its use is probably most appropriate for achieving a just outcome" [1987: 33].)

The threat exists by virtue of actions and statements made by the abuser, regardless of whether he is awake or asleep when the woman acts in her own self-defense. In this respect, the court in *State v. Norman* ruled that "a jury, in our view, could find that decedent's sleep was but a momentary hiatus in a continuous reign of terror by the decedent, that defendant merely took advantage of her first opportunity to protect herself, and that defendant's act was not without the provocation required for perfect self-defense" (*State v. Norman*, 5).

Judges have the authority to give instructions to the jury so that the woman's actions can be understood within the context of the battering.

Through this channel, the concept of what is "imminent" and what is "reasonable" could be understood in this broader sense, taking into consideration the history and pattern of abuse, and not simply the brutality that immediately preceded her killing her partner.

This broader approach will allow the law to accommodate the relevant contextual considerations of the battered woman's situation while keeping to the spirit of a self-defense justification. In this respect, the justice and compassion that Justice Blackmun saw missing in the *DeShaney* case can be incorporated to avoid the "sterile formalism" of rigidly holding to the law while sacrificing the more vulnerable members of the society.

It would be best if a battered woman did call the police, did seek a restraining order when her partner was violent or threatened her and others close to her, and that she pursued community channels to address the levels of violence she has been living with. But what if she does most or all of these and is still being tormented, threatened, or stalked? If the police do not respond or cannot be counted on to come when called, if communities lack resources for victims of domestic violence, and if we continue as a society to overlook the extent and severity of wife-battering, then we have, effectively, left it entirely up to the woman to defend herself. (But even with prompt police action and a supportive community, women are still being stalked and killed, and it is unrealistic to think they can be fully protected.)

We should not hold battered women to a higher standard of self-defense than others whose lives are threatened in such a way that they must take action in order to preserve those lives. In assessing whether her action is justified, we need to consider the relevant details of the relationship, the history of abuse, the specific context, whether her action was born out of revenge or other responses to the battering, and whether she had a legitimate reason to fear for her life. If we acknowledge that the traditional notion of self-defense needs to be modified to extend beyond a one-time attack model in which people of more or less equal strength are pitted against one another, then there seems to be no reason why a broader sense of what constitutes imminent danger, and what is a reasonable response to that danger, could not be applied to the battered woman who kills.

LEGAL CASES CITED

DeShaney v. Winnebago County Department of Social Services, 489 US 189 (1989)

Maher v. People, 10 Mich. 212 (1862)

People v. Aris, 264 Cal. Rptr. 167 (Cal. Ct. App. 1989)

People v. Christian S., 7 Cal. 4th 768, 872 P. 2d 574, 1994 Cal. Lexis 2196, 30 Cal. Rptr. 2d 33

People v. Emick, 128 Misc. 3d 129, 488 N.Y.S. 2d 358 (Sup. Ct. 1985)

People v. Odum, 3 Ill. App. 3d 358, 279 N.E. 2d 12 (1972)

People v. Powell, 102 Misc. 2d 719, 442 N.Y.S. 2d 645 (App. Dic. 1981)

People v. Torres, 448 N.Y.S. 2d 358 (N.Y. 1985)

State v. Hundley, 693 P. 2d 474 (Kan. 1985)

State v. Kelly, 97 N.J. 178, 478 A.2d 364 (1984)

State v. Norman, 89 N.C. App. 384, 366 S.E. 2d 586 (1988)

Violence in Bangladesh

ROKSANA NAZNEEN

The purpose of this paper is to describe and attempt to understand the most common forms of interpersonal violence in Bangladeshi society. These are found in a family context where a bride or wife and her family are normally abused by violent in-laws. The perspective of this paper is simple: that emotional and physical violence between husbands and wives and their families is socially patterned and strongly backed by cultural norms. Although the paper demonstrates the existence of pro-violence cultural norms, the question how such norms came into existence in the first place is not answered.

I selected this specific type of violence to write about, a phenomenon which I call "in-law syndrome," for two reasons. First, this is the most common locus of interpersonal violence in Bangladeshi society, one which can be identified in every social class and every region of the country. And secondly, I myself was a victim of this kind of violence, though not physically. But I think emotional violence is no less damaging than physical. I fled my country and came to Canada to escape from my in-laws—to live like a human being and to be treated like one. This paper is an attempt to analyze how the family structure and the cultural norms permit violence against women in an unhealthy social environment.

Reprinted from *Interpersonal Violence, Health, and Gender Politics*, 2d ed., ed. S. G. French (Dubuque, Iowa: Brown & Benchmark, 1994).

INTERPERSONAL VIOLENCE AND
RESEARCH IN BANGLADESH

Any attempt to understand why emotional and physical violence
occurs so often in Bangladeshi marriages must take into account the way
society structures the interaction between two families—the husband's
and the wife's—at an interpersonal level. As French states, "violence is any
act that causes the victim to do something she or he does not want to
do, or prevents her from doing something she wants to do, or causes her
to be afraid" (1994: 3). The available evidence suggests that, with rare exceptions, family members using violence are not mentally ill (Hotaling
and Straus, 1980). French (1994) also rejects the medical model. Instead,
as this paper argues, violent acts by one family member against another are
the result of socially learned and socially patterned behavior which can be
explained by a world view or Weltanschauung.

But unfortunately, in Bangladesh, interpersonal violence has never been
a subject of serious academic research. Some papers have been written on
political violence, but none on interpersonal violence—specifically, violence against women. The main reason for this, I think, is that this concept
has a strong religious flavor. Everything people do against women is done
in the name of Islam. The academics or the intellectuals do not have the
courage to upset the religious political groups. Also, people usually are interested in abnormal or unnatural things. What I call "in-law syndrome" is
not considered abnormal; it is the way of life. As a consequence, research
into this particular type of social problem remains totally neglected in
Bangladesh.

In the West, research has sought often to explain how culture, social
structure, and social behavior affect violence. Despite the plethora of literature regarding cultural influence on violence, most of the studies have
been limited to the history and culture of the developed countries. Two
reasons can be given to account for the apparent lack of interest. First, the
developing nations, specifically in Africa and Asia, lack national statistical
data on violence essential for scientific research. Secondly, in the developing nations, research on violence has not yet reached the same stage of
academic acceptance as in the developed countries. To minimize the in-
sularity and parochial nature of research work done in this area, several
sociologists, including Opolot (1976, 1979), Clinard and Abbott (1973),
Chang (1976), and Arthur (1991), have called for comparative analyses of
violence to assess the extent to which theories of violence based on Western culture will hold for nations with different socioeconomic structures
(Wolf, 1971).

INTERPERSONAL VIOLENCE IN BANGLADESH

Despite the fact of poverty and illiteracy, Bangladeshi society lacks some specific forms of interpersonal violence which are common in the Western societies. But at the same time, in Bangladesh, there are some unique causes of interpersonal violence, alien to Western society, which can only be described by cultural norms and values. Bangladesh has norms and values that positively sanction the use of violence in the family setting. And this legitimization of aggressive behavior is likely to increase the extent to which violence is actually used as a "problem-solving technique" within the family.

The term "culture" means something roughly similar to social heredity, that is, the total legacy of past human behavior effective in the present or what is available to be learned from others (Williams, 1970). In large part, cultural norms account for differences between the family patterns of people in different societies.

Cultural norms regulate almost all aspects of family life. They provide a blueprint of the behavior appropriate for husbands, wives, children, grandparents; in fact, for each of the relationships within a family. Thus, the culture contains norms specifying how marriages are to be arranged (and, if necessary, dissolved), who is to be regarded as a member of the family, what activities a husband should carry out in relation to the wife and vice versa, how children should be brought up, and so on. The degree of control exercised by family members over one another is an element of family structure affected by and in turn affecting many other aspects of family integration and interaction (Kolb and Straus, 1974: 757). It is the family structure and cultural norms that instigate violence in Bangladeshi society as they do in many other societies; but some causes of violence in this society are unique and the objective of this paper is to describe them.

Rape, abuse against servants (a "neo-slavery system" exists in the cities, where young girls and boys between the age of six to late teens, from the poorer classes, work in almost all households for low wages), and domestic violence are very common in Bangladesh. On the other hand, the concept of father-daughter incest is unknown in this traditional society. Alcohol- and drug-related violence is also very rare. But who needs alcohol and drugs to justify their actions when there are cultural norms to legitimize violence?

IN-LAW SYNDROME: A SOCIAL DISEASE

The most common type of interpersonal violence in Bangladesh stems from the conflicts related to the idea of so-called "rights" over the wife by the husband and his family. I shall call this "in-law syndrome," as this type of violence starts when a bride steps into her husband's house to live with his family. From the first day of her married life, the bride is bound to obey not only her husband, but also his mother, father, sisters, and brothers. They all have the "right" to "discipline" the bride; and it is the bride's family that will try its best to keep the groom's family satisfied by fulfilling their financial demands.

I was twenty-three when I got married. My parents raised me as an independent person, provided me with the best education available, but taught me values totally different from those of my in-laws. The first thing I lost on my wedding day was my freedom. From that day, my mother-in-law took over my life and started deciding what to do with it. I could not eat or sleep without her permission. I had to have her permission to go to sleep at night when everybody else was in bed; and early in the morning my brother-in-law used to wake me up when everybody else was asleep. I was not allowed to eat anything unless my mother-in-law gave me permission, and snacking between meals was totally forbidden for me because "brides are supposed to eat less." I was ordered to put a veil on my face when my father-in-law or other house guests were around. My job was to cook, clean, and baby-sit for my other sisters-in-law all day long. And I was constantly reminded that my mother did not teach me anything. I did not know how to cook and serve three times a day for a family of twenty-five. I did not even know how to spend day after day in a dark tiny kitchen. My mother-in-law found my mother responsible for all my faults.

The structure of the family plays an important role in accommodating the cultural norms. It is the structure of the family which creates a hierarchy where elderly members hold power over younger members. In Bangladesh, households are often composed of an older man and his wife, their adult sons with their wives, unmarried daughters, and the grandchildren. The head of the family is usually the eldest male or female. In my case, it was my mother-in-law. Along with other members of the family, the bride or wife is supposed to obey him or her without questioning. As a newcomer in the family she is also a subordinate to every member of that family. Though this extended family structure is in decline in the urban areas, it is still universal in the rural areas.

After our marriage my husband lived in another city, but I was never allowed to live with him. I had to live with my in-laws and was forbidden to go to my parents' house.[1] My husband used to visit us once a month for two days; not only that, I could see him in private only when we went to sleep at night.

I had never been in an extended family before. So the lifestyle in my in-laws' house was a total shock for me. There was no respect for privacy, individuality, or even for basic human needs. Those nine months I spent in my in-laws' house can only be compared with a life in prison.

There are two major areas of conflict between wives and in-laws. The first, which all in-laws love, is dowry. And the other, which they hate, an infertile wife.

Dowry: An Obligation Involving Violence

It is particularly interesting to see how the people of Bangladesh, who claim to be very "Islamic," do not hesitate to practice a very non-Islamic system which has its roots in Hinduism. Dowry plays a major role in a marriage in this Islamic country. "The term dowry means the property that a bride brings with her at the time of marriage" (Teays, 1991: 29). Teays confirms that this is a pure Hindu religious tradition widely practised in India, where the growing trend of dowry murders reflects the socio-economic crisis. Teays's picture of India provides a mirror image of Bangladeshi Islamic society.

The dowry system is illegal in Bangladesh. But in reality, state law has little impact on social practices. Violence begins when the bride or the bride's family fails to comply with the demands of the groom's family. The victims often are the bride and her family. The common belief is that the family of the groom "deserves" dowry, as they have agreed to take the bride into their family and, by doing so, they do "a great favour" to the bride's family. Many of the acts of violence could be avoided if the groom's family remained satisfied with the amount of dowry they agreed upon initially. But usually they want more and more as the days go by, and they use violence as a tool to get what they want:

> Muslim and Selina got married in 1990. Selina's poor father bought new furniture, kitchenware and jewellery for them and gave his son-in-law some cash money as his family demanded. Everything went well for six months. Then Muslim started to send Selina to her parents' place asking for money. Every time Selina returned empty-handed, she was beaten severely. Finally, on September 6, 1993, Muslim sent Selina to her parents' home asking for 50,000 taka. Unable to satisfy the demand, her

mother asked Selina not to go back to her husband's home. Fearing more abuse, Selina declined. She returned home where her husband was waiting. Muslim asked about the money and Selina remained silent. Muslim started kicking her. She fell to the ground. He punched and kicked her for half an hour. Selina was pregnant with her first child. She passed out lying on the floor. That night, she could not get up to eat supper. So she slept on the floor. Early in the morning, at 2 A.M., while she was asleep, Muslim poured gasoline on her body and set it on fire. Neighbours woke up as she was crying for help. They saw Selina come running out of her home with her body on fire and Muslim standing in front of the house watching her. Neighbours came to her rescue and took her to Dhaka Medical Hospital at 5 A.M. that morning. Selina died on September 11, 1993. Muslim disappeared when Selina's family filed a complaint.[2]

Considering what happened to Selina, I was fortunate. My in-laws did not ask for dowry, because they knew that my mother would take them to court if they did. Later I came to know that they expected my mother to pay a large amount of dowry since my family is rich. Disappointed by my mother's decision, my mother-in-law took all the jewellery my mother and my relatives had given to me as wedding gifts and later sold it without even telling me. But that did not stop her from blaming me or my mother for being "inconsiderate" and for "cheating." I was cursed constantly for having a dark skin,[3] too much education, and a "rich attitude." After nine months of living in that hell, when I finally moved out to live with my mother, I was not allowed to take my clothes or any of my other belongings.

The occurrence of dowry-related violence is related significantly to the existence of patriarchal norms and values, where men control the wealth and have, thereby, a power advantage over women. And surprisingly, many women encourage this system by their behavior. In most families it is the mother-in-law who has the ultimate power over a bride. There is no doubt that mothers-in-law also were abused as brides. She takes her revenge when the time comes.

The dowry system is a tool to secure men's position in the society. The socialization process teaches every woman to be humble, to accept everything in-laws do, to obey them without any question. This learning process begins from a very early age when girls are in their parents' home. When a mother gives birth to a daughter, the whole family starts preparing itself for the possible abuse and harassment waiting down the line.

Unlike Western societies, the wedding day seems to be a sad occasion where the bride and her family say goodbye to each other. This is the day the daughter ceases to be a member of her father's family, the day she loses her freedom to her in-laws. Like most brides, I was forbidden to go to my parents' house, though they lived only two miles away, and my family was never welcomed in my in-laws' house. Starting with the wedding day, it is either the father-in-law or the mother-in-law who decides what the bride eats, when she goes to sleep, who she meets, where she goes and with whom. I was allowed to go out of the house only when my mother-in-law thought it was absolutely necessary, and I had to bring one of my brothers-in-law along to "guard" me. In fact, the in-laws control every aspect of a wife's life. If the wife or her family fails to satisfy her in-laws, often it is not the husband, but an older member of the family who punishes her:

> Rina's father agreed to give 3,000 taka as dowry. But due to a very poor financial condition, he could not provide that money after the wedding. So the father-in-law started to abuse Rina (age 17) physically and emotionally. But still Rina's father was unable to give the money. So, on July 14, 1992, the father-in-law took Rina to the Marriage Registry Office and forced her to sign the divorce papers. Later, when they returned home, the father-in-law tore her cloths, left her naked and then spilled pesticides on her head. Rina lost all her hair forever. (*Weekly Chitrabangla*, August 28, 1992, p. 49)

Often it is not only the wife who is the victim of violence related to dowry, but also her family members are exposed to this type of violence:

> Alok did not ask for a dowry when he married Nipa. Nevertheless his father-in-law gave him a costly motorcycle, an expensive wristwatch and some jewellery worth 100,000 taka as gifts. Alok started asking for money after the wedding was over. On several occasions Nipa's father provided him with large sums of money. Alok used to beat Nipa every time her father refused to give money. Soon Nipa's father had used up his savings and stopped giving money. So Nipa started to receive emotional and physical abuse from her husband and her in-laws on a regular basis. On August 13, 1993, Nipa's brother went to see Nipa with the news that he had passed the school final examinations with good standing. Pleased by the news she asked her brother to have lunch with her. Alok came home from work in the afternoon. Nipa asked for his permission to go to her parents' house along with her brother. Alok refused to let her go and told her that she would not be allowed to see her parents ever. Nipa started to argue and Alok attacked her with a vicious punch on her face. Nipa's bewildered brother tried to cover his sister with his arms. Alok started to beat

him too. . . . Nipa begged her brother to leave. "Please, leave! Otherwise he is going to kill us both! Don't worry about me, I'll call you later." The beating continued even after her brother had gone. The neighbours said that Nipa's mother-in-law also took part in the beating. That same evening Nipa was strangled to death with a telephone cord. Nipa's family was not allowed even to see the dead body. The police declared it a case of suicide, though the coroner's report indicates there were signs of beating all over Nipa's body. Alok was never arrested. (*Weekly Chitrabangla*, September 23, 1993, p. 16)

This kind of violence is what Gelles and Straus (1978) call "legitimate-instrumental" violence, violence that is permitted or required by the norms of society when physical force is used to induce some desired act or to prevent some undesired behavior. The in-laws think that dowry is their right, and they do whatever they can to get what they want. Alok's father is a rich and famous person in his region, and as happens all the time, the police were on his side.

Infertility: A Biological Crime

Women in technologically simple societies are valued above all for their fertility. Bangladesh is no exception. Not only are cultural values overwhelmingly pronatalist, but people say explicitly that they want children because of the economic value their work will contribute to the family and because they represent a form of social security to parents in their elder years (Mamdini, 1972). A wife, aside from characteristics of her health or personality, is valued for her ability to bear and rear children. Women in highly patriarchal societies achieve social esteem because of their role as mothers of the children claimed by their husbands' descent groups. Women know that, through their fertility and their ability to nurture children, they can claim tolerance and support from their in-laws (Caldwell, 1976, 1978, 1980). But if they have trouble becoming pregnant, then it is only the wife who is to be blamed. There never seems to be any doubt about the husband's ability:

When Mosharraf and Champa got married in May 1988, Champa's father gave 30,000 taka as dowry to his son-in-law. But Champa could not make her in-laws happy because she could not get pregnant immediately. So Mosharraf demanded 50,000 taka more as penalty. Champa's father, Wazed Ali, is a taxi driver. He had already spent all his savings for the wedding. He told his son-in-law that it was impossible for him to pay another

50,000 taka on such short notice. At his mother's suggestion, Mosharraf started physically assaulting his wife almost every night after coming home from work. Often he would bring his friends and forced her to have sex with them. On several occasions he let his friends beat her. Mosharraf's parents knew everything and never tried to stop their son. Not only that, they used to curse Champa all the time for not being able to produce a child. Often the mother-in-law and father-in-law, along with the sisters-in-law, would beat Champa. They thought Champa was evil. This went on for a period of five years. Finally, one night, after being beaten severely, Champa left her husband's home and went to live with her parents. On August 17, 1993, Mosharraf went to see Champa and told her that he wanted to divorce her because she was infertile. He gave her the divorce papers to sign. Champa refused to sign them. Then Mosharraf started to beat her. When she lost consciousness, Mosharraf left the house. Two blocks away he met Wazed Ali who was coming home from work. Mosharraf attacked his unsuspecting father-in-law, who was later taken to the hospital with severe head and bone injuries. Champa filed a complaint accusing her husband, mother-in-law, father-in-law and his brother of emotional and physical abuse. (*Weekly Chitrabangla*, September 23, 1993, p. 22)

An infertile wife and a wife who gives birth only to girls are considered to be similarly inadequate. Girls are an economic burden, but boys are potential wage earners, and they carry the family's name. The wife who gives birth to girls is often abandoned by the husband, or the husband gets married again. Husbands are allowed to keep four wives, though the previous wives must approve the marriages. The wife has little choice but to give permission; because if she does not, the husband will divorce her, which means poverty and insecurity for the rest of her life.

SEXIST ORGANIZATION OF SOCIETY

The cultural norms and values permitting and sometimes encouraging violence against the wife and her family reflect the hierarchical and male-dominant society typical of the Indian subcontinent. The right to use force exists to provide the ultimate support for maintaining the power structure of the family when those low in the hierarchy refuse to accept their place and roles. Some specific ways in which the male-dominant structure of the society and of the family create and maintain a high level of violence are described below.

Taboo on Divorce

The divorce rate in Bangladesh is strikingly low. During a twelve-year period (1975 to 1986) the number of registered divorcee women was only 607,199 (United Nations, 1987), and it is likely that most of these were abandoned by their husbands. This number is low considering the population size of 113.01 million (United Nations, 1990–91). The divorce rate is low, but not because the couples are extremely happy. The main reason is that, financially, the wives are completely dependent on their husbands.

Many women continue to endure physical attacks from their husbands and in-laws because the alternative, to divorce, means poverty and insecurity. According to both Islamic and state law, women can get a divorce any time they want. But the concept of alimony is unknown in this society. In a divorce, the husband is not obligated to pay any financial support to his ex-wife. And also, the social norms do not encourage divorce, even when the wife is in total agony.

This practice also has its roots in Hindu culture, where divorce was totally forbidden, both for the husband and the wife. According to A. S. Altekar, in Hinduism "the wife's marital tie and duty do not come to an end even if the husband were to sell or abandon her" (1973: 83). The "Islamic" society of Bangladesh made some "convenient adjustments" to this Hindu notion by permitting a man to divorce his wife at any time; but when a wife divorces her husband, she is usually condemned by the society. A woman divorces her husband only when she or her family is rich and only when her family agrees to support her. Even in those cases, relatives and neighbours reject the whole family and treat them as immoral and as sinners.

There are two major reasons why wives tend to stay married even when they are abused. The first is fear of losing the children. Another cultural norm that helps to maintain the subordination of women is the idea that children, especially boys, cannot be adequately brought up by the mother. The father has the sole right to his children and gets to keep them when divorce takes place. In the city, where the mother has access to the justice system and is rich enough to hire a lawyer, she may get the custody of the children, though only temporarily. The father regains custody automatically when the male child is seven and the female thirteen years old.

The second reason that most women hesitate to divorce is the fear of losing property. In Bangladesh, according to both Islamic and state law, a daughter may claim some of her parents' property (half of what her brother gets), but usually she does not. According to cultural norms, married women are considered to be members of the husband's family and they cease to be a part of their parents' family. This is also a traditional

Hindu custom, where women were prohibited from inheriting land (Teays, 1991: 30). A woman is allowed to have her share only when a divorce takes place, and only if her parents and brothers support the divorce. But a wife also owns one-eighth of her husband's property, according to the Muslim Family Act introduced in 1969. And in the case of her husband's death, she also gets to take care of her children's share, if they are minors. But the wife loses her share if a divorce takes place. So women choose abuse over divorce, hoping to get power later in life, rather than being considered a burden in their parents' home for the rest of their lives.

The social system also discourages a woman from getting a divorce without any support from her family. Women are not allowed to live alone. They always have to live with some elderly relative, preferably a man, no matter how well educated or wealthy the woman may be. Taslima Nasrin is a thirty-one-year-old physician and divorcee.[4] In her autobiography she criticizes this kind of social injustice while describing her experiences when she was transferred to a hospital in Dhaka and had to leave her parents' home: "I was looking for a place to live in this city. . . . The first question asked by all the landlords was, 'Who else is going to live with you?'. . . They want a man to live with me. They would not care if that man abused me, because that is not their concern. They just want a man to live with me. . . . So I could not find a place of my own in this city. I am living with my relatives and friends, one day here and one day there" (1993: 54).[5]

Divorce is an unattractive choice for a woman unless she has the moral support of her family, even when she is highly educated and economically independent.

Male Orientation of the Criminal Justice System

Not only is much male violence against wives attributable to the sexist organization of society, but the final indignity is that the male-oriented organization of the criminal justice system virtually guarantees that few women will be able to secure legal relief. According to state law, the husband is not bound to provide financial support to his ex-wife in case of a divorce. Also, a wife cannot claim any portion of her ex-husband's property. If the wife gets the custody of the children, the husband has to pay child support, but the children have to ask for that in front of a judge. There is no law to make him pay or to penalize him if he fails to pay. The father is always the legal guardian, no matter who gets the custody of the children.

In the villages the situation is even worse. People have no access to the justice system, because the villages are almost completely isolated from the cities. The village head (usually the richest or the oldest man in the village) plays "the judge" and decides the fate of the children. Needless to say, it is the father who gets to keep the children, because that is the custom. These village heads hold immense power over every villager:

> Somed was abusive to his wife. So his wife decided to divorce him. But the villagers became angry (women who divorce their husbands are considered immoral) and arranged for a "trial" in front of the village head. After listening to both sides, the village head ordered that the wife be beaten in front of all the villagers. The order was carried out. Then she was thrown out of the village. (*Weekly Chitrabangla*, August 28, 1992, p. 48)

Ignorance

In Bangladesh most of the women are not aware of their rights. This is natural when one considers that only 5 percent of the women of this country have secondary-level education. (United Nations, 1990–91) The socialization process women go through is also responsible for this kind of ignorance. Women are raised to believe everything their husbands say. Taslima Nasrin describes a perfect example:

> It was in the afternoon. I heard a cry. I was not sure whether it was an animal or a human. After listening for a few minutes I found that it was a young woman, my neighbour. . . . Later I got to know the young woman. She was eighteen years old, had finished high school, and was newly married to a bureaucrat. . . . We became friends and she began to tell me her story. Her husband made her have sexual intercourse five or six times every day. At first she did not deny her "husband's right," but then the pain became too much to take and she could not help crying. Every time she refused to go to bed, her husband used electric cords to beat her.
>
> I asked her, "Don't you get angry? Why don't you leave him?" "Leave him? Why? He has the right to beat me. It's in the Hadis [religious code]," she replied.
>
> "Who told you this?"
>
> "My husband."
>
> "He lied to you. Hadis does not permit a husband to beat his wife."
>
> With disbelief in her eyes, she just said, "Not only my husband, everybody says so" (1993: 27).

This is a woman who lives in a major city, has some education, and comes from a higher-middle-class family. So the situation in the villages, where women have little or no education, may easily be imagined. A popular belief in the villages is that a woman who goes to school loses her husband. Village women do not have access to the media and know nothing about the justice system.

Negative Self-image

Under the present social structure women tend to develop negative self-images. From early childhood a girl finds herself cursed by her mother for not being a boy. It is "shameful" to give birth to a daughter who can only be a burden to a family. The family has to pay a large amount of dowry when the daughter gets married; not only that, they have to be ready to take every possible abuse from her in-laws. So a daughter is never appreciated in a family. Taslima Nasrin writes from her experience: "A mother always loves her son more than her daughter. She always gives the son the better portion of the food, but never cares for the daughter. . . . We used to have some big trees in our backyard. One day, I was in my early teens, I was about to climb a tree and my mother forbade me to do so, saying 'trees die if a girl touches them—girls are evil'" (1993: 62).

Girls grow up knowing that they are "nature's accident" and, as a consequence, feelings of guilt develop which result in women tolerating "in-law syndrome" and the violence related to that.

However, in Bangladesh, as Wolfgang and Ferraciti suggest in their "subculture of violence" theory (1967), the degree of violence related to "in-law syndrome" varies somewhat within society. In some segments of society violence may be regarded as more culturally acceptable than it is in others. The values I learned in my parents' home are totally different from the values that my in-laws have. The main reason is that my husband and I came from two different social classes. The basic differences in our two family cultures are in the level of education and in the family structure itself. In my family everyone, regardless of gender, is highly educated, and the women are encouraged to pursue professional careers. I have never heard of taking or receiving dowry in any of the marriages in my family. On the other hand, my husband is the only member of his family who has a university degree. The jobs for the women in my in-laws' family are to cook and to clean. Also, I was raised in a nuclear family, but my in-laws live in an extended family and they have a close tie with their village roots.

In the cities, where women have more independence and economic freedom, and where the justice system is more accessible, physical violence against women is not as common as it is in the villages. But emotional abuse is always there. I was a graduate student when I got married. Soon I was asked by my husband's family not to go to the university because my classes were hampering my duties at home—cooking and cleaning. That was the first time I stood up against my in-laws. I left their house and went to live with my mother. My in-laws asked my mother to force me to return to their house. My mother simply said, "She is an adult, I have no right to force her. She can make her own decisions." I can still hear my brother-in-law shouting, "She is a married woman now, she is not supposed to make any decisions. It is we whom she should obey." So it is important to point out that human aggression need not take the form of overt physical damage; violence can be manifest in verbal, indirect, passive, and subtle forms of psychological harm.

Established notions that husbands and fathers have authority over women and children are found in the Judeo-Christian traditions and among other world religions such as Islam, Buddhism, Confucianism, and Hinduism. A high proportion of societies imbue the adult male role with authority to coerce the behavior of dependent women and children. Women and children, because of their economic and physical limitations, have always been in a weak position to take an individual stand against domination by one male or several allied males or sometimes even elderly females. The situation is more intense in Bangladeshi society as the cultural norms permit wives to be abused by every older member of the in-law family. Family interpersonal violence must be seen as a mode of behavior acquired through years of cultural and family socialization. As it is portrayed in this paper, neither cultural norms nor family structure alone can account for the high rate of violence related to "in-law syndrome." But together they form an explosive combination.

Important as are the cultural norms that make it legitimate for in-laws to use physical force on the wife and her family, they do not fully explain "in-law syndrome." These norms are guidelines more for culturally "permissible" actions than for culturally "required" actions. So the question remains as to why some families do and others do not engage in such permissible violence. We must also examine how or why norms legitimizing violence within the family came into being, and why such norms continue to exist.

Violent acts are the same in every society. It is the "justifications" that may differ from society to society. In Bangladesh, Islam is used as an excuse to abuse women. But as I have tried to explain in this paper, it is not the religious codes, but the cultural norms which permit women to be abused in this particular social setting. State law is not enough to prohibit the dowry system. Society needs social awakening. The examples of in-law violence in Bangladesh show us that changes must occur in the social fabric itself, together with shifts in attitudes, beliefs, and the sense of individual self-worth. I consider myself lucky; I had the courage and the financial ability to flee my country and to come to Canada to begin a new life. But my heart goes out to the women of Bangladesh who have nowhere to run.

Female Genital Mutilation: Violence in the Name of Tradition, Religion, and Social Imperative

SEMRA ASEFA

This paper provides an overview of female genital mutilation (FGM), from its historical roots and cultural underpinnings to the identification of this practice as a custom that perpetuates violence against women, with grave physical and psychological results. FGM is commonly known as "female circumcision" by the communities where it is practised, so I may occasionally refer to it by these terms. However, the term "circumcision" implies male circumcision, where the foreskin is removed without damaging the organ itself. On the contrary, the damage to females is much more extensive. A male/female comparison will highlight the differences. "Sunna" circumcision of females is equivalent to cutting off the head of the penis. The male equivalent of clitoridectomy would be the amputation of most of the penis. The male equivalent of infibulation is the removal of all the penis, its roots of soft tissue, and part of the scrotal skin. But while a man would not normally experience further complications once the wound heals, the scars created by the female operation lead to terrible problems at childbirth as normal dilation is prevented (Toubia, 1993: 9; Hosken, 1982: 36).

The Bobbitt case generated an international media mania and yet, amazingly enough, the communications networks around the world ignore the fact that globally, 6,000 girls are at risk of genital mutilations every day, two million every year (Toubia, 1993: 5). This practice has af-

Reprinted from *Interpersonal Violence, Health, and Gender Politics*, 2d ed., ed. S. G. French (Dubuque, Iowa: Brown & Benchmark, 1994).

fected 85 to 114 million women and girls to date. It is clear that FGM has received, and continues to receive, a grossly inadequate amount of the attention it fully deserves.

I first became interested in FGM when my mother, a consultant for UNICEF, casually handed me a booklet by Nahid Toubia on the subject. I read through it, alternately horrified and fascinated, noting with surprise the percentage of female populations circumcised in the countries I had grown up in and considered my second home. I came to my own country, Ethiopia, paused and blinked: 85 percent. I did not know the word for "circumcision" in my language. Nor has female circumcision come up during any conversation I could recall with my family or the African friends I grew up with. Eighty-five percent? Beginning to question the validity of the statistics, I started calling Ethiopian friends and relatives in my peer group. They all seemed to share my ignorance and did not believe the figure I quoted. My mother being absent on an extended tour of Asia, I called my aunt in Virginia, who confirmed that almost all Ethiopian groups circumcise.

As I probed deeper with an older cohort of family friends and relatives, the more I sensed that this was a rarely discussed topic, almost verging on a taboo. Most Ethiopian circumcisions are not associated with a rite of passage (particularly for the Christian groups) and girls are generally circumcised while they are between seven days and several months old, which no doubt contributes to the secretive nature of the topic that I initially found so mystifying.

My curiosity had been piqued. Armed with some recent documentation supplied by my mother, and the active encouragement of Stanley French, I got my research underway.

THE HISTORY AND TYPES OF FGM

FGM dates back at least 2,000 years, but opinions vary as to whether it originated in one area and spread to other regions, or whether it was developed by ethnic groups in different places at different times independently. Although the amount of research done on its history is surprisingly scant, considering its social impact on behavior, family life, health and economic development, the practice has existed on all continents in different forms. Cultures that practised FGM in the past include Hittites, Phoenicians, the ancient Egyptians, the Aboriginals in Australia, and some Pacific island inhabitants. FGM was also practised by modern physicians in Canada, England, and the United States as recently as the

1940s to treat masturbation, hysteria, lesbianism, and other female "deviances." Currently FGM is widespread in Africa, the southern part of the Arab peninsula, along the Persian Gulf, and among the Moslem populations of Malaysia and Indonesia (Abdalla, 1982: 11; Hosken, 1982: 51). This paper will draw its case histories from Africa, particularly from the horn of Africa.

In medical literature there are three definitions of the operations encompassed by female circumcision.

Type 1: Sunna Circumcision: The mildest form, sunna consists of removing the prepuce and the tip of the clitoris. This is wrongly believed by many to be an Islamic requirement. The word "sunna" means tradition in Arabic.

Type 2: Excision/Clitoridectomy: Considerably more severe, excision entails the removal of the entire clitoris as well as the adjacent tissues of the labia minora (small lips) leaving the outer labia majora (large lips). The gaping wound is allowed to heal without closure of the vulva.

Type 3: Infibulation: Infibulation or pharonic circumcision, as the Sudanese call it in reference to the ancient Egyptians who used to practise it, is the most drastic and severe form of genital mutilation. It consists of the removal of the clitoris, the labia minora and, depending on the ethnic group involved, either the removal of a thin ribbon of flesh from either side of the labia majora or the "roughing" of the labia majora by a series of small cuts to create an open wound. These two wounds are brought into contact and made to adhere by various means. Adhesive substances such as sugar, egg, and cigarette paper are used in Eastern Sudan, while thorns are utilized in Somalia. Stitching with silk or catgut sutures are other common means. The aim is to create a hood of skin that covers the urethra and most of the vagina. A reed or thin stick is placed such that when the wound heals and forms a tough scarred tissue, a small opening, sometimes as small as a match head, is left to allow passage of urine and menstrual flow. Note that with infibulation, recutting or defibulation is inevitable in the future. For example, it has to be performed: (1) to treat the immediate complication of urine or menstrual retention arising from an inadequate opening; (2) to allow intercourse after the marriage ceremony; and (3) in all cases of infibulation, recutting takes place with each childbirth so the baby can crown without tearing the tough tissue (El Dareer, 1982: 1; Toubia, 1993: 10).

In regions where infibulation is the prevalent form of FGM (N. Sudan 89 percent, Somalia 98 percent, parts of Ethiopia, Eritrea), refibulation is also common for divorced women who want to remarry and women who have given birth. Often, they are refibulated to the same size as before the marriage so as to create an illusion of virginal tightness for their husbands. In addition, an intermediate form of infibulation has recently been developed, especially in or close to urban areas, by families who believe it will avert some of the drastic health consequences. Different grades of intermediate have come about because midwives follow the instructions of the girl's relatives who stand around ordering, "take this and leave that." Since the health and psychological effects are virtually the same, intermediate is not considered separate from infibulation.

THE CONSEQUENCES OF FGM ON HEALTH

The memory of their screams calling for mercy, gasping for breath, pleading that those parts of their bodies that it pleases God to give them be spared. I remember the fearful look in their eyes when I led them to the toilet, "I want to, but I can't. Why Mum? Why did you let them do this to me?" Those words continue to haunt me. My blood runs cold whenever the memory comes back. It is now four years after the operation and my children still suffer from its effects. How long must I live with the pain that society imposed on me and my children? (*Testimony of Miami.* Toubia, 1993: 8)

The damages to children's and women's health resulting from genital mutilations are considerable, though of course the severity of the complications depends on the types of circumcisions performed and the sanitary conditions. Also, as the passage above illustrates, a child undergoes extreme psychological trauma before, during, and after the operations, a fact that has been neglected by researchers in the past, conveying the impression that the children have bodies but no psyche (Toubia, 1993: 19; Abdalla, 1982: 27).

The immediate health effects for all types of circumcisions include difficulty in passing urine due to swelling, and burning pain leading to urine retention. In the case of infibulation, this condition lasts for years (including menstrual retention). Fadumo of Somalia related how "it used to take us hours to finish our morning urine . . . but it was always hard to get rid of all the urine because it always came in drops and never finished properly. We envied our mothers and grandmothers when they went to urinate in the forest in their turn and came back quickly. We looked forward to the day when we could do this. Marriage was a new problem and a solution at the same time" (Abdalla, 1982: 107).

Urine and menstrual retention can be treated in hospital by decircumcision for the lucky few with access and means to pay for it. But in most cases families have little knowledge of anatomy and attribute complications to metaphysical forces, thus they are reluctant to seek medical help. While conducting her research for *Woman, Why Do You Weep?* in Sudan, Dr. Asma El Dareer relates how a family brought their four-year-old daughter in. After examining her, the doctor told the girl's relatives that she needed decircumcision and that he would do it. Apparently, the relatives thought that "decircumcision" would spoil the girl's circumcision and they escaped with the child while the staff was preparing for the operation (El Dareer, 1982: 32).

The second most common complication is haemorrhaging, primarily from injuries to arteries and veins, or from infection. Other related complications include fever, and shock, of which there are two types: neurogenic, from terror and pain, and haemorrhagic (from loss of blood). Infection in most cases is inevitable in light of the unhygienic way the operations are performed. The instruments (stones, knives, razors, scissors) are simply washed in oil or water, which leads to blood poisoning (septicemia), and tetanus, which can be fatal. Harmful practices worsen the situation. For example, in Western Sudan, pulverized animal excreta is applied to the wound to stem bleeding (El Dareer, 1982: 33). In West Africa, the operators throw dirt. In Nigeria, the Hausa, in addition to excising their teenage brides, make cuts in the vagina to facilitate intercourse for the polygamous husband. They also believe it makes childbirth easier, but frequently end up with the opposite result. Long-term complications include chronic pelvic infections, malformations such as keloid formations (hardening of the scars), cysts which sometimes grow to the size of oranges, painful intercourse, and lack of orgasm.

More complications follow with childbirth, with difficulty in dilating as a result of excision scars, delay in labor and second-stage labor, all of which necessitate recutting. Traditionally, in Sudan, the woman in labor hangs from a rope attached to the roof beam of the hut while the midwife "assists" by making cuts from below, with serious risks of injuring the newborn as well as increasing the suffering and damage to the mother. The continuous pressure of the baby's head sometimes causes death in the tissue, leading to fistula (abnormal passage) between the bladder and vagina or between the vagina and the rectum. The fistula causes incontinence and an unpleasant smell leading the husbands of these women to abandon them (El Dareer, 1982: 38). These are only a few examples of the horrors involved.

With regard to the psychological complications of FGM, there hasn't been any systematic effort, to date, to study the traumatic effects of FGM on children and women. However, many children do exhibit behavioral changes, whereas with other children, the problems are not evident until adulthood. These psychological symptoms, according to Taha Baashar, a senior psychologist from Sudan, include "anxiety state," which is lack of sleep and hallucinations caused by fear of the operation. The other two examples listed were "reactive depression," by women who have on-going health complications arising from childbirth and recircumcision, and "psychotic excitement." As Nahid Toubia, a Sudanese surgeon, put it, "Many women who may be traumatized by their circumcision experiences, worried about a physical complication, or fearful of sex, have no acceptable means of expressing their feelings and suffer in silence. When the pressure reaches a certain level, their condition can progress to psychopathological levels" (Toubia, 1993: 19).

There are few qualified psychotherapists and psychologists available and, in the majority of cases, traditional remedies and rituals are administered without any understanding of the deep-rooted problems. In Nahid Toubia's experience in the public hospitals of Sudan, thousands of women went to the Ob/Gyn outpatient clinics complaining of vague chronic symptoms such as general fatigue, backache, loss of sleep, and pelvic congestion. Since they have no medically detectable pathology, they are considered to be a nuisance by the doctors and the hospital establishment—a drain on the system. However, for those who do take time to listen, it becomes apparent that the vague symptoms described in a depressed voice are a subdued appeal for treatment of a deeper felt pain. With some probing, the women talk about fear of sex, of infertility after infection, and about their genital condition, as they have no means of assessing whether they are normal. Yet in most cases they are labelled as hysterical and their feelings are dismissed.

FGM AS AN ACT OF VIOLENCE:
THE GIRL CHILD AND SOCIETY

In his paper "Interpersonal Violence: Power Relationships and Their Effects on Health," Stanley French defines interpersonal violence as: "the exercise of physical or emotional force so as to inflict injury on or damage to persons (or property). . . . It may be said that violence is any act that causes the victim to do something she or he does not want to do, or causes her to be afraid. There are several types of interpersonal violence:

physical, verbal, emotional, sexual" (1994: 3). Female genital mutilation certainly exhibits all aspects of interpersonal violence—verbal, emotional, physical, and sexual. The health complications mentioned above present only one aspect of violence that hints at the psychological trauma involved. In order to understand the damage to the girl's core identity, the "why?" of the mutilations, one must explore the social underpinnings of the communities, women's roles and power positions, and that of the men, that is the *Weltanschauung*, which French defines as "the collection of beliefs, attitudes and values that an individual or a group holds" (French, 1994: 14).

Throughout history patriarchal societies have sought to control women's sexuality and reproduction by one means or another. And circumcision has long been justified by the belief that women are unable to control their own sexuality, that they are ruled by sex. Religions have been interpreted to support this view. Thus, rules and laws were made to enforce man's control and "tradition" used to perpetuate it. As anthropologist Ashley Montagu wryly stated: "Never was the truth so madly inverted. The truth is that men are possessed by sex, while women possess it" (Hosken, 1982: 3).

Hence a little girl child learns that her genitalia are a source of preoccupation to her family, a thing of shame that has to be "cleansed" and "purified." She hears horror stories that cause her to be afraid, to have nightmares, yet she notices the taunts and insults that uncircumcised girls receive and may in turn endure. Thus a conflict of feelings is created, between wanting to please her parents and relatives by doing something that is highly valued, being "normal," and the terror of the anticipated pain.

CASE: Anab, with other girls her age, used to go out to look after the sheep of her community in Somalia. While out herding the girls would talk among themselves about their circumcisions and compare who had the smallest opening. Since she had not been infibulated yet, Anab always felt ashamed that she had nothing to show the others. Whenever she touched the hair of the infibulated girls, they screamed at her not to touch them, taunting her with being "unclean" for she had not been circumcised and shaved (after infibulation the girl's hair is washed and shaved as a rite of purification) hence her hair was dirty. One day she finally snapped and, taking a razor and string from her home, she went to an isolated spot where she tied the string around her clitoris and, pulling the string with one hand, tried to cut her clitoris with the other. She stopped when she saw the blood. Racked with pain, she sought out her paternal aunt (her mother had died). Her grandmother told her she had done the same thing to hasten the process. A few weeks later, at the age of seven, Anab was infibulated with several other girls. After a month she regained enough strength to resume her normal work and she expressed pride at not having to hide her genitals when asked if she was infibulated (Toubia, 1993: 41).

Anab's story illustrates the tremendous pressure to belong, particularly in African societies where conformity is the rule.

I believe that, although female genital mutilation exhibits all the dynamics of interpersonal violence according to the definition given by French, it cannot be classified in such a simple manner. The enormity, the impact of female mutilations is too complex to be encompassed by the narrow definition of interpersonal violence. Although it may be the relatives or a midwife that carry out the act of mutilation, the whole society, particularly the leaders (who are men), are actively involved and equally responsible for the act of mutilation, for they set the social norms. By destroying an essential part of the girl's anatomy, they annihilate forever the girl's rights to her body's integrity, her self-esteem, her initiatives. Her potential to bloom to the full extent of her personhood is nipped in the bud.

With the act of circumcision there are two primary elements that will come to govern her life as a woman. First, fertility (and polygamy). Her capacity for sexual enjoyment destroyed or diminished, she will be a breeding machine to perpetuate her husband's line. In turn, his virility increases proportionately with the number of children he has, which explains the prevalence of polygamy in most traditional and Islamic African communities. Hence she is punished severely for adultery while he is encouraged to acquire as many wives as he can afford to pay the bride prices for. Secondly, her domestic confinement, which stems directly from the above to enforce her husband's control.

Two other elements, though not directly linked to FGM, contribute to her second-class status, and may be indicative of why she and her mother accept their lot fatalistically. One is that she has no property rights. She is excluded from owning and disposing of property. Furthermore, she has no rights to her children. They are her husband's. She is bound emotionally and economically. She passes from her father's tutelage to that of her husband and finally her son. Secondly, she has no political/civic role. She is excluded from the public sphere (Hosken, 1982: 2).

I contend that female genital mutilation is not just *an* act of violence. It is an initiation into life-long violence and abuse, including future genital mutilations.

CASE: For a month after their marriage "Zena" and her husband were not able to consummate their marriage because Zena had an extremely tight circumcision. Her husband refused to let her go to the nearest hospital to be decircumcised because he feared that people would gossip and believe that he was not a real man to need such assistance. The repeated attempts were painful for Zena. Finally he followed the advice of his friend to use acid (moyat al nar). He poured the acid on her vulva, which affected all the area to the anus. Zena started to cry from the pain while her husband tried to effect penetration. His penis became affected also and he jumped off her crying. They called a midwife but omitted to tell her that the injury was due to acid. The midwife stitched the wound, but it festered, and Zena's relatives took her to the hospital. Her husband was so embarrassed that he took off to a distant hospital for his own treatment (El Dareer, 1982: 46).

Another striking feature of FGM, which is of utmost importance, is that it is not recognised as an act of violence. After all, the reasoning goes, how can what parents do out of concern for their daughters be a crime? It is shrouded in the mystifying guise of "the loving act."

MYTHS AND BELIEFS

Ultimately, FGM is a generalized form of violence aimed at controlling female sexuality. Societies that practice FGM use different justifications to rationalize this violence. Some of these justifications are briefly described below.

From a moral point of view FGM is said to safeguard virginity by preventing wayward behavior. There is also an economic aspect in that FGM protects the owner (i.e., the father) from potential "disgrace" until his daughter is safely married and the bride price collected. FGM also cures sexual "deviances" such as lesbianism, frigidity, and excessive sexual arousal. The general view being that women do not have a right to enjoy sex.

FGM is an initiation into womanhood and into the tribe. Hence the uncircumcised cannot be married. The worst insult in these communities is to be called "son/daughter of an uncircumcised woman." Also, FGM enhances the husband's sexual pleasure and makes vaginal intercourse more desirable than clitoral stimulation. This last point is interesting because it is the same argument used by Freud, who labelled clitoral orgasm as "immature," hence imposing psychological castration on Western women for decades.

It is commonly held that female genitals are dirty and need to be cleaned, that they are ugly and will grow if they are not cut back. FGM is necessary for one to become a real woman. The latter two views especially apply in West Africa, where the clitoris represents male characteristics, and the prepuce of the penis represents female characteristics, thus both have to be removed before one becomes a true male or female.

FGM is believed to allow conception and to prevent infant and maternal mortality.

Wherever it is practised FGM is a religious requirement.

In combination, the beliefs listed above only partially explain the persistence of FGM, for the practice continues to be common in urban areas and among the educated who are aware that the myths are just that—myths. Other traditional practices such as face scarring disappeared quickly enough when the men ceased to perceive them as beautiful. However, FGM is a tradition that is deeply entrenched in communities because of its fusion with religion. Men are not playing the same role in eradicating circumcision because they too are trapped in the tradition. Their virility and manhood hinge upon achieving the difficult task of penetrating the circumcised woman. Thus, many who do not fear religious fanaticism are afraid of social criticism, of being considered incompetent. As Nahid Toubia notes, "the fear of losing the psychological, moral, and material benefits of 'belonging' is one of the greatest motivators of conformity" (Toubia, 1993: 37).

Even parents who are opposed to circumcision may circumcise their girls for fear of criticism, or may resort to cheating, making all the preparations, inviting guests but instructing the midwife to just make a scratch or apply adhesive plaster in a pretence that the child has been circumcised. This does not always work, for grandmothers and other relatives may insist upon seeing the circumcision and may take matters into their own hands, often taking the child to be circumcised themselves. The case of a professional woman in Mali illustrates this.

> After I became conscious of all the trouble and problems that result from genital operations, my husband and I decided that we would not allow our children to be either excised or infibulated. My children were born in France, where both my husband and I finished our studies. When we returned to Mali my mother asked if I had the girls operated . . . I said no . . . that I am opposed to it. During the children's vacation, after I had found some work, I left them with my parents. One day, coming home from work, I stopped by my mother's house. . . . "Where are the girls?", I asked my mother. "Oh, they are in their room," she said. They were lying on the floor on some straw mats. Their swollen eyes and faces took

my breath away, and I screamed: "What has happened to my children?"
But before they could even answer, my mother replied: "Don't trouble
yourself about *my* little girls. I had them excised and infibulated this
morning." I cannot say what I felt at this moment. What could I do against
my mother? I felt revolt rising in me, but I was helpless against her. My
first reaction was to cry. She said: "You should be very happy. Everything
went well with the girls." Rather than being disrespectful, which is very
badly taken in our society in Mali . . . I quickly left the house (Hosken,
1982: 205).

ERADICATION OF FGM

For those individuals and activists who have labored in isolated
battles to eradicate FGM, it has become increasingly clear that, in order to
do so, a linking of efforts and resources is mandatory at the grassroots, national, and international levels.

Starting at the grassroots level, the steps to eradicate FGM would involve
education, legislation, religious authorities, and social responsibility. To
elaborate, education relating to anatomy and sexuality, which in most African societies are taboo topics, has to be made widely available to women
and men, through family care centres, the midwives, and other communal
centres. Missionary and public schools must include sex education as part
of their curricula. Legislation must be introduced to support such initiatives. The legislation that has been introduced to ban FGM has been ineffective, for example in Sudan, because it was introduced by a colonial
power and did not expressly forbid FGM. Sunna was allowed. Midwives
who did end up in court claimed that their knives slipped.

One practical suggestion by Asma M. A'Haleem (1992) is a civil law that
allows a child the right to sue, after puberty, her parents and/or the midwife for a civil remedy. A woman who is hesitant about seeking a judgment
against her parents will have no problem initiating a lawsuit against the
midwife or the physician, knowing this may deter the practitioners.

Other suggestions include revoking practitioners' licences and prison
terms for parents of the victims. The former will target physicians primarily, since most midwives have no formal training. This proposal is very important because there is a recurring theme of justification by doctors who
practice FGM, and by lawyers who want to legally designate a group that
may be allowed to practice FGM, claiming that it will ensure that FGM is
hygienically done, resulting in fewer complications later on. The real question is, how can physicians medically justify a practice that has no medical

benefits, and indeed inflicts injury on their patients? How can they, in good conscience, make money by inflicting bodily and other damage to unconsenting patients? To do so is a clear violation of the Hippocratic Oath.

Another important aspect is that all the legitimacy and respect reserved for physicians is transferred to the practice of FGM itself, entrenching the custom even further. Somalia, with a 98 percent FGM rate, is a good example of this. Modern medicine is being used by hospitals in Somalia to efficiently churn out mutilated girls at an assembly-line pace.

Religious authorities acknowledge that FGM is not a requirement in Islam or Christianity. Such authorities must be actively involved in denouncing this practice. The silence of the past is not good enough. Religious silence is taken to be tacit approval, as indicated in a nationwide survey by Dr. Asma El Dareer (1982) in Sudan.

Finally there is the issue of social responsibility, particularly for men who, because of their social status, are at present in a better position to learn about the nature and consequences of FGM. They, and the educated women, should encourage the elimination of FGM among their own family members.

National governments are beginning to realize that their goals of modernization cannot continue to exclude 50 percent of their populations. This is especially true given the fact that African women carry a disproportionate burden in food production as well as family care. Women who are kept ignorant cannot teach their children to cope with the changing face of Africa. The governments cannot afford the medical drain of their scarce resources as a result of complications caused by FGM. Thus eradication should be given high priority. Governments can sponsor and encourage the grassroots initiatives mentioned above.

One must take a closer look at the initiation rites with which FGM is usually associated. These rites are a way in which guidance and knowledge are transmitted from one generation to the other. Yet the fact that a harmful practice such as FGM is associated with these rites has led some people to denounce both. They are then bewildered by the opposition from the women in the communities that they are trying to help. Women (particularly the older ones) are the propagators and holders of tradition, and have been loud in their protests against what they perceive to be an attack on their cultural identity. Therefore care has to be taken to find ways to transmit positive cultural values while taking measures to eliminate the harmful ones.

International organizations have to participate more actively than they have in the past. The argument that they cannot interfere in a "cultural" practice unless invited to do so by the governments involved is not acceptable. FGM is a health epidemic and therefore deserves the global mobilizations that smallpox and polio generated in the past. It is a human rights violation—an individual rights violation—the right to be born free and equal and to live with dignity. It is a medical ethics issue as modern medicine plays an increasing role in FGM operations. With the widespread immigration to the West in the last two decades, FGM cannot be conveniently swept under the rug as an "African" or "Arab" problem. These mutilated girls and women now include French, American, Dutch, and Canadian citizens. Though most Western countries where it is a problem have passed legislation, or are in the process of doing so (e.g., U.S.A.), their publics are a huge potential resource in advancing the elimination of FGM. By raising awareness through mainstream media, public opinion can be crucial in maintaining pressure on development and aid organizations to fully use their influence in eliminating FGM.

I would like to point out that some recent initiatives are encouraging. In February 1994 there was an international meeting held in Anand, India. The meeting involved representatives from several non-governmental organizations, officials from various governments, UNICEF, and the Inter-African Committee, which was set up in 1984 as a steering committee for FGM eradication. Among the initiatives evaluated and discussed were a training and information campaign, the training of traditional birth attendants, production of educational material, coordination between non-governmental organizations and governments, and surveys started by certain non-governmental organizations to assess the impact of previous campaigns aimed at changing attitudes.

The focus seems to be on education and changing social attitudes. Interestingly enough, the materials from the Anand meeting give no indication of whether legal initiatives are being undertaken as well. Progress is slow. It was noted at the Anand meeting that one of the core trainers in the Eradication of Harmful Traditional Practices program for midwives had herself recently submitted to family pressure and had her daughter circumcised.

SECTION 3

SEXUAL HARASSMENT IN
LEGAL AND MEDICAL CONTEXTS

CHAPTER SEVEN

Identifying Sexual Harassment: The Reasonable Woman Standard

DEBRA A. DEBRUIN

On the topic of sexual harassment, people in our society agree *only* about the claim that there is tremendous and heated *disagreement* over what kinds of behavior ought to count as sexual harassment. We are all familiar with how the "discussion" of this issue typically goes: Some people contend that others are uptight or hypersensitive. Others insist that some "just don't get it." This kind of conversation amounts to a mere clash of perceptions that does little, if anything, to advance our understanding of the issue.

We need a different kind of conversation—a philosophical discussion about what kind of criteria we should adopt for classifying behavior as sexual harassment. There is precious little public discussion of this issue among professional philosophers, but a fairly active debate about it has been taking place in our courts. In recent years at least a handful of judges have contended that our society should adopt what has been called "the reasonable woman standard" for identifying sexual harassment. Roughly, this standard establishes "that a female plaintiff states a *prima facie* case of hostile environment sexual harassment when she alleges conduct which a reasonable woman would consider sufficiently severe or pervasive to alter the conditions of employment and create an abusive working environment" (*Ellison v. Brady*, 626). Judges who have rejected this standard have done so because they believe that its gender specificity violates fundamental norms of justice. My aim in this paper is to demonstrate that justice demands a gender-specific standard.[1] I shall do so by defending the adoption of such a standard against the leading objections advanced by the courts.

[107]

A BRIEF JUDICIAL HISTORY

The courts recognize two distinct forms of sexual harassment: quid pro quo harassment, and hostile environment harassment. Quid pro quo harassment, as the name suggests, involves the demand that sex be provided in exchange for some employment or educational benefit (such as job promotion or good grades) or the avoidance of some detriment (such as dismissal). The courts first recognized that quid pro quo sexual harassment constitutes a form of sex discrimination in 1976 (*Williams v. Saxbe*; MacKinnon, 1979: 57–99, esp. 60).[2] Since 1981 courts have also allowed claims for so-called hostile environment sexual harassment— sex-based harassment that creates an "intimidating, hostile or offensive environment" (*Henson v. City of Dundee*, 903; Abrams, 1989: 1183).[3] However, as the Supreme Court of New Jersey acknowledged in *Lehmann v. Toys 'R' Us, Inc.*, "quid pro quo sexual harassment is more easily recognized and more clearly defined and well-established as a cause of action. Hostile work environment sexual harassment, on the other hand, has only recently been recognized as actionable sexual harassment. Because of the relatively recent recognition of the harm, some confusion remains in the minds of employers and employees concerning what sorts of conduct constitute hostile work environment sexual harassment" (452).

Thus our search for a criterion for identifying sexual harassment focuses on hostile environment sexual harassment. The disagreement in the courts concerning the adoption of such a criterion primarily turns on the choice between a gender-neutral *reasonable person standard* and the gender-specific *reasonable woman standard*. Since the debate has centered on the concepts of gender neutrality and gender specificity, we must get clear on those concepts. It may seem obvious that the reasonable woman standard is gender-specific while the reasonable person standard is gender-neutral. However, the reasonable woman standard actually requires that we judge whether conduct is severe or pervasive enough to create an intimidating, hostile, or offensive environment from the perspective of *a reasonable person of the same gender as the alleged victim*. It has been named the reasonable woman standard because, in the vast majority of cases, the alleged victims of sexual harassment are women. While both standards apply to members of both genders, one is gender-specific and the other is gender-neutral. The reasonable woman standard is gender-specific because it specifies the gender of the reasonable person from whose perspective we are to judge matters; it *requires* that we view matters from a perspective that is gendered in a particular way. Thus, for example, the standard requires a man to view the situation from the perspective of a reasonable woman when thinking about a case in which the alleged victim is a woman. The reasonable person standard, on the other hand, is gender-neutral, because it makes no specifications about the gender of the person from whose perspective we are to judge matters. It requires that our perspective be genderless—that we abstract from considerations of gender, that we filter out the influence of gender on our perspective—when we think about an alleged case of sexual harassment. So the reasonable person standard *forbids* us from asking, "How would I have felt if I had been *of the same gender as the alleged victim* and subject to the treatment in question?" when trying to judge alleged cases of sexual harassment.

From whose perspective should we judge whether conduct is severe or pervasive enough to create an intimidating, hostile, or offensive environment—the (allegedly) genderless perspective of the reasonable person, or the (clearly) gendered perspective of the reasonable woman? The dispute began in *Rabidue v. Osceola Refining Co.* In this case, the Sixth Circuit Court of Appeals assumed that "to accord appropriate protection to both plaintiffs and defendants in a hostile and/or abusive work environment sexual harassment case, the trier of fact, when judging the totality of the circumstances impacting upon the asserted abusive and hostile environment placed in issue by the plaintiff's charges, must adopt the perspective of a reasonable *person's* reaction to a similar environment under essentially like or similar circumstances" (*Rabidue v. Osceola Refining Co.*, 620; emphasis added).

On this basis, the court ruled that Vivienne Rabidue had not suffered hostile environment sexual harassment. It concluded that the behavior to which Rabidue had been subjected did not create an intimidating, hostile, or offensive environment because (as we shall see below) it judged that such behavior would have nothing more than a negligible impact on a reasonable person in Rabidue's circumstances. Judge Keith, in his dissenting opinion, argued that courts should reject the reasonable person standard and adopt the reasonable woman standard. Since then, some courts have embraced the reasonable woman standard—most notably the Third Circuit Court of Appeals in *Andrews v. City of Philadelphia*, the Ninth Circuit Court of Appeals in *Ellison v. Brady*, the Eighth Circuit Court of Appeals in *Burns v. McGregor Electronic Industries, Inc.*, and the Supreme Court of New Jersey in *Lehmann v. Toys 'R' Us, Inc.* However, during this time other courts have insisted upon relying on the reasonable person standard—most notably the Sixth Circuit Court of Appeals in *Davis v. Monsanto Chemical Co.*, the Fifth Circuit Court of Appeals in *DeAngelis v. El Paso Municipal Police Officers Association*, the Supreme Court of Michigan in *Radtke v. Everett*, and the United States Supreme Court in *Harris v. Forklift Systems, Inc.*

REASONABLE PERSON OR REASONABLE WOMAN?

Courts object to the gender-specific nature of the reasonable woman standard for two main reasons:[4] (1) only gender-neutral standards can be acceptably uniform (the Uniformity Objection); and (2) gender-specific standards "could entrench the very sexist attitudes" (*Radtke v. Everett*, 167) they are meant to counter (the Entrenching Sexism Objection). I shall take these up in turn.

The Uniformity Objection

The Uniformity Objection goes like this:[5] (1) The reasonable person standard is a community standard. That is, the reasonable person is "a personification of a community ideal of reasonable behavior, determined by the jury's social judgment" (*Radtke v. Everett*, 166). (2) The reasonable woman standard, on the other hand, "eliminates community standards and replaces them with standards formulated by a subset of the community" (*Radtke v. Everett*, 166).[6] (3) Justice requires that the law treat everyone equally; "the law can have no favorites" (*Radtke v. Everett*, 166). (4) Allowing a subset of the community to set standards of behavior for the community violates the dictum that the law must treat everyone equally. (5) Thus, we must reject the reasonable woman standard and embrace the reasonable person standard. The fundamental idea in this argument is that justice must be blind (in this case, gender-blind).

Must justice be blind? Among other things, justice must require that we strive to eliminate oppression. It is commonplace to think that gender oppression is simply the privileging of one gender over another, and so that striving to eliminate oppression means striving for gender neutrality. Is the privileging of the perspective of women inherent in the reasonable woman standard unjust? Does justice require that we embrace the reasonable person standard instead?

No. To see why, we must get a clearer understanding of the nature of oppression. People commonly think of oppression as something that takes place entirely in the sphere of action: in the distribution of benefits and burdens to persons in society. But one central aspect of oppression concerns how groups, and individuals in those groups, are conceived of in society. Oppressive societies take the dominant group's identity and experience to be not the particular identity or experience of one group in society, but universal identity and experience—that is, the norm.[7] I shall call this aspect of oppression "false universalism." This account of false universalism does not presuppose that members of dominant groups hate members of subordinate groups, or that the former conspire to use their power to keep the latter in "their place." Rather, the idea is that people in oppressive societies are acculturated to conceive of groups and the individuals in them in certain ways. One virtue of this account is that it recognizes that people often participate in oppressive practices without consciously choosing to do so or even being aware that they are doing so. The upshot of false universalism in male-dominated societies is that men's identity and experience serve as the standard of what it is to be a person. This is true only of men's identity and experience; it is not true of women's.

According to sociologists Kimmel and Messner, there is a sociological explanation for this conceptual phenomenon. "The mechanisms that afford us privilege are very often invisible to us. . . . Thus, white people rarely think of themselves as 'raced' people, rarely think of race as a central element in their experience" (1992: 2–3). Hence, I contend, we use the phrase "people of color" to refer to everyone but white people—as though whites have no color or race. Moreover, with respect to ethnicity (and ethnocentrism), we use the phrase "ethnic food" to refer to many types of cuisines—e.g., Chinese, Thai, Indian, Ethiopian, soul food—but not western European cuisines such as French or Italian food—as though only people and food that are not of western European descent have ethnicity. According to Kimmel and Messner, the same point holds for gender. That is, men rarely think of themselves as gendered persons, rarely think of gender as a central element in their experience. Indeed, Kimmel and Messner suggest, when asked what kind of being they see when they look at themselves in the mirror, white men tend to respond "a person" or "a human" (race- and gender-neutral), but white women tend to respond "a woman" (race-neutral but gender-specific), and black women tend to respond "a black woman" (race- and gender-specific) (2).

Our use of language bears out the point that our society takes men's identity and experience as the standard of what it is to be a person. The way we talk reflects the way we think. In our language, terms such as "he" and "man" serve as gender-neutral terms; terms such as "she" and "woman" do not. Also, we qualify gender-neutral occupation terms when women, but not men, hold the occupation in question. For example, we speak of "women doctors," "female professors," and "lady cops" but not "male doctors," "men professors," or "gentlemen cops." Her gender is irrelevant; his is not.[8] She is conceived of in gendered terms; he is not. His identity and experience serve as the standard of what it is to be a doctor, professor, police officer—or even a person.

False universalism is reflected in our behavior as well. Some of the most interesting examples of false universalism in action come from scientific research; I shall mention two such cases here.

First, medical research has traditionally been conducted on all-male study populations, even when the research concerns conditions that affect both men and women and is used as a basis for treating both men and women. One of the main reasons given by researchers for this exclusion of women has been their claim that women's hormonal cycles "'confound' or confuse research results" (Herman, 1992: 10–16). By appealing to this argument, scientists (perhaps not consciously) take men's physiology as paradigmatic for humans, and view women as not merely different from men, but as deviant or problematic.[9] Second, about the dominant theories of the psychology of human development, Carol Gilligan writes:

> These observations about sex differences support the conclusion reached by David McClelland . . . that "sex role turns out to be one of the most important determinants of human behavior; psychologists have found sex differences in their studies from the moment they started doing empirical research." But since it is difficult to say "different" without saying "better" or "worse;" since there is a tendency to construct a single scale of measurement, and since that scale has generally been derived from and standardized on the basis of men's interpretations of research data drawn predominantly or exclusively from studies of males, psychologists "have tended to regard male behavior as the 'norm' and female behavior as some kind of deviation from that norm." . . . Thus when women do not conform to the standard of psychological experience, the conclusion has generally been that something is wrong with the women.[10] (Gilligan, 1982: 14)

Thus the conduct of our scientific research further bears out the point that our society takes men's identity and experience as the characterization or standard of what it is to be a person.

False universalism has two consequences. First, it makes women invisible in the following sense. When we think "person," we tend to think not of women but of our paradigm persons—men. Women tend to disappear from the conceptual scene when we're thinking in gender-neutral terms, because we tend to think of women only in terms of their gender. On the other hand, men tend not to disappear, because we tend not to conceive of men in gender-specific terms but as the standard of what it is to be a person. Second, insofar as they are different from men, women are conceived of as inferior, deficient, or deviant. If they were not, if their differences were viewed as *mere* differences, this would challenge men's claim to universality, their ability to serve as the standard of what it is to be a person.

False universalism is a central aspect of oppression. In an oppressive society such as ours, purportedly gender-neutral standards such as the reasonable person standard are not truly gender-neutral. When we ask whether a reasonable person would experience a situation of alleged hostile environment sexual harassment as being pervasive or severe enough to create an intimidating, hostile, or offensive environment, we tend to think not of how women would experience the conduct in question, but how men would.

Consider, for example, two cases in which the reasonable person standard was applied:

In *Scott v. Sears, Roebuck and Co.*, 798 F.2d 210, 212 (Seventh Circuit 1986), the Seventh Circuit analyzed a female employee's working conditions for sexual harassment. It noted that she was repeatedly propositioned and winked at by her supervisor. When she asked for assistance, he asked "what will I get for it?" Co-workers slapped her buttocks and commented that she must moan and groan during sex. . . . The court did not consider the environment sufficiently hostile.

Similarly, in *Rabidue v. Osceola Refining Co.*, 805 F.2d 611 (Sixth Circuit 1986), *cert. denied*, 481 U.S. 1041, 107 S.Ct. 1983, 95 L.Ed.2d 823 (1987), the Sixth Circuit refused to find a hostile environment where the workplace contained posters of naked and partially dressed women, and where a male employee customarily called women "whores," "cunt," "pussy," and "tits," referred to plaintiff as "fat ass," and specifically stated, "All that bitch needs is a good lay." Over strong dissent, the majority held that the sexist remarks and the pin-up posters had only a de minimis [i.e., a negligible] effect. (*Ellison v. Brady*: 877)

The purportedly gender-blind reasonable person standard *is* blind, but it is blind, not to gender altogether, but to the perspectives and experiences of women. Moreover, insofar as women's experience of allegedly harassing conduct differs from men's—and we all know that it does—women's experience tends to be characterized as deviant or deficient: women are deemed uptight or hypersensitive or worse. Thus, the concept of false universalism makes sense of not only the conceptual and linguistic phenomena discussed above, but also the conduct of the public debate about sexual harassment.

Since, in an oppressive society such as ours, purportedly gender-neutral standards are not truly gender-neutral, both the reasonable person standard and the reasonable woman standard privilege the perspective of one gender over the other.[11] Justice cannot require us to adopt a gender-neutral standard if one is not available. So whose perspective ought we to privilege in adopting a standard for identifying hostile environment sexual harassment—men's or women's? The answer is, women's.

> Adopting the victim's perspective ensures that courts will not "sustain ingrained notions of reasonable behavior fashioned by the offenders." *Lipsett*, 864 F.2d at 898, *quoting Rabidue*, 805 F.2d at 626 (Keith, J., dissenting). Congress did not enact Title VII to codify prevailing sexist prejudices. To the contrary, "Congress designed Title VII to prevent the perpetuation of stereotypes and a sense of degradation which serve to close or discourage employment opportunities for women." *Andrews*, 895 F.2d at 1483 (*Ellison v. Brady*, 880–81)

It is a misdescription of the situation to say, as the Uniformity Objection does, that the reasonable woman standard "eliminates community standards and replaces them with standards formulated by a subset of the community" (*Radtke v. Everett*, 166). So-called community standards, such as the reasonable person standard, are not uniform standards. Rather, they too are the standards of a subset of the community, the dominant group. We cannot eliminate oppression if we continue to privilege the perspectives and standards of dominant groups over those of oppressed groups. Thus, given a choice between adopting a criterion of sexual harassment that privileges men's perspective and one that privileges women's, justice requires that we privilege the perspective of women.

The Entrenching Sexism Objection

The other main argument courts give against the reasonable woman standard goes like this:

> Although well-intentioned, a gender-conscious standard could reintrench the very sexist attitudes it is attempting to counter. The belief that women are entitled to a separate legal standard merely reinforces, and perhaps originates from, the stereotypic notion that first justified subordinating women in the workplace. Courts utilizing the reasonable woman standard pour into the standard stereotypic assumptions of women which infer women are sensitive, fragile, and in need of a more protective standard. Such paternalism degrades women and is repugnant

to the very ideals of equality that the [civil rights] act is intended to protect. (*Radtke v. Everett*, 167)

This argument, too, calls for a gender-blind standard, which, the argument implies, will contain no stereotypic assumptions about women and so will promote equality.

Rather than providing a gender-neutral standard with no stereotypic assumptions about women, the reasonable person standard reflects the perspective of the dominant gender in our society, which is laden with such stereotypes. Rather than providing equal protection for men and women, the reasonable person standard privileges the perspective of men and renders the perspective of women invisible; recall the first consequence of false universalism.

The reasonable woman standard, on the other hand, provides equal protection for both men and women. At the most general level, it prescribes the same treatment for men and women. It identifies as sexual harassment conduct that a reasonable person of the same gender as the alleged victim would judge to be sufficiently severe or pervasive to create an intimidating, hostile, or offensive environment. Gender-specific differences in protection arise only when a reasonable man and a reasonable woman disagree about whether they would judge that such an environment had been created, were they (gendered as they are, not imagining themselves with the gender of the alleged victim) subject to the conditions in question. Of course, such differences do arise. Women often think that sexual harassment has occurred in situations in which men feel that it has not.[12] The commonplace nature of such disagreements accounts, in large part, for the character of the public debate about sexual harassment with its familiar generalizations: women insisting that men just don't get it, and men charging that women are hypersensitive and uptight. If we were to apply the reasonable woman standard, certain conditions would qualify as sexual harassment when women are subject to them, but not when men are subject to them. So the reasonable woman standard does, indeed, protect women from conditions from which it does not protect men. (I am not saying that the reasonable woman standard protects men from none of the conditions from which it protects women. By this standard, some conditions count as sexual harassment when experienced by either women or men.)

Does the reasonable woman standard thus establish a higher level of protection for women than for men, so treating women "as if they remained models of Victorian reticence" (*DeAngelis v. El Paso Municipal Police Officers Association*, 593) who are "sensitive, fragile, and in need of a more protective standard" (*Radtke v. Everett*, 167)? When we protect a woman from specific situations from which we would not protect men, we thereby treat her as sensitive and fragile only if what we are protecting her from is not really serious enough to qualify as sexual harassment. If we were to adopt these gender-based differences in protection, would we be sheltering women from situations that do not qualify as sexual harassment? To assume that the answer to this question is "yes" is to treat the man's perspective as capturing the objective truth about the situation and the woman's perspective as being clouded by hypersensitive subjectivity. But that would be to fall into the trap of false universalism. Recall its second consequence: that insofar as women differ from men, they are deemed inferior or deficient. Could we not assume instead that women are objective and men are hampered by an inability to truly understand? Or we could believe that men and women are both correct: that what he judges not to be sexual harassment indeed is not for him, but is for her.

We should embrace this relativistic option. It can be reasonable for a woman to object to treatment that a reasonable man would find unproblematic (or less problematic) were he subject to it, given that men and women tend to occupy different places in the social order. Not only do norms of masculinity and femininity affect nearly every aspect of our lives and identities, but men belong to a dominant group, and women belong to a subordinate group, by virtue of gender, rather than some other attribute (such as race, economic class, sexual preference, etc.). This difference in social position affects men's and women's lives in a myriad of ways—ways that must be understood if we are to comprehend what our norms of reasonableness ought to be. For instance, in our culture, women face a far greater risk of rape and sexual abuse than men do. Thus behavior such as unwelcome touching, or hostile sexual comments, which may seem harmless, or amusing, or inappropriate, or annoying, or perhaps even shocking to a man, may well seem highly threatening to a woman. It is one thing to be subjected to behavior that reasonably makes one feel shocked and offended, and quite another, and a more serious thing, to be subjected to behavior that reasonably makes one feel threatened.

Let us consider the behavior at issue in *Ellison v. Brady*. Kerry Ellison and Sterling Gray both worked as revenue agents with the IRS in San Mateo, California. They did not become friends, and they did not work closely together, though Gray's desk was only twenty feet from Ellison's. Gray persistently asked Ellison out; she consistently declined and avoided him. He "pester[ed] her with unnecessary questions and [hung] around her desk" (873). One day, Gray handed her a note which read, "I cried over you last night and I'm totally drained today. I have never been in such constant term oil [sic]. Thank you for talking with me. I could not stand to feel your hatred for another day" (874). When Ellison read the note "she became shocked and frightened and left the room" (874). Gray followed her out and demanded that she talk to him, but Ellison refused. Ellison then showed the note to her supervisor (a woman), who told Ellison that Gray's behavior constituted sexual harassment. Ellison requested that she be allowed to handle the situation informally; she asked a male co-worker to tell Gray that Ellison was not interested in him and she wanted him to leave her alone. The male co-worker did so. The next day Gray called in sick. Before Gray returned to work, Ellison began a previously scheduled four-week training course in a city halfway across the country.

Gray tracked her down and mailed her a three-page, single-spaced, typed letter. It included the following message: "I know that you are worth knowing with or without sex. . . . Leaving aside the hassles and disasters of recent weeks. I have enjoyed you so much over these past few months. Watching you. Experiencing you from O [sic] so far away. Admiring your style and elan. . . . Don't you think it odd that two people who have never even talked together, alone, are striking off such intense sparks. . . . I will [write] another letter in the near future" (874). The letter "made repeated references to sex" (880). It frightened Ellison; she thought Gray was crazy and was worried about what he might do next. She immediately contacted her supervisor, who repeatedly demanded that Gray leave Ellison alone. Gray responded by transferring to the IRS office in San Francisco.

However, after Ellison returned to the San Mateo office from her training course, Gray filed a union grievance and demanded that he be allowed to transfer back. The IRS acquiesced. This worried Ellison. Two further developments made her even more fearful: Gray requested joint counseling to patch things up, and Ellison received yet another letter from Gray in which he made it clear that he was still thinking of her in the way he had been at the time of his previous missives. Ellison then filed a sexual harassment complaint against Gray.

One can imagine that, had it been a man in Ellison's place, he might have reacted quite differently than Ellison did. He might well not have felt threatened. He might have been annoyed; he might even have been flattered. (A teaching assistant I knew received letters from a male student similar to the letters Ellison received from Gray. She was advised by her supervisor to report the letters to her dean. The dean dismissed her worries, telling her that he would be flattered if he received such attentions from a student.) Indeed, the District Court that initially heard Ellison's case decided that she had not been sexually harassed; it ruled that Gray's behavior was "genuinely trivial" (876). Only when the appellate court applied the reasonable woman standard was it decided that Ellison had been sexually harassed.

The appellate court ruled appropriately. Not only did Ellison react differently in her situation than a man might have, it was reasonable for her to have done so. To understand why, we must consider the social context in which the situation occurred. Given that women face a far greater risk than men of sexual assault, stalking, rape, and other forms of violence, including murder, it is reasonable for women to experience fear or feel threatened when a man might not. Had Ellison been a man and Gray a woman, it would have been reasonable for him not to take her behavior as seriously. Since Gray's behavior was persistent and made a reasonable woman's work environment frightening and threatening, we must conclude that it created a hostile, abusive, or offensive environment— that is, that Gray's behavior was not "genuinely trivial" but rather sexual harassment.

Thus reasonable women can experience as sexually harassing behavior that reasonable men would not experience as such. Since this is so, we do not establish a higher level of protection for women if we protect them from behavior from which we do not protect men. But what if we adopted a gender-neutral standard for sexual harassment, protecting men and women only from the same behaviors? Then we would find ourselves in one of the following two scenarios.

In the first scenario we protect everyone only from the behavior that reasonable men would experience as sexually harassing. That is, given false universalism, we adopt the reasonable person standard, by which men receive full protection from sexual harassment, since they are protected from everything that reasonable men would experience as sexually harassing. But women would not be fully protected, because it is possible for reasonable women to experience as sexually harassing behavior that reasonable men would not experience as such. If we protect women only from behavior that reasonable men experience as sexually harassing, then we fail to protect women from some behavior that is sexually harassing to them. In this first scenario we do not provide equal protection for men and women, but rather appropriate protection for men and inadequate protection for women.

In the second scenario we protect everyone from all the behaviors that reasonable women would experience as sexually harassing. Women would thus receive full protection from sexual harassment, and men would be protected from some behavior that really was not sexually harassing to them. In this second scenario we do not provide equal protection for men and women, but appropriate protection for women and a higher level of protection for men.

Uniform standards that are blind to gender differences could provide equal protection for men and women only if gender differences were irrelevant. But gender differences matter significantly to the issue of sexual harassment. Therefore only a gender-conscious standard can protect men and women from all and only those behaviors that are sexually harassing to them. Contrary to the claims of the Entrenching Sexism Objection, the reasonable woman standard does not treat women "as if they remained models of Victorian reticence" who are "sensitive, fragile, and in need of a higher standard."

Although it does not discuss false universalism, or indeed provide any analysis of sex discrimination to ground its claims, the Ninth Circuit Court recognizes in *Ellison v. Brady* that

> The reasonable woman standard does not establish a higher level of protection for women than men. . . . Instead, a gender-conscious examination of sexual harassment enables women to participate in the workplace *on an equal footing with men*. By acknowledging and not trivializing the effects of sexual harassment on reasonable women, courts can work toward ensuring that *neither men nor women* will have to "run a gauntlet of sexual abuse in return for the privilege of being allowed to work and make a living." *Henson v. Dundee*, 682 F.2d 897, 902 (11th Cir. 1982). (*Ellison v. Brady*, 879–80; emphasis added)

The court rightly insists that "adopting the victim's perspective ensures that courts will not 'sustain ingrained notions of reasonable behavior fashioned by the offenders'" (880–81). On the other hand, adopting a falsely gender-neutral perspective ensures that we will perpetuate male dominance and fail to protect women from sexual harassment. Thus, it is not the reasonable woman standard but the reasonable person standard that "degrades women and is repugnant to the very ideals of equality that the [civil rights] act is intended to protect" (*Radtke v. Everett*, 167).

ON REASONABLENESS

My aim in this essay has been to defend the gender specificity of the reasonable woman standard, and that I have now done. A complete account this standard must explain how we ought to understand the notion of reasonableness.

We are committed to developing some account of this notion; any acceptable standard for determining what types of behavior count as sexual harassment must involve the perspective of the *reasonable* woman. We cannot legitimately sidestep the difficulties involved in developing standards of reasonableness by appealing instead to the perspective of the "average" woman (the standard used by the U. S. District Court in *Rabidue v. Osceola Refining Co.*, 433) when deciding what counts as sexual harassment. In the first place, it is not clear that such a maneuver saves us any trouble, since we would then need an account of the "average woman." Also, since women are as subject to sexist acculturalization as men are, the so-called average woman might not classify as sexual harassment behaviors that other women would reasonably consider to be sexual harassment. Thus, if our legal standard appealed to the perspective of the average woman, some cases that should be decided in favor of the plaintiff would instead be decided in favor of the defendant. The average woman standard would yield unacceptable results from the point of view of justice.

Similarly, we cannot sidestep the difficulties involved in developing standards of reasonableness by appealing instead to the perspective of *any* woman when deciding what counts as sexual harassment. Such a criterion would classify as sexual harassment any behavior that at least one woman found to be intimidating, hostile or offensive, no matter how unreasonable or hypersensitive she was. (I am not saying here that women tend to be overly sensitive; I am merely pointing out the conceptual consequences of the adoption of such an "any woman" standard.) We cannot legitimately proscribe behavior that appears intimidating, hostile, or offensive to only the most unreasonable, hypersensitive person. Thus, we need an account of reasonableness.

An acceptable account of reasonableness must acknowledge, contrary to the findings of the courts, that it is reasonable for a woman to find such behaviors as those described in *Scott v. Sears, Roebuck and Co.* and *Rabidue v. Osceola Refining Co.* to be sufficiently intimidating, hostile, or offensive to classify them as sexual harassment: repeated propositioning by a supervisor, jokes about quid pro quo exchanges, co-workers' explicit comments and questions about the woman's private sexual behavior, and touching of the woman's private parts; having to work in an environment containing posters of naked and scantily clad women with a male co-worker who regularly engages in vulgar, sexual name-calling ("whore," "cunt," "pussy," "tits," "fat ass") and making hostile sexual suggestions ("All that bitch needs is a good lay.").

In general, an acceptable account of reasonableness must be based on an adequate understanding of what it is like to be a woman in this society.

That is, an account of reasonableness must be developed relative to the relevant context. Since men and women occupy different places in the social order, it can often be reasonable for a woman to object to treatment that a man would find to be relatively unproblematic were he subject to it. The gender difference in risks of rape, stalking, and sexual abuse or violence by no means exhausts the innumerable ways in which our lives are affected by our gender. We must keep in mind that, despite gains, women remain subordinated in our society. Consider the example of the display of pornography in the workplace.[13] Given women's risk of sexual victimization, such a display could understandably make a woman in that setting uncomfortable, worried about the possibilities of sexual exploitation. It would be reasonable for a woman who had to work in such a setting to feel that she, too, was conceived of by her male co-workers as a "piece of meat," and not taken seriously as an equal partner. The important general point is that information about how gender affects our lives is crucial if we are to determine whether it is reasonable to judge that certain treatment is severe or pervasive enough to create an intimidating, hostile, or offensive environment, and thus is hostile-environment sexual harassment.

Much more needs to be said before we have a full account of reasonableness, but this discussion indicates an important criterion of adequacy for such an account. The development of such an account will be no simple task; it will require an understanding of the pervasive and complicated effect that gender has on our lives in our society.

It is unwise simply to have faith that individual judges have sufficient understanding of the effects of gender to make acceptable judgments about reasonableness. Nor should we be content that we are solving this problem if we simply work for the appointment of judges in whom our faith is justified. Such an attempt at reform, though valuable, is too slow and piecemeal to be a sufficient strategy. Our society should not leave judgments of reasonableness completely up to judges, as it does now. Instead, sexual harassment regulations should codify guidelines for making such judgments. These guidelines should be as specific as possible—including specific types of behavior that it is reasonable to classify as sexual harassment. Such guidelines should help to insure that proper decisions are given in sexual harassment cases.

But in addition to developing such guidelines, we should develop educational programs designed to prevent sexual harassment. Such programs would disseminate information about what kinds of behavior constitute sexual harassment, and in so doing increase awareness of the relevant ways in which gender affects our lives. As the *Ellison* court put it, "we hope that over time both men and women will learn what conduct offends reasonable members of the other sex. When employers and employees internalize the standard of workplace conduct we establish today, the current gap in perception between the sexes will be bridged" (*Ellison v. Brady*, 881). Thus the reasonable woman standard should not only govern legal action concerning sexual harassment, it should also inform our public discussion of it. We must reject both of the judiciary's main arguments against the gender specificity of the reasonable woman standard. We must see that, at least at this point in our history, embracing a gender-neutral ideal of justice damns us to the perpetuation of gender oppression.

LEGAL CASES CITED

Andrews v. City of Philadelphia, 895 F.2d 1469 (3d Cir. 1990)

Burns v. McGregor Electronic Industries, Inc., 989 F.2d 959 (8th Cir. 1993)

Davis v. Monsanto Chemical Co., 858 F.2d 345 (6th Cir. 1988)

DeAngelis v. El Paso Municipal Police Officers Association, 51 F.3d 591 (5th Cir. 1995)

Ellison v. Brady, 924 F.2d 872 (9th Cir. 1991)

Harris v. Forklift Systems, Inc., 114 S.Ct. 367 (1993)

Henson v. City of Dundee, 682 F.2d 897 (11th Cir. 1982)

Lehmann v. Toys 'R' Us, Inc., 626 A.2d 445 (NJ 1993)

Meritor Savings Bank v. Vinson, 477 US 57, 91 L Ed 2d 49, 106 S Ct 2399

Rabidue v. Osceola Refining Co., 584 F.Supp. 419 (1984)

Rabidue v. Osceola Refining Co., 805 F.2d 611 (6th Cir. 1986)

Radtke v. Everett, 501 N.W.2d 155 (Mich. 1993)

Scott v. Sears, Roebuck and Co., 798 F.2d 210, 212 (7th Cir. 1986)

Williams v. Saxbe, 413 F. Supp. 654 (D.D.C. 1976)

CHAPTER EIGHT

"Her Body Her Own Worst Enemy": The Medicalization of Violence against Women

ABBY L. WILKERSON

Philosopher Susan J. Brison (see Chapter 1) writes of an experience that "undermined [her] most fundamental assumptions about the world": "walking down a quiet, sunlit country road one moment and . . . battling a murderous attacker the next" (1995: 38). After being "beaten, raped, strangled, and left for dead at the bottom of a ravine," Brison attempted "to rebuild my shattered system of beliefs," which included searching the philosophical literature on the subject. She concludes that "other philosophers (with a few, rare, feminist exceptions) have not been able to face the fact of violence against women."

From this personal perspective Brison identifies the central philosophical concerns related to rape: "the undoing of the self," an "inability to feel at home in the world," a "paradox of practical reason: I can't go on. I must go on," and "a radical undermining of trust" (1995: 38). She contends that women's perspectives are a central, necessary aspect of the philosophical analysis of rape.

I believe such an analysis is called for in the context of health care. To some, violence against women may not seem to be an issue acutely in need of the guidance of bioethics; it does not, on the face of it, give rise to the dilemmas of medical practice that are the staples of bioethics. Many phy-

I thank Sandra Bartky, Lisa Heldke, Timothy Murphy, and Pat McGann for their painstaking readings of earlier versions of this paper, and their very helpful suggestions. I also thank the women of Sarah's Inn, a domestic violence service agency in Oak Park, Illinois, who shared with me many valuable insights and experiences when I volunteered there from 1988 to 1990.

sicians or bioethicists might agree that violence against women is indeed a very complex, perhaps even an intractable social problem, yet view the appropriate medical response to the issue as both limited and clear-cut, consisting primarily of treating and documenting injuries (in a compassionate manner), and perhaps providing referrals to social service agencies. I will argue, however, that violence against women, a neglected topic in bioethics, not only is an important issue for the field, with the potential to shed light on a number of current questions, but is also urgently in need of feminist bioethical analysis.[1]

The experience of rape, or of battery in intimate relationships, constitutes an existential crisis which can be exacerbated by a woman's treatment by professionals—an aspect of violence which is often recognized, yet not adequately addressed in either medical practice or bioethics. Although medicine is regarded as a benign, even humane institution for responding to the crisis of rape or battery, a respected body of literature has provided evidence (discussed below) that the institution of medicine contributes in subtle ways to the perpetuation of violence against women. If this is indeed the case, then moral analysis of standard medical practice is sorely needed.

Moreover, many women have some contact with the health care system as a result of rape or battery, and even those of us who do not experience such assaults must nonetheless reconcile ourselves in some way to these issues as important features of the social world, influencing our views of ourselves and how we are viewed and treated by others. It is therefore very important to understand the impact of medical authority on these experiences. I argue that it often functions to pathologize and thereby stigmatize women,[2] and to legitimize a characterization of female selflessness as both an implicit behavioral norm and an existential categorization. At the same time, the medical profession maintains an image of the physician (likely male) as detached and objective, yet compassionate and beneficent.

In this paper I advocate a "biosocial" approach[3] to the moral analysis of health and health care, examining the social and political contexts that influence the experience of health and illness, as well as the institution of medicine. Second, I argue that the cultural status of medicine must be analyzed along with the specific practices that more typically are the objects of moral analysis.

The role of normative commitments in medical theory and practice has become an important philosophical topic. Modern medicine, because of its grounding in biomedical science, purports to be value-free. But this is an illusion; medicine is not purely descriptive, and the specific values that it expresses are deeply problematic. I begin with an overview of the mainstream medical paradigm, both in terms of the scientific paradigm that is

the foundation for medical knowledge and practice, and in terms of medicine as a model or foundation for broader social and political knowledge
and practice. I then examine the consequences for women of this mainstream paradigm as it influences current medical conceptualizations and
treatments of rape and battery.

MEDICINE AS SOCIAL PARADIGM

Over the past twenty-five years a diverse group of consumer activists and radical academics, including the Boston Women's Health Book
Collective (1992), Mary Daly (1978), Angela Davis (1981), Barbara and
John Ehrenreich (1970), Ivan Illich (1977), and Thomas Szasz (1974),
have offered critiques of the United States health care system. Many of
these critics are particularly concerned with the role of medicine in justifying, reinforcing, or contributing directly to specific forms of oppression
(heterosexism, sexism, classism, racism, ageism, and so on) that are pervasive in society.

Illich describes "medicalization" as a "medical and paramedical monop-
oly over hygienic methodology and technology . . . a device to convince
those who are sick and tired of society that it is they who are ill, impotent,
and in need of technical repair" (Illich, 1977: xvii). Medicalization, in
short, is a way of reducing a broad array of human behaviors and social
problems to malfunction or individual pathology.

It has become widely accepted that, in the past, medical conceptualizations of many diseases were based on moral norms rather than on "pure
science," and that these norms were often inegalitarian. Present medical
practice, particularly the interactions of female patients and male physicians, continues to promote moral norms in the guise of medical advice.
Medical sociologist Kathy Davis's analysis of four hundred tapes of clinical
interactions identifies frequent paternalism in the form of "general practitioners making moral judgments about women's roles as wives and mothers, psychologizing women's problems, not taking their complaints seriously, massive prescription of tranquilizers, [and] usurpation of women's
control over their reproduction" (1988: 22). Davis finds this kind of paternalism particularly insidious given the apparent benevolence of doctors: "It was precisely the intimate, pleasant quality of the medical encounter itself that made issues of power and control seem like something
else" (ibid.).

Medicine as power and control, both within the doctor-patient relationship and in its broader social functions, depends not only on the social

roles of doctor and patient, but on the social construction of science as the foundation of modern medicine. The scientific grounding of medicine provides a base of knowledge, but a deeper analysis reveals that the detached epistemology of medicine, rather than liberating it from the "tyranny of values," instead legitimizes medicine's implicit moral/political judgments.

Michel Foucault's *The Birth of the Clinic* (1975b) clarifies the relationship between the epistemology of medicine and its moral authority, tracing the processes by which the medicalization of society began to remap the moral domain from the soul onto the body. What emerged in the modern era of medicine, "the clinic," was a mode of knowledge not so much grounded in empirical information, which could be apprehended directly through the senses, but in quantifiable and precise data made possible through the use of an ever-increasing array of instruments—utterly detached knowledge, removed from the distortion not only of emotion but of the senses.

Foucault summarizes the epistemic principle of the clinic in the following way: "That which is not on the scale of the gaze falls outside the domain of possible knowledge" (1975b: 166)—with the gaze representing not ordinary human vision, but a grasp of knowledge that seems indisputable in its technological grounding (instruments cannot lie), its precision and quantification, its detachment and objectivity. Thus, by association, the moral and political judgments reflected in medicine gained the status of objective truth as well.

The twentieth-century manifestation of "the scale of the gaze" is evident in Donald Seldin's defense of the Flexnerian model of medicine and medical education as based strictly in physics, chemistry, biology, and related subdisciplines. Seldin, a prominent medical administrator, professor, and consultant, limits the role of medicine to the following task: to "bring to bear an increasingly powerful conceptual and technical framework for the mitigation of that type of human suffering rooted in biomedical derangements" (1984: 62). According to Seldin, medicine "must by definition become dissociated from concerns of a social nature, the solutions of which lie outside those boundaries" (57).

This epistemological model structures medical discourse at the level of practice as well. Suzanne Poirier and Daniel Brauner (1988) argue that the objectivity and detachment in "the daily language of medical discourse" obscure the humanistic concerns of patients and doctors: individual values, personalities, relationships, needs and circumstances—the "nonmedical" aspects of life, which nonetheless have great bearing on the subjective experience of illness and healing, as well as on the medical diagnosis and treatment of disease and injury.[4] I see this expulsion of humanistic concerns from the daily language of medical discourse as a result of the narrow framework of the Flexnerian model. To adapt Foucault's metaphor to the argument of Poirier and Brauner: that such concerns are "not on the scale of the gaze" only exacerbates the power imbalances in the interaction of doctor and patient, because the patient's perceptions and desires and other "nonmedical" aspects of health and illness are not necessarily translatable into that discourse.

In the context of violence against women, this medical framework— its knowledge strictly scientific, its values objectivity and detachment— (1) produces significant medical inaccuracies and mistreatment; (2) stigmatizes women; (3) defines women in terms of our relationships with others, which leads to the erasure of selfhood; and (4) obscures power relations.

MEDICAL TREATMENT OF
VIOLENCE AGAINST WOMEN

In examining this issue, I rely on certain tenets shared by activists, practitioners, and theorists associated with the women's health movement:

(1) a social context of patriarchy, racism, classism, and homophobia is harmful to women's health;

(2) the health care system as presently structured reflects and reinforces society's devaluation of women;[5]

(3) to address these two problems adequately, not only must they be understood in relation to an inegalitarian social context, but the social structure must be transformed in many ways as well;

(4) thus, health care must incorporate the goal of promoting women's interests and agency, as workers, professionals, and clients, in medical and other contexts.

These beliefs provide background for my argument that the medical treatment of violence against women reveals the harmful consequences of the narrow medical paradigm defended by Seldin. Mainstream medicine often treats the symptoms of violence while ignoring and even obscuring the causes, isolating a specific injury from the context in which it occurred and (in the case of domestic violence) is likely to recur; fails to reduce the risk of medical treatment's retraumatizing patients; and in some cases relies on conservative notions of "women's place." The paradigm Seldin defends is not only inadequate for the needs of women, but is not altogether objective, nor free of moral norms, as it purports to be.

The clinical paradigm may conceal the nature of the injury. A 1990 *Jour-*

nal of the American Medical Association report notes that "only 5 percent of 107 victims of domestic violence at a metropolitan emergency department were identified in the physicians' records as abused" (Parsons, 1990). Similarly, Stark, Flitcraft, and Frazier show that injuries from domestic violence are likely not to be identified as such in medical care. Their study identifies features of domestic violence that clearly distinguish it from most other types of injury seen in emergency rooms, yet injuries from domestic violence are often characterized as accidents (1983: 187–88).

Unfortunately, a distinguishing feature of domestic violence is that its victims may not be in a position to explain the cause of their injuries. Debbie Burghaus, a social worker in a Chicago hospital, states, "a lot of times, the victim isn't going to offer to tell you she was beaten up, because he's waiting for her in the hall, or she's just not empowered to leave him yet" (Parsons, 1990).

Understanding the nature of domestic violence or the difficulty of pressing charges or leaving an abuser requires knowledge of patients' social and economic circumstances, such as the compounding of the effects of battering for women who face additional forms of oppression, including lesbians, women of color (Richie and Kanuha, 1993), and disabled women (Warshaw, 1994). Yet, as Dr. Carole Warshaw of Cook County Hospital states, physicians "see their job as fixing the physical problem, and they don't see the person or their life context as part of the problem, so that's not their job" (Parsons, 1990). Thus Warshaw and other feminist analysts call for a broader clinical approach that would recognize the social nature of the problem in order to facilitate prevention and intervention.

The medical paradigm pathologizes victims, obscuring structural features of medicine which perpetrate violence and hinder treatment, such as the authoritarian aspects of standard doctor-patient interactions. While women are sometimes unable to discuss battering because they fear retribution by the batterer, at other times they may actually be prevented by the doctor or other medical professional who is privileged to control communication with patients; this systemic feature of medical interactions often disadvantages battered women when they attempt to voice their concerns (Warshaw, 1994).[6] According to Lori Heise, however, "providers have found that, contrary to their expectations, women have proven quite willing to admit abuse when asked directly in a nonjudgmental way" (1994: 245).

Stark, Flitcraft, and Frazier found that many survivors seeking treatment for injuries were given "pseudopsychiatric labels in the medical records such as 'patient with multiple vague medical complaints' or 'multiple symptomatology with psychosomatic overlay'" (1983: 195). Yet battered

women have long been known to experience the physical manifesta-
tions of chronic stress, such as "severe tension headaches, stomach ail-
ments, high blood pressure, allergic skin reactions, and heart palpitations"
(Walker, 1979: 61), along with anxiety and depression. A woman's body
manifests the daily assaults on her sense of self through chronic tension
and anxiety, prompting her to seek a medical remedy that may be her only
safe outlet for addressing the multiple harms, medical and otherwise, that
the batterer inflicts on her. Yet when she attempts to articulate her situation in "the daily language of medical discourse" (Poirier and Brauner,
1988), her perceptions can be stripped of their meaning. This aspect
of medical practice undermines the social authority of women who have
been battered. Moreover, psychiatric pathologization not only diverts attention from chronic, stress-related illnesses, but fails to address the real
cause of the problem.

Pathologization also serves to obscure the group identity of women who
are battered, perpetuating the sense that their suffering is an isolated personal problem, due to bad luck or their own inadequacy—rather than a
common manifestation of relationships between men and women in this
society. Many battered women have changed their lives through participation in support groups with other battered women, learning that they are
not alone and that they can begin to exercise greater control over their
lives. Fortunately, some hospitals do refer patients identified as battered
women to such groups. But psychiatric pathologization substitutes a diagnosis for real assistance, a diagnosis that can only stigmatize, compounding the hopelessness and shame that battering often causes (Walker, 1979)
by eroding women's self-regard and their identification with and regard
for other women who have survived domestic violence.

Not only does the pathologization of domestic violence present an image to women of themselves as the ones with the "problem," it also serves
to mask institutional responsibilities. A survivor who frequently returns to
the emergency room may be labeled a chronic complainer or hypochon-
driac, such characterization functioning "to suppress the 'inappropriate'
demands for help of those victimized elsewhere. . . . The label explains the
failure of the medical paradigm and the continued suffering of the abused
woman in a way that is intelligible, even acceptable, to the physician"
(Stark, Flitcraft, and Frazier, 1983: 187). In fact, Stark, Flitcraft, and Frazier argue convincingly that the medical profession indirectly supports systemic violence against women by failing to acknowledge assault as such, at
the same time protecting its own interests in the face of the difficulties the
women present.

Failure to identify the cause of an injury may not count as misdiagnosis in the usual sense, yet if domestic violence or sexual abuse is understood as a pattern in a woman's life, rather than as discrete, unconnected incidents, a kind of misdiagnosis—and ultimately mistreatment, or inadequate treatment—does occur. Symptoms are addressed, but not their underlying causes. In my view, this failure is a result of the medical/cultural assumption that heterosexuality and marriage are biologically certified as "natural"—hence appropriate, hence safe.

This point can be understood by exploring the medical understanding of domestic violence that is acknowledged as such. Domestic violence education for the medical profession tends to rely on research on "the violent family," which obscures a widespread social problem by focusing on "an aberrant subtype" of the family rather than on problems with "the American family as such" (Stark, Flitcraft, and Frazier, 1983: 194). Clearly, the notion of "the violent family" contains an unstated norm, a belief that "the family," with heterosexuality and marriage at its core, is nonviolent, a benign institution. Here, then, is one manifestation of the set of relational norms I have alluded to in the medicalization of women's health: the belief that women belong in relationships with men, belong in "the family"— a normative assumption which denies that heterosexuality and family life constitute a context of risk for women, and implies that such risk is occasioned by aberrations from the norm, rather than being part of a continuum of various forms of violence (not necessarily physical battering) that affect all women's lives.

The medicalization of rape also poses difficulties for women, as evidenced by Peter Cartwright's "Sexual Violence" chapter in *Novak's Textbook of Gynecology* (Cartwright, 1988), which is clearly well-intentioned, yet problematic nonetheless.[7] On the positive side, Cartwright addresses the relationship of sexual assault to the social context, citing well-known feminist social science literature (528). He also alerts the physician to psychosocial issues that victims face, recommends that physicians take the opportunity to "initiate crisis intervention" (531), and emphasizes the need for "reestablishing the victim's sense of control over her own life situation" (532)—one implication being that victims must be allowed to make their own decisions about whether to report the crime.

But neither Cartwright's treatment of psychosocial issues nor his effort to link rape to the social context is ultimately successful. The physician's first task is the initial interview, which Cartwright alludes to many times without specifying either questions to ask or techniques for helping to reduce the survivor's stress during the interview. Cartwright defines medical management to include "the treatment of physical injuries, the prevention of venereal disease and pregnancy, the initiation of crisis intervention, and the collection of forensic specimens and data" (531). For those who have just been violated and traumatized, undergoing this extensive set of procedures is likely to be quite difficult, yet nowhere does Cartwright acknowledge the potential traumatizing impact of the procedures nor suggest strategies to make them more tolerable.

Furthermore, when Cartwright does address psychosocial issues, he offers little in the way of guidance. The physician is told to ask the woman where she will go after leaving, as well as "how will [her] husband or family view her now that she has been 'violated'" (531), yet Cartwright fails to discuss what sorts of answers to look for, or how the physician is to respond. Cartwright also recommends a six-week followup, at which time the physician is to assess how well the woman is coping, and "refer those in need of more intensive therapy" (533). The basis for this assessment, however, is not specified, nor are criteria given for the relevant qualifications of these professional referrals.

Cartwright's discussion of the social context is obviously well intended, its tone sympathetic both to women and to feminist analysis. Yet he individualizes the act of rape as a random aberration even as he acknowledges its prevalence. Ultimately his approach pathologizes women themselves, ignoring the agency of rapists and the social context which supports it. In a section on the "etiology" of rape—a telling example of the medicalization of social relations—Cartwright rejects the claim that rape is inherent in males, and yet, in his one-paragraph discussion of rape "as a social issue," he notes that "potential rapists seem quite common in our society" (528). He then proceeds with a five-paragraph examination of individual characteristics of rapists, immediately undercutting the feminist social analysis of rape which he has just cited with seeming approval.

Perhaps the most unsettling passage is the chapter's opening:

Women are the preferred victims of violence in all societies. Most sexual violence is violence with sexual connotations that is directed toward women. Rape and sexual abuse of women and children is an ancient problem that has plagued all socioeconomic and educational levels in the Western world. Sexual assault is so common in the United States that all women are touched by fear, thinking perhaps they may become a victim. This fear dictates how a woman holds her arms, dresses, or speaks, where she goes and with whom. She knows a misinterpreted gesture may provoke a violent, hateful, perhaps fatal attack upon herself. *Her body and her own sexual desires become her own worst enemy.* (525; emphasis added)

Note the passive constructions: women "are the preferred victims" of a violence that "is directed toward women" like an approaching thunderstorm, "an ancient problem" that has always "plagued" society, and perhaps will eternally. Cartwright speaks of rape as if it were beyond all human agency or intervention, rather than a conscious, deliberate act by specific men.

In fact, Cartwright presents rape as a force emanating from the bodies of women themselves, rather than a choice made by particular men. Invoking women's sexual desires in the context of rape only rejuvenates the woman-blaming myths (she must have wanted it if she dressed that way, went to his hotel room, was out alone after dark, and so on), which Cartwright *seems* to want to avoid. Surely most rape survivors would be surprised to learn that their own bodies are worse enemies than their assailants themselves.

Cartwright presents women as tragically and inevitably preoccupied with their own dangerous bodies, and at the same time he erases his own gender and physicality, along with that of the doctor or medical student reading his text: the medical "view from nowhere."[8] But it is exactly this awareness that is vital: not a woman's alleged fear of her own body, but a physician's awareness of the impact of the medical gaze and the medical touch—quite likely a male touch—for a rape survivor. Cartwright's approach to sexual violence exemplifies the confinement of the medical paradigm, which does not extend beyond the boundaries of the patient's body. Yet the medical gaze must encompass other bodies and other social forces as well, if women are to receive the treatment we need.

MEDICINE, PHILOSOPHY, AND "THE UNDOING OF THE SELF"

The medical treatment of violence against women has significant implications for ongoing debates in the field of bioethics. First, the call to increase access to health care has come from many quarters—not only the philosophical literature,[9] but also from activists in the women's health, lesbian/gay/bisexual liberation, and AIDS movements, as well as from mainstream political discourse. Activists are equally concerned with injustices arising from the social power of medicine, however, including its ability to define and control people by calling them sick. If medicine does contribute significantly to the oppression of women, then simply increasing access without addressing this problem may well serve to perpetuate injustice even as it alleviates the crisis of access. Discussion must be broadened to address eradication of the oppressive aspects of the existing system.

Second, recent bioethics discussions address a broad array of questions about the role of health care in response to social group differences, and relations between individuals and communities.[10] My contention is that a biosocial understanding of human health is a necessary aspect of this analysis. I have argued that the appropriate medical treatment of women who have survived violence can only be defined, using diverse perspectives of women, in relation to a social context that shapes and influences the health status of women and our experiences of health care as well. An analysis of the medicalization of violence against women illuminates the complex relations between individual lives, the health care system, and the broader social context—exemplifying an approach that can and should be used for other specific topics in health care.

The medicalization of violence against women also requires reflection on important epistemological questions. It will be useful not only to consider this issue in the context of the critique of objectivity construed as detachment, but to consider further the relation of this episteme to "the undoing of the self" (Brison, Chapter 1) for women.

I have discussed many problematic impacts of medical discourse and practice on violence against women: assaulting women's integrity; alienating women from our own bodies; undermining women's agency; erasing the interests of individual women as they are distinct from others'; and eroding women's self-regard, as well as our identification with and regard for other women. Paradoxically, medicine simultaneously relegates women to the category of Other as it radically individualizes us; it presents oppressive social relations as facts of nature. Medical discourse often pathologizes women, and pathology carries stigma—in this case the stigma of one's gender, a central component of identity. Experiences of violence, always enmeshed within a complex of social relations, are reduced to "female problems"—physiological or psychological inadequacies associated with *being a woman*. In a social context in which women face a variety of disadvantages, these aspects of medical care reinforce other oppressive beliefs and practices, such as the patriarchal conception of femaleness that trains the medical gaze upon the presumed disruptiveness of women's own bodies, obscuring the social forces that break those bodies, spirits, and lives.

Medicine regulates many experiences of women, enforcing its definitions of reality over women's own perceptions. Women need to be able to trust our own perceptions of our bodies and our experiences, a goal that medical theory and practice should respect and support. Along with the attack on her body, a rapist or batterer assaults a woman's sense of competence and efficacy. Standard medical conceptualizations and treatments of violence may erase or undermine women's agency and selfhood, exacerbating the "undoing of the self" that results from violence—yet it is precisely this strong sense of selfhood that is needed in order for a woman to leave a batterer and make a new life, or regain a sense of safety and control in the world again.

Women may be treated for physical injuries, while psychological injuries, which may be even deeper, are ignored, or addressed only superficially, invisible to the clinical gaze or outside its parameters, as if these subjective states of suffering, the damage to women's self-esteem and sense of agency, were insignificant.

On "the scale of the gaze," Foucault's metaphor for the epistemic principle of modern medicine, knowledge is valued for its precise quantifiability, its detachment, which is understood to render it pure, objective, and untainted by the body or the idiosyncrasy of individual consciousness. Clearly this epistemic norm does not accommodate the subjectivity of health, illness, and injury, which I have argued must be included in the construction of knowledge. At the same time, the norm functions to obscure the impact of professional (typically male) subjectivity role in oppressive power relations.

These considerations show the need for a model of knowledge that not only incorporates subjectivity, but does not radically separate epistemological questions from moral ones.[11] In the context of medicine there are distinct advantages to an epistemological perspective that incorporates egalitarian norms. My opposition to certain norms in medicine is part of a broader defense of just norms.

Yet the modern medical paradigm—the Flexnerian model defended by Seldin—defines any such moral commitments as the corruption of "pure" science with alien values. Should we therefore reject the medical gaze and refuse, for example, the diagnostic arsenal of x-rays, endoscopes, ultrasound, and magnetic resonance imaging? Some critics may indeed reject the institution of medicine altogether, or nearly so,[12] but this is not my position. Instead, I argue that the scale of the gaze, as a basis for medicine, is unnecessarily and inappropriately reductionist, excluding the inherent moral, social, and political aspects of the embodied human concerns defined as medical, even as it obscures the tacit (and often inegalitarian) moral commitments already present. What I argue for is a biosocial understanding of health.

The women's health movement and the domestic violence and rape survivors' movements have generated knowledge with the potential to correct and inform traditional medicine in two ways: through their contribution to "better science," contextually based, and thus to more accurate understandings of health, illness, and injury, which in turn provide a better basis for treatment; and through facilitating morally preferable conceptualizations and treatments of women that can help rectify some aspects of an oppressive social context. Both the institution of medicine and the discipline of bioethics can and must contribute to the survivor's remaking of the self, and to the prevention of violence, by working with these movements to transform material conditions and give women greater voice in the social definition of reality.

SECTION 4

Pornography and Prostitution

Media Liability for Personal Injury Caused by Pornography

EDITH L. PACILLO

O n July 17, 1981, David Herberg forced a 14-year-old girl into his car, tied her hands with his belt, and pushed her to the floor. With his knife, he cut her clothes off, then inserted the knife into her vagina, cutting her. After driving a short distance, he forced the girl to remove his clothing, stick a safety pin in the nipple of her own breast, and ask him to hit her. He then orally and anally raped the girl. He made her burn her own flesh with a cigarette, defecated and urinated in her face, and compelled her to eat the excrement and to drink her own urine from a cup. He strangled her to the point of unconsciousness, cut her body several times, then returned her to the place where he had abducted her. In reviewing Herberg's criminal appeal, the Supreme Court of Minnesota noted that when Herberg committed these acts, he was "giving life to some stories he had read in various pornographic books." Officials seized these books from him during his arrest.[1] The court, however, was not asked to address whether the publishers of the pornographic material bore any responsibility for the injuries the young girl suffered as a result of Herberg's "giving life" to their stories.

Feminist legal scholars have long debated whether pornography plays a role in perpetuating cultural permissiveness of violence against women.[2] Some liberal feminist scholars argue, for instance, that pornography advances women's rights by sexually liberating women.[3] On the other hand, anti-pornography feminist legal scholars argue, for instance, that pornog-

Reprinted by permission of the *Suffolk University Law Review*.

raphy frequently acts as an instruction manual for perpetrating real-life sexual violence against women.[4] These scholars also assert that pornography propounds the harmful message that women enjoy, deserve, or secretly desire sexual violence.[5] To ameliorate this perceived harm, antipornography feminist legal scholars and activists have attempted to articulate a theoretical approach to holding the pornography industry liable when their products cause the type of harm that David Herberg's young victim suffered.[6]

In a broader context, courts have similarly struggled to determine whether imposing civil liability on the media for physical injury caused by broadcasts and publications violates the First Amendment right to freedom of speech.[7] In these cases, courts have attempted to resolve the considerable tension between individuals' expectations of physical safety and their right of free speech.[8] Despite the number of cases dealing with this issue, commentators contend that courts have provided inadequate and inconsistent guidance for balancing these two important interests.[9] Anti-pornography advocates argue that judicial indifference toward pornography's harmful effects further prevents relevant case law from advancing the feminist effort to eliminate pornography's threat to women's safety.[10]

Although the intra-feminist debate surrounding pornography has created a wealth of feminist jurisprudential theory worthy of examination, rather than enter the debate, this paper proceeds from the concept on which both liberal and radical feminists agree: legally enforced and socially constructed subordination of women contributed to the evolution of a legal system in which the experience of women remains invisible.[11] This paper first discusses the public policy underlying negligence and the development of current First Amendment doctrine.[12] Next, this paper examines several judicial decisions involving pornography and sexual violence in which courts have attempted to appropriately balance the competing interests of free speech versus compensation for injuries.[13] The paper then discusses recent attempts to create a statutory civil rights cause of action against pornographers.[14]

This paper argues that the First Amendment should not shield pornographers from liability when their publications[15] allegedly cause bodily harm.[16] Instead of traditional First Amendment analysis, this paper advocates that courts should use a negligent publication standard that incorporates free-speech interests into a negligence balancing test.[17] This paper will address only publisher liability for death and bodily injury allegedly caused by pornography, although pornography may cause other types of harm[18] and negligent publication may lead to other types of liability.[19]

HISTORY

Public Policy Underlying Negligence as a Cause of Action

The negligence cause of action protects individuals' physical safety by deterring risky conduct and compensating individuals for injury caused by another.[20] Injured parties must prove four elements to succeed on a negligence claim: duty, breach, causation, and injury.[21] When their conduct creates an unreasonable risk of harm, actors have a duty to act with the care of a reasonably prudent person under the circumstances.[22] Conduct creates an unreasonable risk of harm when the magnitude of its risk outweighs its social utility.[23] When determining whether this duty of care exists, courts also consider public policy factors such as the plaintiff's need for compensation, deterrence of dangerous conduct, punishment for moral culpability, and loss spreading.[24] A breach of this duty of care occurs when an individual fails to act reasonably to prevent harm to a class of foreseeable plaintiffs.[25]

To be legally actionable, conduct must also bear a reasonably close causal connection to the injury.[26] In determining whether this causal connection exists, courts consider both cause-in-fact and proximate cause.[27] Because of the potentially infinite results of an act, the proximate cause concept limits liability to only those harms which the actor could have reasonably foreseen.[28] To receive the compensation for their injuries, individuals harmed by a form of speech must overcome the substantial obstacle of the First Amendment right to free speech in addition to proving the four elements of negligence.[29]

The Social Value of Continuum in Free-speech Analysis

Courts apply First Amendment scrutiny to any challenged state regulation of speech.[30] Imposition of civil liability against the source of the speech constitutes state action.[31] The First Amendment, therefore, may shield tortfeasors from liability for harm resulting from a form of speech.[32] Under contemporary First Amendment analysis, the level of constitutional protection afforded speech depends on the assigned social value of the speech in question.[33] Courts analyze freedom of speech abridgements by placing the challenged speech in one of three categories: core speech, speech with limited social value, or speech with no social value.[34] Courts provide a greater or lesser degree of protection depending on the category in which the speech falls.[35]

Core speech includes political, religious, and philosophical speech.[36] Core speech receives the greatest constitutional protection because it promotes free expression and contributes to the system of self-government by informing the public and encouraging public debate on important issues.[37] States may proscribe this type of speech only upon a strong showing of government interest.[38] States must show an important governmental interest to avoid imposing prior restraints on speech, even in the form of self-censorship for fear of incurring liability.[39] Nonetheless, the Supreme Court of the United States has consistently rejected an "absolutist" approach to free speech by placing numerous limitations on freedom of speech.[40] For example, states may regulate the time, place, and manner of core speech when necessary to promote an important governmental interest, such as public safety.[41]

Speech of limited social value receives less protection than core speech because it has less intellectual content and, therefore, does not further the free exchange of ideas.[42] Commercial speech such as advertising, for example, traditionally receives an intermediate level of First Amendment protection.[43] The commercial speech doctrine provides that states may regulate speech that merely proposes a legal economic transaction if the regulation serves a substantial government interest, the government carefully tailors the regulation to meet its objective, and the regulation is not impermissibly overinclusive.[44]

Finally, states may proscribe only certain limited categories of speech which courts assign little, or no social value.[45] Courts have placed fighting words,[46] defamation,[47] incitement,[48] obscenity,[49] and child pornography[50] in this category.[51] Courts reason that because these types of speech do not significantly contribute to the system of free expression, proscription presents no danger of chilling the free exchange of ideas which the First Amendment protects.[52]

Liability for Speech Causing Bodily Harm

INCITEMENT

Publishers generally raise the First Amendment as an absolute bar to liability when plaintiffs allege that the publisher's speech caused bodily harm.[53] Injured parties, however, argue that the injurious speech constituted incitement and, consequently, the First Amendment defense should not apply.[54] Because states have a compelling interest in maintaining order and public safety, they may prohibit incitement, which by definition creates a risk of immediate breach of the peace.[55]

In *Brandenburg v. Ohio*,[56] the Supreme Court of the United States defined incitement as speech which advocates the use of force or unlawful activity which incites or produces "imminent lawless action and is likely to incite or produce such action."[57] Subsequent cases added the requirement that the speaker must intend to produce the lawless activity.[58] Because the incitement test focuses on the content of the speech and the likelihood and imminence of harm, it allows prior restraint on speech, even if the threatened harm does not occur.[59] Injured parties, however, rarely succeed in proving incitement because of the difficulty in meeting the strict definition of incitement and in showing that the speaker intended the speech to cause harm.[60]

Incitement Test Applied to Pornography and Sexual Violence

Two principal cases, *Olivia N. v. National Broadcasting Company*[61] and *Herceg v. Hustler Magazine, Inc.*,[62] illustrate how courts apply the incitement test in the context of pornography and sexual violence.[63] *Olivia N.* involved an NBC broadcast of a television movie depicting a young girl being raped with a plunger.[64] Four days after watching and discussing the broadcast, a group of juveniles raped Olivia N., a nine-year-old girl, with a bottle.[65] The trial court dismissed the action after viewing the broadcast and determining that it did not constitute incitement.[66] The California Court of Appeal concluded that the lower court's viewing of the film violated Olivia N.'s right to trial by jury because only a jury may determine whether the broadcast constituted incitement.[67]

On remand, Olivia N.'s counsel unsuccessfully attempted to circumvent the incitement test by alleging simple negligence on the part of the defendant television broadcaster.[68] Citing Olivia N.'s admitted inability to prove incitement, the trial court granted NBC's motion for judgment of nonsuit under the applicable statute.[69] Reasoning that Olivia N. could not prove incitement and that the broadcast did not fall into any other unprotected category of speech, the California Court of Appeal afforded full First Amendment protection to the broadcast.[70] The court reasoned further that imposing traditional negligence liability on a broadcaster of protected speech would impermissibly inhibit television broadcasters' programming selections and essentially chill free speech.[71] Accordingly, Olivia N. did not recover for her physical and emotional injuries.[72]

The Court of Appeals for the Fifth Circuit reached a similar result in *Herceg v. Hustler Magazine, Inc.*[73] *Hustler* magazine printed an article entitled "Orgasm of Death," detailing the practice of autoerotic asphyxiation in which participants deplete their oxygen supply while masturbating as a means of enhancing sexual pleasure.[74] The article appeared in a column devoted to educating readers about sexual activities and lessening their sexual inhibitions.[75] Troy D., a fourteen-year-old boy, attempted auto-erotic asphyxiation and, as a result, died of strangulation.[76] Andy V., a friend of Troy's, found him the next day, hanging in his closet, with the *Hustler* magazine opened to the article "Orgasm of Death," lying on the floor beside him.[77] Andy V. and Troy's mother, Diane Herceg, sued *Hustler* magazine for emotional harm that they suffered as a result of Troy's death.[78]

Troy's mother and Andy V. claimed the *Hustler* magazine article incited Troy to perform a potentially fatal act, and, alternatively, they argued that the court should apply a less stringent standard than the *Brandenburg* test because the case did not involve core speech.[79] The court first examined the article to determine whether it incited Troy to commit a lawless act.[80] Because the article did not create an imminent threat of danger, the court found that even if the article had encouraged autoerotic asphyxiation, the encouragement did not rise to the level of culpable incitement necessary to impose liability on the publisher.[81] The court also declined the alternative argument, stating that mere negligence does not comport with First Amendment values or the incitement test.[82] The court held that the article received full First Amendment protection, barring Diane Herceg and Andy V. from recovery.[83]

Concurring in part and dissenting in part, Judge Edith H. Jones criticized the result of First Amendment jurisprudence that protects citizens from defamation, obscenity, and the threat of mob violence, but denies compensation for bodily injury or death caused by speech.[84] Moreover, Jones argued that because pornography has no cognitive element and does not contribute to a free exchange of ideas, the majority erred in assuming that the "Orgasm of Death" article should receive full First Amendment protection.[85] Instead, Jones contended that the majority should have examined the underlying goal of the First Amendment when determining what degree of First Amendment protection to afford *Hustler* magazine.[86] Specifically, the dissent asserted that, regardless of whether the pornographic article was technically obscene, it should receive a lower level of protection because *Hustler* magazine is a commercial enterprise designed to appeal only to the reader's prurient interest.[87]

The dissent further asserted that *Hustler* magazine knew or should have known that adolescents make up a significant portion of its audience, that pornography has been causally linked to sexual violence, and that, accordingly, the article created an undue risk of harm.[88] Jones additionally reasoned by analogy that because courts balance the state's interest against individuals' interests in defamation cases, the majority could have similarly balanced the interests in this particular instance.[89] Discounting the majority's "slippery slope" argument, Jones' dissent asserted that courts should base their decisions on the specific facts of a case, not on unfounded speculation about the decision's potential impact.[90] Jones reasoned that placing pornography in a less protected category along with commercial speech would have the desirable effect of protecting society from injury and would hardly restrict debate on public issues or other modes of core speech.[91]

Cases Imposing Civil Liability

The preceding discussion illustrates cases in which courts protected free speech interests at the expense of the injured parties' rights to receive compensation for their injuries.[92] Two other cases, however, illustrate the converse problem for protecting injured parties' interests without adequately protecting free speech concerns.[93] In *Weirum v. RKO General Inc.*,[94] a radio disc jockey encouraged listeners to follow the car of another disc jockey who promised cash prizes to the first listener to reach him.[95] In their efforts to reach the disc jockey, two motorists forced another motorist into the highway divider, killing him.[96] In a wrongful death action brought by the motorist's wife and children, the Supreme Court of California upheld the verdict after finding that the radio station's encouragement caused the accident.[97] The court summarily dismissed the radio station's First Amendment defense without elaborating on how it reached its result.[98]

In *Hyde v. City of Columbia*,[99] Hyde, a kidnapping victim, sued a newspaper which published her name and address before authorities had captured the kidnapper.[100] Hyde sued the newspaper for negligent publication and recovered for the mental anguish she suffered as a result of receiving telephone calls from the kidnapper following her escape.[101] In allowing Hyde to recover damages, the Missouri Court of Appeals stated that other interests outweighed the newspaper's First Amendment rights, but did not specify which interests it considered more important than free speech.[102] Courts have addressed these factors—the burden imposed on plaintiffs, the inherent ambiguities in the incitement test, and the possibility of content-based restrictions on free speech—more adequately in cases where courts have applied a comprehensive balancing test and allowed a negligence cause of action.[103]

NEGLIGENT PUBLICATION AND THE *SOLDIER OF FORTUNE* CASES

Recently, the financial burden of litigating publication cases forced the paramilitary magazine *Soldier of Fortune* to discontinue publication of classified advertisements.[104] In the first such case, *Norwood v. Soldier of Fortune Magazine, Inc.*,[105] Norman Douglas Norwood alleged that an assassin hired through a "gun for hire" advertisement in *Soldier of Fortune* shot and wounded him.[106]

The United States District Court for the Western District of Arkansas denied the magazine's motion for summary judgment, holding reasonable jurors could find that the advertisement posed a substantial risk of harm.[107] The court also stated that "gun for hire" advertisements do not relate to the type of public debate that the First Amendment seeks to protect.[108] In addition, the court reasoned that Norwood did not seek to abridge free speech, rather, he sought to recover damages for his personal injuries.[109] The court concluded, therefore, that the magazine could incur liability for injury caused by its classified advertisements.[110]

Two years later, in *Eimann v. Soldier of Fortune Magazine, Inc.*,[111] the United States Court of Appeals for the Fifth Circuit avoided a First Amendment analysis by finding as a threshold matter that the magazine did not act negligently.[112] *Eimann* involved the following advertisement which John Hearn ran for three months in *Soldier of Fortune*'s classified section: "EX-MARINES—67–69 'Nam Vets, Ex-Di, weapons specialist—jungle warfare, pilot, M. E., high risk assignments, U. S. or overseas."[113] In response to this advertisement, Robert Black hired Hearn to murder his wife, Sandra Black.[114] Following the murder, Sandra Black's son and mother sued *Soldier of Fortune* for wrongful death, alleging the magazine negligently published the advertisement.[115] Applying Texas tort law, the court used a risk-utility balancing test to determine the defendant's liability.[116]

Under this test, courts weigh the burden of taking precautions and the product's social utility against the product's foreseeable risk and gravity of potential harm.[117] If the risk and gravity of the harm outweigh the burden of adequate precautions and the utility of the product, the court considers the activity unreasonable and may, therefore, impose liability.[118] Although *Soldier of Fortune* owed a duty of reasonable care to the public, the *Eimann* court reasoned that the magazine could not reasonably have foreseen that Hearn's ambiguous advertisement would result in harmful conduct.[119] The court also considered the First Amendment protection afforded to classified advertisements as evidence of their social utility, thereby incorporating free speech concerns into the risk-utility test.[120] As a result, the court denied the plaintiff's recovery, reasoning that the burden of requiring publishers to refrain from publishing ambiguous advertisements, combined with the social utility of classified advertisements, outweighed the risk of foreseeable harm.[121]

Applying the same risk-utility test, the United States Court of Appeals for the Eleventh Circuit reached a different result in *Braun v. Soldier of Fortune*.[122] The advertisement in *Braun* read: "GUN FOR HIRE: 37 year old professional mercenary desires jobs. Vietnam Veteran. Discrete [sic] and very private. Body guard, courier, and other special skills. All jobs considered."[123] In response to this advertisement, a man hired Savage to murder his business partner, Richard Braun.[124] Braun's sons sued *Soldier of Fortune*, alleging negligent publication of the advertisement.[125] The court weighed the risk of harm from Savage's advertisement against the magazine's burden of adequately preventing the harm, and determined that the magazine owed a duty to refrain from publishing the advertisement.[126] The court also incorporated First Amendment concerns into its balancing test by modifying the negligence standard to require a clear threat of harm on the face of the advertisement in order to impose liability.[127]

After holding that the magazine negligently published the advertisement, the court considered whether the First Amendment should bar the imposition of liability.[128] The court acknowledged that liability might have a chilling effect on commercial advertising, but held that the "modified" negligence standard adequately protects publishers' First Amendment interests because of the heightened degree of risk required to impose liability.[129] In reaching this conclusion, the court analogized to defamation law.[130] Specifically, the court relied on *Gertz v. Robert Welch*,[131] in which the Supreme Court of the United States held that states imposing liability on publishers must do so on the basis of fault.[132] Noting that *Gertz* involved noncommercial core speech, the *Braun* court applied the same principle to classified advertisements, which receive less protection than core speech.[133] As a result, the court held *Soldier of Fortune* magazine liable for negligently publishing an advertisement which clearly presented an unreasonable risk of harm.[134]

Attempts to Create Statutory Cause of Action for Injury Caused by Pornography

In 1983, feminist legal scholars introduced a civil rights theory and Model Ordinance based on the premise that pornography subordinates women as a class, thereby creating sex discrimination, and proposed a civil cause of action against pornographers based on actual harm.[135] Specifically, the Model Ordinance provides four causes of action: coercion into pornography, forcing pornography on a person, assault or physical attack due to pornography, and trafficking in pornography.[136] The Model Ordinance defines pornography as "graphic sexually explicit pictures or words that subordinate women," and include one or more of a number of scenarios which typify pornography.[137] The theory first became law in Minneapolis, Minnesota, after extensive public hearings which included the testimony of survivors of harm caused by pornography.[138]

In *American Booksellers Ass'n v. Hudnut*,[139] the United States Court of Appeals for the Seventh Circuit held that the ordinance violated pornographers' First Amendment right to free speech.[140] Simultaneously, however, the court acknowledged that pornography threatens women's rights to equality and physical safety.[141] The majority's oxymoronic holding stated that although pornography fosters aggression against women, "this simply demonstrates the power of pornography as speech," and, therefore, the need to constitutionally protect pornography.[142] The *Hudnut* decision exemplifies the difficulty courts experience in adequately balancing individuals' right to live free from bodily harm against a system of free expression.[143]

ANALYSIS

Inadequacies of Contemporary First Amendment Doctrine

Most courts apply the incitement test to allegations that some form of speech caused an individual to suffer bodily injury.[144] Courts developed the incitement theory, however, to protect the state's interest in controlling crowd behavior.[145] Not surprisingly, then, the incitement theory has proven to be an inadequate means of adjudicating personal injury cases not involving mob violence.[146] The incitement test additionally requires the injured party to prove that the speaker intended to produce the harmful result.[147] In certain cases alleging negligent speech, proving negligence and intent poses an impossible task for injured parties.[148] As a result, the incitement test usually prevents injured parties from recovering for their injuries.[149]

Besides being an inappropriate and unduly burdensome test for personal injury cases, the incitement test also fails to provide adequate protection to free speech interests.[150] In particular, by requiring injured parties to prove only imminent harm rather than actual harm, the test poses a threat of prior restraint, the antithesis of freedom of expression.[151] Similarly, as the *Hyde* and *Weirum* cases illustrate, the confusion surrounding current First Amendment case law also threatens free speech interests because of its failure to articulate the precise factors that will result in the imposition of media liability.[152] These unpredictable results might impermissibly chill free speech by forcing publishers, broadcasters, and other speakers to limit their editorial choices to avoid liability.[153]

Courts have recognized that states have a strong and legitimate interest in allowing parties to recover damages when slanderous speech injures their reputation.[154] In cases alleging bodily harm caused by speech, however, courts often apply the rigid categorization scheme, unfairly precluding victims from litigating claims against the source of their injuries.[155] Although the plaintiffs in *Olivia N.* and *Herceg* suffered grave harm, for example, the courts barred their suits because the speech involved did not fall within an unprotected category.[156] Moreover, in these two negligence actions, the courts applied defamation law, which was developed to curb prior restraints on public speakers, not to deter risky conduct or compensate injured parties.[157] As a result, this categorization approach leads to anomalous and often inequitable results.[158] The inappropriateness of the rigid categorical analysis is further compounded in cases involving pornography because of the difficulty courts experience in defining pornography.[159]

Pornographers should not automatically receive full First Amendment protection merely because their product does not constitute incitement or some other unprotected type of speech, especially if the pornography caused actual bodily harm to an individual.[160] Considering the principles underlying the First Amendment, the justification for favoring pornographic speech becomes even more obscured because First Amendment doctrine was originally developed to protect political minorities from majoritarian oppression.[161] In contrast, the multi-billion dollar pornography industry currently misuses the First Amendment as a shield against incurring liability for the considerable harm it causes.[162] Pornography neither contributes to a democratic society by debating issues of public concern nor seeks to communicate an idea to its consumers.[163] Rather, pornographers aim to produce the physical result of sexual arousal, often using photographs depicting sexual abuse of women.[164] In fact, in its most graphic forms, pornography depicts acts of violence, degradation, torture, and mutilation, frequently with a female victim.[165]

Balancing the Competing Interests

The risk-utility test applied in *Braun v. Soldier of Fortune Magazine, Inc.*[166] provides an equitable and flexible means of balancing free-speech concerns with a woman's right to recover for bodily injury.[167] The *Braun* balancing test protects plaintiffs' interests in recovering for their injuries because it does not utilize a rigid categorical scheme for defining speech.[168] Instead, courts using this balancing test determine liability on a case-by-case basis, considering the overall social utility of the speech and whether the speech legitimately concerns issues of public interest.[169] Under this approach, injured parties stand a better chance of getting past the First Amendment barrier and litigating claims on their merits.[170] This balancing test also provides more protection to publishers' free speech interests than the traditional First Amendment approach provides.[171] The test requires a case-by-case examination of the particular speech in question to determine whether the speech poses an unreasonable risk of harm.[172]

Accordingly, courts will often find that publishers of the most egregious "how to" type of pornography have breached their duty of care while other non-violent pornography frequently will remain protected.[173] Because juries determine whether publishers have breached their duty of care, publishers can also rest assured that community standards will guide consideration of their product.[174] The balancing test further increases victims' burdens in negligent speech cases by requiring proof of a clearly identifiable and unreasonable risk of harm on the face of the publication.[175] Finally, a negligence cause of action protects publishers from prior restraints on speech because, unlike incitement, negligence actions require plaintiffs to show actual harm as a result of the speech.[176]

Implications for Feminist Legal Theory

Feminist legal scholars correctly assert that legal reforms have historically had only limited success in advancing women's substantive social equality.[177] Most notably in the pornography context, in spite of pornography's documented harms, courts and legislatures have consistently rejected efforts to create statutory actions against pornographers.[178] Tort actions such as negligent publication, however, have the potential of promoting women's social status by removing the most damaging forms of violent pornography from the marketplace.[179]

Negligence law functions to deter risky conduct that has little or no social utility.[180] Pornography fits this description, especially considering the wide range of harmful effects it causes.[181] Because injured parties must prove actual harm as an element, negligent publication cases against pornographers will raise societal awareness and understanding of the unacceptable amount of violence inflicted upon women, violence which the pornography industry perpetuates solely for financial gain.[182] The negligence cause of action has the additional benefit of allowing female survivors to define pornography's harm in their own terms, using their own voices, a prerogative which courts have long denied to women.[183]

Perhaps most important, pursuing the negligent publication strategy addresses both sides of the feminist pornography debate.[184] Resolving this source of division within the feminist movement represents an especially worthwhile goal for feminists, because the pornography debate has divided feminists for more than a decade.[185] By targeting only violent pornography that poses a facially unreasonable risk of harm, the negligent publication strategy will not limit the range of material available to both men and women who enjoy non-violent erotic publications.[186] Additionally, because the *Braun* test requires injured parties to show an unambiguous threat of harm on the face of the publication, courts cannot discriminatorily censor non-violent gay, lesbian, or heterosexual erotica.[187]

Anti-pornography feminists seek to use civil litigation to legitimize women's real-life experiences with pornography.[188] The negligent publication strategy also meets this goal because it forces courts to recognize and redress the actual harm pornography causes to women on the same basis as any other personal injury claim.[189] Unlike earlier, unsuccessful anti-pornography strategies, litigating negligence claims requires no new legislation.[190] Suing pornographers for negligent publication will further empower women survivors of sexual violence to promote their right to equal protection under the law, the common goal of both the liberal and radical feminist movements.[191]

Courts must reconsider the current free speech doctrine that inequitably considers pornographers' free speech interest more worthy of judicial protection than a woman's right to sue the source of her injuries for compensation. Instead, courts considering negligent speech cases, particularly those involving pornography, should utilize the case-by-case risk-utility balancing test applied in *Braun v. Soldier of Fortune Magazine, Inc.* Although pornography causes other, equally objectionable types of harm in addition to physical injury, successful negligent publication claims would, nonetheless, constitute an important first step in holding pornographers accountable for the damage their products cause. This strategy would ultimately lead to greater judicial and societal recognition of pornography's role in maintaining the subordination of women. Rather than continue the rhetorical debate, therefore, feminists must focus their collective energies on locating female survivors willing to bring their claims of negligent publication against pornographers who cause their injuries.

CHAPTER TEN

The Myth of the Happy Hooker: Kantian Moral Reflections on a Phenomenology of Prostitution

CLELIA SMYTH ANDERSON AND YOLANDA ESTES

This essay represents an attempt to bring prostitutes' and clients' voices into the philosophical discourse about prostitution.[1] The prostitute's subjective position has been expressed by prostitute rights organizations such as CORP, COYOTE, PONY, prostitute rescue organizations such as WHISPER, and prostitute performance artists such as Annie Sprinkle, Gwendolyn, Scarlot Harlot, and Veronica Vera. We wish to add the voices of individual prostitutes and clients in order to expand the contemporary philosophical understanding of prostitution[2] as a complex and problematic ethical concern.

The first section of this essay explains the conceptions of subjectivity, sexuality, and violence that underpin our analysis of prostitution.[3] The second section scrutinizes the prostitute's and the client's motivating goals and the means they use to accomplish them. The third section presents a phenomenological description of prostituted sex from the prostitute's and the client's respective viewpoints.[4]

Prostitution is the performance of a sexual act for material gain. Many forms of prostitution occur, a large number of which are legal, condoned, or even encouraged.[5] Our focus is on the explicit, verbally consensual, voluntary exchange of a sexual act involving direct physical contact for money. We will address only the prostitution of women to men.[6]

SUBJECTIVITY, SEXUALITY, AND VIOLENCE

From a Kantian perspective, prostitution is morally wrong because it violates the "principle of humanity."[7] It is "not good" to treat other human beings as if they were nothing more than tools or things to be used to accomplish the objects of our desires. Our concept of human subjects identifies subjectivity and dignity with the self-determining will and locates the will within the limited willing activity of embodied individuals.[8] Sexuality is one manner in which embodied subjects are mutually determined as individuals. Regardless of gender, sexual orientation, or sexual practice, individuals are partly determined by their relation to sexuality, their choices regarding sexual expression, and their integration of sexuality within life as a whole.[9] All human activities, including sexual activities, express subjectivity, but not all involve mutual recognition of subjectivity and mutual respect.

Without respect, sexual activity objectifies the participants and violates human dignity by withholding recognition of their subjectivity.[10] Respect for persons in the sexual context requires the minimum criteria of mutual consent, concern, and desire to relate as individual subjects.

Respect for others requires an explicit or implicit expression of willing participation in sexual acts. Consent alone fails to safeguard an action from moral reproach.[11] While one need not accommodate others' desires, one ought to take their desires and aversions into account.[12] In addition, respect requires that one's actions exhibit concern for others' interests, needs, and general well-being.[13]

Sexual activity does not express a person's desires if she engages in it without consent, or if the act is coerced or forced. Furthermore, if a person performs sexual acts for another without any interest in or desire for connection to that person, without any response to sexual needs of her own, or solely to accomplish some end extraneous to her sexual and emotional satisfaction, then her actions express no desire to interact sexually with her partner. If one engages in a sexual act solely to preserve one's life, physical safety, or standard of living, and at the cost of an unreasonable degree of physical or emotional well-being, then performance of the act does not itself express desire. Sex in such a context may be voluntary and consenting, but it demonstrates that the participants are using one another as mere means for some other end.

Without mutual consent, concern, and desire for sexual contact with a particular individual, bodily acts become bodily intrusions that obscure the distinction between a human body and a thing.[14] The relevant issue is not merely that such acts can damage or destroy the human body, but that they appropriate it without concern for its subjectivity. Such encroachment on the individual through the body pervades the entire interaction of the prostitute and her client, and reflects a disrespectful and violent attitude on the part of both.

Violence becomes sexualized when sexuality serves as a medium for expressing the violent attitude. Prostitution attempts to justify sexualized violence through the provision of a monetary substitute for desire and concern.

MEANS AND ENDS:
THE MOTIVES FOR PROSTITUTION

The prostitute uses sex as a means for obtaining money. This factor would be secondary only if the prostitute were willing to engage in the act without it. Her toleration of sex in the prostitution encounter occurs without expressing a sexual desire to relate to her client, just as the submission of a woman forced or coerced into performing a sexual act occurs without expressing her desire to relate sexually to her molester.

The prostitute's client understands that something other than sexual desire and concern for him motivates her actions. His primary motive for seeking gratification with a prostitute is less apparent, because many other outlets for sexual expression exist. Many liberal accounts of prostitution compare sexual needs to physical needs, and sexual work to service work. Presumably, a man buys the services of a prostitute to sate his sexual appetite. The prostitute's client wants something other than a mere orgasm or even an especially good orgasm. He wants sexual relations with a woman. This, however, does not explain why he buys the sexual services of a woman. Most men who seek prostitutes have, or could obtain, other willing, unpaid sexual partners. In other words, the prostitute's client demands more than sexual relations with a woman.

Perhaps he wants a particular sort of woman, such as one who is more comely, obliging, or sexually adventurous. Initiating, building, and working for the sort of sexual relationships he desires involves an inconvenient, time-consuming, and arduous endeavor. Sexual relationships offer potential delight, relief, and joy, but also contain the potential for rebuff, chagrin, and feelings of inadequacy. Moreover, even so-called casual relationships require some work, time, and obligations. Sexual partners may fulfill our desires, but usually have their own desires that they want obliged in turn. Maintaining these relationships burdens the client with responsibilities, demands, and needs that he prefers to avoid.

The prostitute does not satisfy the need for a woman or even the desire for a particular sort of woman. She accommodates men's desires for women who cease to exist when they are no longer wanted.[15] Indeed, she fulfills the wish for a woman who does not exist, as a human woman would exist for him, because she is paid to disguise the subjectivity expressed through her individual needs, sexual desires, and interests. A man seeks a prostitute in order to avoid the inconvenience of sexual relations with another subject. With a prostitute, a man can have sex when and how he wants it. He can choose on the basis of appearance, charm, or willingness to engage in particular acts. He need not exert himself to attract her attentions and arouse her desires. The consequences she bears for their sexual encounter need not concern him. Prostituted sex requires nothing more than the asking price. It delivers a woman-thing without the responsibility of dealing with a woman.[16]

The prostitute must attend to her client as would a woman who desires him. Her sexual performance must exhibit recognition for his individuality, his person (Pateman, 1994: 131). He wants his woman-thing, body, mind, and soul. As noted by John Stuart Mill in a somewhat different context: "Their masters require something more from them than actual service. Men do not want solely the obedience of women, they want their sentiments. All men, except the most brutish, desire to have, not a forced slave but a willing one, not a slave merely, but a favorite" (1970: 141).

In prostitution, as in slavery, the "master's" desires must remain unfulfilled, for obedience is bought rather than given. The prostitute's consent to engage in sexual relations need not express her sentiments, and indeed her client has every reason to suspect that it does not. Her sexual identity and desires are entangled in a net of familial and social ties, personal interests, and activities that constitute her life beyond prostitution. Individual interests, projects, and personal facticity structure her empirical, sexual self, but the nature of prostitution demands that she exclude these aspects of herself in her encounter with the client.

MEAGER MEANS: A PHENOMENOLOGY OF PROSTITUTION

The prostitute's role as woman-thing veils her selfhood. The client expects this hidden subject to recognize his subjectivity, but that would require acknowledging her subjectivity as well. To feign, or even convince himself that he feels an interest in her individual person, compromises the nature of prostituted sex. Prostitution exists to relieve him of the inconvenient trappings of subjectivity, such as commitments, emotional bonds, and another person's needs and desires. Nonetheless, the desired recognition of his subjectivity depends on mutual recognition.

The prostitute finds herself in an equally problematic position. She wants to preserve the integrity of her personal life and assert her subjec-

tivity without jeopardizing her agreement with the client. An attitude of indifference would manifest her individual subjectivity. Passionate reference
to her personal life would assert her womanhood in the face of her role as
woman-thing. Soliciting his concern for her desires, interests, and needs
might force him to view her as a subject. These modes of disclosing her
subjectivity may repel the client or impose demands on him beyond the
scope of their agreement. A compromise more aptly preserves both her
professional role and her sense of self, and thus she might present an image of sexual desire by means of small talk, flirtation, and other theatrical
devices. Because no pretense can assimilate this man within the larger
context of her life, she must dissociate herself from her sexual activity in
order to maintain the illusion.

Their sexual activity evokes feelings and emotions that threaten the illusion. Her repugnance must not appear to him as disgust. Submitting to
any pleasurable sensation, on the other hand, jeopardizes her sense of
control, and the pretended irrelevance of her own bodily needs. Every visible reaction evinced by the handling of her body addresses the client's desires rather than her own. In order to attend to her client, she must detach
herself from the bodily event without separating herself from her body. By
means of abstraction, alcohol, or drugs, she anesthetizes herself to function as animate thing.

Prostitution cultivates a perverse stoicism that nullifies every emotion or
sensible reaction threatening to engage the prostitute in the bodily event.
Unlike the stoic who seeks to control emotion in order to guide her activity according to reason, the prostitute attempts to annihilate her very presence within a sexual activity by extinguishing her reaction to it. As woman-
thing, she presents the specter of a subject with a sensibility that she, as
subject, cannot acknowledge herself to possess. She maintains control of
her prostituted body and appears to herself as an active but nonsubjective
body. Initially, this discipline facilitates her sexual performance, but it
poses the threat that she might become conditioned to respond similarly
to all sexual stimulation.

A violent fragmentation of self permits the compartmentalization of her
sexual activity with the client. She maintains the self-deception that her
"real" self is shielded and that this body is not her *self*. "This is not me," she
tells herself. She assumes many different personalities and simulates sexual involvement. When the illusion dissolves, she expects to reintegrate
her "real" untouchable self and her body. This unification is impossible,
however, because she never actualizes the distinction between her real self
and herself as woman-thing. Her alienation within the sexual performance

is not a separation from her body. Try as she may to deny it, her bodily experience is her own.

The prostitute's fragmentation into woman-thing and concealed woman mirrors the client's conflicting demands. His attempt to obtain the recognition of a woman without incurring an obligation to the woman perpetuates her dissolution. Plunging through the female body before him, he seeks to reach beneath the surface and wake the woman concealed within the thing. His endeavor to reach her may take a variety of forms, embroiling him in a mimicry of seduction or rape.

Attempts to coax the prostitute into dropping her defenses perpetuate an illusion of trust, understanding, and mutual recognition, which the mercenary nature of their encounter renders impossible. In order to identify with her, the client might suggest to himself that the prostitute is really a "good girl" come on hard times. Concerned-sounding questions about her personal life or attempts to carry out the sex act in a diligent, gentle manner, as would a "good lover," might create the appearance of a connection based on mutual concern, desire, and respect. The need to maintain this illusion might inspire the client to be attentive to the prostitute's responses and expressed needs. He might manifest his courtesy through a variety of behaviors, such as frequently asking what pleases her, showing great interest to avoid causing distress, or making the most determined efforts to bring her to climax. From outward appearance, this seduction of a reluctant mistress imitates an act of considerate lovemaking prohibited by the inherent deceptions of prostitution and seduction.

Rather than seducing, the client may attempt to provoke a genuine response from the prostitute by deliberately degrading her, by trying to revolt or injure her. He may insist on "getting his money's worth," or denigrate her services by stating that she does not know how to please a man. In short, he may indulge in brutal sexual intercourse resembling rape in every respect other than her consent.

Unless the client is willing to forgo his original objectives, everything he does is destined to fail. On the one hand, the harshness of a brutal client makes it difficult for the prostitute to retain her self-respect and composure. As his intrusions become more persistent, her efforts to separate herself from the encounter become more desperate. On the other hand, kindly gestures compel her to view herself and her client as persons. Her task might be easier if the client were to leave her the option of viewing him as nothing more than a vicious animal, a man-thing, that services itself on her woman-thing. In avoiding feelings of compassion or respect for the client, she avoids acknowledging his capacity to touch her.

In other contexts, those to whom the prostitute is bound by more complex patterns of emotions, loyalties, and responsibilities may touch her as a person. By what right does the client try to force his way into the inner recesses of her mind and soul? One can imagine that the client also feels somewhat disgruntled. She denies him what he most desires, a recognition of his power over her through a surrender of body and soul. The client seeks to control the prostitute's sexual expression without stifling the candid spontaneity of her sexual responsiveness. He wants her to get caught up in the moment despite herself, to elicit from her a genuine response, albeit one that he can predict. It is conceivable that the client might penetrate her defenses, for despite her attempts to dissociate herself, the prostitute remains aware of her bodily involvement. However, even if he succeeds in this endeavor, the contradictory basis of their encounter gives the client reason to question the candor of her response.

When climax has been reached, neither can deny that he has been moved by her touch to pleasure and orgasm. His orgasm is a physical manifestation of a mutual presenting of subjectivity. Yet this realization provides no comfort or joy, for it likewise reveals the violence they have done to one another. Despite their objectification of one another, the bodily nature of the encounter forces them to recognize their mutual humanity. This recognition is simultaneously a revelation of the harm they have done to one another and the harm they have done to themselves. In the prostitution encounter, both the prostitute and the client attempt to use the other as a mere means to an end. Neither participant achieves his or her original objective, because the objectives are self-contradictory. Each intends to leave with something gained. But each walks away having given up more of themselves than was agreed to in the bargain.

SECTION 5

POLICIES AND PERSPECTIVES

ON VIOLENCE

CHAPTER ELEVEN

Violence and Transcultural Values

ARNOLD R. EISER

Understanding the cultural basis of violence requires a working definition of violence. Sidney Hook, for example, defined it as "the illegal employment of physical coercion for personal or group ends" (as quoted in Ogle, 1950: 115). Political philosophers argue the degree to which legitimization renders physical coercion something less than violence; physical harm may, for instance, have legitimate applications, as in defensive war or personal self-defense. The process of defining violence depends upon the social and cultural matrix that underlies the legitimization of an act of physical coercion. Talcott Parsons observed that a society uses the threat of legitimate force to encourage conformity to regulations and as a symbol of security in the social system (1964: 63). But violence can undermine both the sense and reality of security; Grundy and Weinstein, for example, point out that violence damages the social structure by undermining the requisite sense of security (1974: 18–24). A government may commit violence by betraying its trust if it enforces policies that are venal and unjustified.

Social theorists such as Rosenberg and Mercy (1991: 25) or S. T. Reid (1979: 173–224) categorize causes of violence as cultural, structural, economic, and interactionist. Under the cultural category, the normative values imbued in members of a society through socialization in turn affect the nature of social interactions. In transcultural comparisons all four cate-

This essay was first presented at a conference organized by the Mount Sinai School of Medicine. A shorter version was published in the *Mount Sinai Journal of Medicine* (vol. 63, no. 2, March 1996). Reprinted by permission of the Mount Sinai School of Medicine.

gories matter, but cultural valuation takes priority. Structural factors influencing a proclivity toward violence include family structures, such as presence of the father, which also relate to cultural values. Given that males commit most violent acts, the socialization of males is of especial cultural significance. Violence against girls and women is particularly important in medical and sociological contexts.

This analysis tries to elucidate the basis for transcultural differences in what constitutes violence. Because our working definition of violence requires that society as a whole delegitimize acts of physical coercion, the role of societal values and institutions in defining violence looms large. This role will become clearer as we examine in greater detail a particular type of violence, female genital mutilation (sometimes called female circumcision).

STAGES OF MORAL DEVELOPMENT
AND TRANSCULTURAL VALUES

A theory of moral development is useful as a heuristic or comparative tool in comparing violence in differing cultures. Lawrence Kohlberg's theory holds that individuals pass through six (potential) stages of moral development as they mature (1981): stage 1 is based on obedience in order to avoid negative reinforcement; stage 2 consists of mutual cooperation motivated by personal self-interest; stage 3 represents conformity to a code of conduct within one's social relationships; in stage 4 social agreement extends beyond one's personal relationships and involves rights and duties within a societal context; in stage 5 certain individual rights such as life and liberty take precedence over majority opinion; in stage 6 an objective criterion of universal applicability takes precedence over social accords and a sense of validity of universal moral principles prevails.

Transcultural studies utilizing this model have been summarized by Snarey (1985). They reveal that, within given societies, the attaining of a given stage tends to be correlated with the age at testing; for example, older subjects were more likely to be in stage 4 or higher. Preliterate societies such as Papuan New Guinea usually reached stage 3, while the Eskimo did not reach beyond stage 2. Only middle-aged members of Israeli kibbutzim, Taiwanese graduate students, and middle-aged upper-middle-class citizens from India reached stage 5 in appreciable percentages. In middle-class Muslim families in Iran, groups from age nine to adult scored at stage 4 regularly, without the usual age distribution. Across countries, scores of urban dwellers were more comparable to one another than were scores of urban dwellers to those of their rural compatriots. Stage 6 was not measurably attained across a wide cross-section of cultures.

These empirical studies indicate that Kohlberg's theory is a useful heuristic probe in understanding cross-cultural moral value systems even though the theory itself is obviously shaped by certain Western philosophical presumptions. The Kantian nature of stages 5 and 6 accounts for their rarity and maldistribution transculturally. The absence of stage 6 from every group studied raises questions of its validity as a category of moral development for groups and individuals. Despite these limitations, I postulate that the framework of the theory will make transcultural comparisons of value judgments regarding violence more understandable, especially in regard to particular examples of violence such as female circumcision.

FEMALE GENITAL MUTILATION

In Africa and the Middle East the practice of female genital mutilation is a widespread cultural practice. It is purported to regulate female sexuality and encourage chastity. Although the practice occurs predominantly among Islamic populations, it is not part of any particular religious doctrine; adherents of other faiths in these regions also follow the practice. The practice has received particular notice recently because of significant immigration to Western countries from countries where it is practiced, and because of the powerful moral repugnance toward this practice in the West.

Stephen James (1994) has noted that male religious elites perpetuate the practice, and argues that it is a human rights violation of international law. Moreover, female circumcision is a violation of the right to health, because its mutilating character engenders illness in the form of clitoridectomy, infibulation, infection, psychic trauma, and complications in childbirth (Toubia, 1994). Because the procedure is generally performed on females before an age where they can consent, it also has been viewed as child abuse.

James asserts that the core of international human rights is universal protection of individual autonomy, but no group studied in either Western or other cultures scored at this stage 6 level of moral development in Kohlberg's scheme. Thus basing an argument against female circumcision on neo-Kantian principles is guaranteed to fall on deaf ears internationally. A cross-cultural analysis of the moral language and conceptualizations of stage 6 thinking reveals that it is confined to Western philosophers and their disciples, whereas the populations from localities where female circumcision is practiced have generally scored at the stage 4 level, where considerations of social accord and system maintenance prevail; at this stage the concern for conformity to tradition is paramount.

I suggest that it is possible to restate the moral critique of this practice on grounds that are accessible to the natives of the lands where it is practiced. In order to do so, one must make a claim of a transcultural moral standard that does not depend upon neo-Kantian universality.

I submit that health and well-being has a claim as such a transcultural value. I have personally observed this *lingua franca* of health, having practiced medicine for eighteen years in the most international community in New York. I have observed that the yearning for health has a force that transcends particular cultural differences. Regardless of country of origin, patients desire a restoration of their health expeditiously.

An international moral standard not to engage in conduct that causes illness does not require a stage 6 assumption. The illness, debility, and death that result from the practice of female genital mutilation make it morally unacceptable by this standard. Although individual and community interests need to be considered and balanced, a non-Western morality still can reject such a practice. The burden of proof would be upon those who defend the practice, because the harm of the practice is objectively documented, while any medical benefit is not. If benefit were demonstrated, such as a significantly lower incidence of AIDS in this population, then a consequentialist deliberation on the practice would be required; health as a transcultural norm still requires methodology for adjudicating conflicting claims of health. At some point the health needs of the person and those of the population must be reconciled.

The conflict between community interests and individual human rights also enters into the consideration of this practice. For example, if certain females are particularly afflicted by this practice, while the majority is not, then the conflict of individual rights versus those of the society is heightened. Western ethics places a priority on individual rights that other cultural traditions do not. But adopting a more substantive notion of the moral imperative for health transcends the issue of personal autonomy while vouchsafing individual health.

One other aspect of this practice that stands out is that the risk-taking is exclusively female. This is consonant with the disproportional degree to which sexual violence is directed against the female. It is beyond the scope of this essay to address the biological basis of violence, but gender differences evidently influence this practice.

TYPES OF VIOLENCE AND KOHLBERGIAN STAGES

It is possible to associate a type of violence with a deficiency at a particular level of moral development. For example, the psychopath or sociopath is unable to comprehend predictable retribution for an act of violence (stage 1). Lack of knowledge of group norms contributes to a stage 2 type of violence. Violent group norms and "group think" constitute stage 3 types of violence, and nationalistic wars, encouraged by cultural norms which embrace violence, are representative of stage 4. Stage 5 ideals can lead to an increase in violence by the loosening and relativization of social mores.

Culture can exert influences on social behavior with regard to violence both contingently and remotely, both formally and informally. An example of a remote influence is that explicated by Nisbett with regard to violence in the Southern United States as related to descendance from sheepherders (1993: 441–49). The pivotal moment in a sheepherder's coming of age involves a violent display or reaction when the flock is threatened. Similar remote influences may exist in such diverse cultures as the Middle East and New Zealand. Remote influences may be ingrained in the folklore and mythology of a people and may not be readily shed by rational discourse alone, but may require alternative, constructive mythology. It is from such cultural determinants that culturally acceptable acts of violence develop.

Culture defines the pattern of daily life and life goals. It is a major determinant as well as deterrent of violent behavior, and it defines what coercion is culturally acceptable. In our multicultural world we can yet reach out for transcultural norms and ideals that do not have to be reduced to the neo-Kantian values of stages 5 and 6. Health/well-being is one such ideal, but it must be construed in a fashion that balances communal, societal, and individual perspectives. The example of female circumcision is an example of how health can serve as a transcultural moral norm to combat a morally objectionable practice in terms that can be understood and rationalized in a variety of cultures.

DESCRIPTION, JUDGMENT, AND VALUE

Kohlberg himself noted that if moral judgment is to survive the proclamations of cultural and moral relativism, it is necessary to refute a received maxim of Western philosophy, the "is/ought fallacy" (1981). Since the time of David Hume it has been widely accepted that one cannot derive "ought" or prescriptive statements from factual information or descriptive statements. The separation of moral philosophy from other humanistic disciplines such as cultural anthropology has long been established in academe. John Dewey challenged this segregation of ethics from biological and humanistic disciplines, asserting that moral judgments are a species of judgment of value, and that judging is not exclusively moral (1960: 122). Moreover, the moral realm is intertwined with the physical and biological through the social nexus. In fact, the thinkers who wrote persuasively in favor of this separation had a very different understanding of moral statements and of the veracity and absoluteness of scientific claims. They believed that science was a process of unearthing ultimate Newtonian truths, not the realm of uncertainty principles. From our postmodern perspective, one can observe that science is not pristine, nor is ethics so discontinuous from other bodies of knowledge. Formalists such as Hare (1981: 25–62) identify behind moral claims a substrata which is analogous to Chomsky's universal syntactical rules (Chomsky, 1965: ch. 1). Ethics like grammar may well be both culture-dependent and culture-transcendent.

HEALTH AS A TRANSCULTURAL VALUE

I submit that health is a transcultural value that can meet the standard of universality. The universal longing for well-being constitutes the *lingua franca* of health. In my medical practice in New York City with over eighty countries represented, the similarity of concerns for expeditious, efficacious, and courteous medical care is striking. Although cultural differences abound in the population I serve, there is a near unanimity about what patients desire from health services. People from developing lands seek out Western medicine, despite its rigors, because of a tacit agreement in its efficacy. Although this approval is not without ambivalence, it is nevertheless meaningful.

In addition, medicine has its own *lingua franca* in the language of medical science and technology. Clinicians and researchers around the globe share common methodologies and objectives. There are some lessons from the universal longing for health and well-being that can inform bioethical discourse here and elsewhere. First, the striving for personal well-being takes priority over issues of autonomy and control of decision-making. Ill patients of diverse cultural backgrounds desire the best decision be made in their case, not primarily that which guarantees the most autonomy—a desire analogous to that found in studies of transcultural nonmedical decision-making (Haidt, Koller, and Dias, 1993). Individual choice and informed consent can remain cherished principles that do not preempt other concerns.

A second observation is that health care invariably concerns community issues as well as strictly private, individual ones. Western minds may more readily perceive this connection when they contemplate far-off famines in the developing regions, but it is no less true here in the United States, and there is no better example than violence itself. Epidemics of violence are a matter that involves the society as a whole and not merely the individual victims and perpetrators. Cultural norms determine the extent to which a society and its subcultures tolerate and encourage organized and individual violence.

Unpermitted acts of physical coercion are politically determined within a specific cultural context. Violence consists of physical coercion that remains outside culturally sanctioned norms. In comparing issues of violence transculturally, Kohlberg's stages of moral development are useful in categorizing types of violence. The practice of female circumcision powerfully illustrates the divergence of moral suasion in differing cultures. In the effort to critique this practice in a manner that "travels" outside of Western presumptions, I have posited that health is a transcultural value that can be applied to both Western and non-Western systems. This claim is based on the experience of health care in a transcultural setting and is charged with the notion of reintegrating prescriptive statements with descriptive ones. Health and well-being have ethical implications that permit one to develop more meaningful transcultural statements of morality than is possible with the Western concepts of universality and autonomy.

CHAPTER TWELVE

International Development Paradigms and Violence against Women

NATALIE DANDEKAR

In this essay I advance a feminist analysis of three international development paradigms: (1) development as large-scale industrialization; (2) development as large-scale industrialization coupled with social justice; and (3) development as efficient use of resources under structural adjustment. The second paradigm includes both the "basic needs" approach and the "women in development" (WID) approach, each of which is discussed separately. For each paradigm I ask, how do these development theories conceive of women? The conceptions of women implicit in these paradigms underlie the increasing impoverishment of women and the denial of rightful options generally available to men, and can therefore be seen as a form of silent institutional violence against women.

DEVELOPMENT AS INDUSTRIALIZATION

Karl Marx wrote, "the country that is more developed industrially only shows to the less developed the image of its own future" (1972: 193). When the United Nations declared the 1960s its First Development Decade, development theorists of every philosophical orientation began by assuming that 108 heterogeneous countries would develop by replacing a traditional (unscientific, preindustrialized) organization of labor with the modern (scientific, technological, industrial, rationalized) organization of

An earlier version of this paper was presented at the North American Society for Social Philosophy meeting at Colby College in August 1995. The discussion there and the comments of the editors of this volume were helpful in shaping the present version.

labor. In a multitude of countries where colonial power had established arbitrary boundaries, where simmering ethnic rivalries had been stoked by colonial policies, and where national unity was still to be forged, governments uniformly aimed at development by way of industrialization. Development aid, regarded as a "pump primer," promoted education and population control as two necessary conditions of successful industrialization.

Procapitalist theorists such as Rostow (1960) assumed that these countries would become stable democratic states through a pattern in which advanced science, technology, and industrialization would effectively create a market economy. Consumer sovereignty would promote individual rights and result in representative democratic government. Everyone, including the poor, would benefit from the prosperous conditions of a liberal democratic capitalist state.

Marxist theorists tended to see development in terms of Lenin's interpretation of history, in which industrialization and subsequent class conflict in capitalist societies were regarded as a necessary phase of the dialectic that would eventually lead to a withering away of the state. Marxist theory promoted investment in large engineering projects, though the societal objectives Marxists aimed at required transformation of a country's "mode of production" that would ultimately trigger wide-ranging changes in the relative importance of social classes.

Since all countries presumably had to enter into scientific-technological industrialized production, development aid workers offered the same advice and promoted similar projects in every country. For example, building a dam seemed the sort of project that could always find funds under this development paradigm.

VIEWS OF WOMEN IN THE INDUSTRIALIZATION PARADIGM

Industrial development has conceived of women as nonautonomous dependents, a characterization that falsified the developing societies in at least three ways. First, women were regarded as nonproductive consumers. Second, poor women were categorized as analogous to the disabled. Third, as women were held responsible for the population explosion, and made the focus of top-down population control schemes, they were conceptually reduced to their reproductive potential.

Development rhetoric professed to respect cultural traditions while recognizing that many of the traditional ways were incompatible with the need for economic growth and would therefore have to be abandoned.

The family, however, was never directly challenged. Instead, family life was presumed to be insulated from the forces that would modernize the market and the labor force; somehow the family was to continue to function as the home of cultural values, even as it became smaller through population control and even as the male head of household adapted to the modern requirements of labor by developing such untraditional habits as personal discipline, punctuality, and responsiveness to monetary incentives.

Industrialization policies aimed at bringing men into the market economy, as if the family consisted of a male head of household earning wages sufficient to support his wife and dependent children. Whether or not this "ideal" family was normal within already developed countries, it was certainly unlike the various extended families that were traditional and normal in many of the underdeveloped countries. Consider, for example, four of these existing traditions: (1) in the polygamous culture of Ghana a wife maintains her own separate household, often by her own efforts; (2) in many Southeast Asian cultures, daughters-in-law are brought to live in patriarchally organized households where the strongest emotional connections link mother and adult son. In an extended, multigenerational Southeast Asian household, the mother-in-law, with the backing and cooperation of her married sons, exercises full authority over any daughter-in-law; (3) traditional Moslem homes of the well-to-do contain a section of the house reserved for women only and respectable women are expected to remain within these sections, shielded from contact with the rest of the world; (4) by contrast, Kerala is a region in India where families and property rights are still traditionally matriarchal.

Policies that presume Western-style social structures in which a male head of household supports his wife and one or two dependent children encourage highly nontraditional outcomes with respect to all four of the family structures listed above. Yet, possibly because these were consistent with patriarchal imperatives, national governments and private citizens simply accepted that Westernized education and work opportunities increased the productive capacity of the male labor force, making it natural for a family to depend upon the wage earned by the male head.

Policies that aimed at increasing earning opportunities of men affected poor women in important ways. These women were not seen as persons who, if they received encouragement, access to education, and employment opportunity, might meet their own needs. Rather, they were seen as having temporarily failed to connect normally with a male wage earner. Women for whom male earnings failed to provide a decent standard of living were not seen as job candidates in their own right but categorized, together with the disabled and the sick, as vulnerable populations. Aid to poor women was regarded as welfare, a temporary way of tiding women over their abnormal failure to connect with the "normal" structures of supply. When women became reconnected with those structures, that is, the family and the market, they would no longer need to depend on welfare.

Welfare provisions understood in this way were a non-productive use of economic resources, a stop-gap until economic progress brought more male heads of household into an increasingly profitable world market. In this way, women's interests were pitted against development interests, with women on welfare seen as competitors draining off resources that could otherwise be directed toward productive industrial investment. Moreover, uncontrolled population growth, seen as a result of women's fertility, was considered a threat that could derail economic growth entirely. Monies which could otherwise be directed toward improving productivity were used for contraception and sterilization campaigns.

In this initial approach, development programs supplied modern technologies directly to men as agents of development. Women were considered consumers whose activities used up economic resources produced by men. It was especially important that women's reproductive potential be controlled so that men's productivity was available as a development resource.

Traditional knowledge, for which women were frequently the repository, was entirely ignored and devalued by experts who believed that such knowledge was nearly worthless (Jazairy, Alamgir, and Panuccio, 1992: 5). Traditional knowledge includes, among other things, recognizing which local plants offer medical benefits, which traditional mix of dishes provide a balanced diet, midwifery techniques, ecologically appropriate forms of planting and harvesting using traditional mixed cropping techniques, forms of water conservation appropriate to the local geography, and the heirloom landrace seed lines developed by the traditional agriculturists of the local regions.

Development aid thus promoted changes formulated in ignorance of the delicate ecological balance sustained by traditional practices. New hybridized crops depended on monoculture cropping and intensive herbicide and petrochemical fertilizer treatments. Monoculture forestry management replaced mixed forestry practices, and dams were sited in terms of Western concepts, without consideration of local ecological lore. Ecological degradations brought about by the resultant "maldevelopment" have been documented by Shiva (1988).

THE "BASIC NEEDS" APPROACH

Under the large-scale industrialization paradigm, progress toward development was measured in gross economic terms. But newly industrializing countries often displayed what is called a dual economy—a minority benefited greatly while the majority was worse off in almost every respect. Measures of per capita income homogenized these disparities, aggregating the earnings of those who benefited and those who failed to benefit, without any indicator for measuring the nonmonetary costs to the latter. Efforts to stimulate enhanced consumption of "modern" goods and services encouraged those men who had wage employment to spend their money on consumption goods.

As Mechthilde Hart notes, "where male status may previously have been associated with hospitality, responsibility for family and village, the owners of the new status symbols . . . become independent from the family as a production unit" (1992: 41). Consumer appetite for modern goods and services also promoted an "exodus of people from rural areas to urban industrial centres," the only place where modern goods were marketed (Mabogunje, 1981: 39). Critical shortages of rural labor brought about agricultural failures leading to rural pauperization, further exodus, and chronic urban unemployment. Ultimately this worsened the divisions of a dual economy so that "underdeveloped countries came to exhibit more sharply the picture of a small minority of extremely wealthy individuals living off, as it were, the backs of a large, poverty-stricken and destitute majority" (ibid.). Where development was conceived of as industrialization, and measured by GNP, life for the majority was visibly worsened by processes that imposed the greatest suffering on the population at the bottom of the income scale (Jazairy, Alamgir, and Panuccio, 1992: 7).

By the end of the 1960s the development community responded to this ever more visible increase in poverty by refining the concept of "modern goods" and using more sophisticated measures of availability. Development continued to be measured by counting goods available to the populace, but in addition to goods that could be purchased in an open market, such as food and shelter, theorists began to include measurements of public goods as well, such as military defense, rich and accessible media, adequate sewage treatment, hospitals, schools, and so forth. Two distributional factors were especially meaningful: the extent to which different social classes had access to public goods, and how the unwanted by-products of development (such as environmental degradation, water pollution, air pollution, and loss of forest) were shared among these classes. The more developed a country, the more public goods are available. But if the poor drink contaminated water because the only available pure water flows to the homes of the rich, the disparity, as measured by the basic needs model of development, is evidence of a "less developed" economy.

In the basic needs approach, the new emphasis on distribution of goods eventually led to a definition of development that stressed the importance of meeting basic needs in a manner compatible with social justice. In the metaphor associated with development at that time, developing nations were baking a national cake. The cake had to be large enough so that, when shared equitably, everyone's basic needs could be met. Groups targeted for special attention to equity included "small peasant farmers, landless labourers and submarginal farmers, urban under-employed and urban unemployed. . . . [T]he new strategy underlined the importance of regional development planning in seeking to even out or at least narrow the gap in the life chances . . . of citizens irrespective of the region of the country in which they live" (Mabogunje, 1981: 42).

WOMEN AND THE BASIC NEEDS APPROACH

The basic needs approach focused on the needy in a "gender-neutral" manner. Information was gathered about "small peasant farmers, landless labourers and submarginal farmers, urban under-employed and urban unemployed," but the use of gender-neutral categories was not, in fact, neutral. Rather, in countries where gender privilege is perceived as "natural," gender-neutral categories effectively perpetuated unrecognized privilege under the guise of gender-neutral law. For example, providing the gender-neutral poor with better access to food, while leaving the gender-skewed intrafamily food distribution pattern untouched, meant that without access to the traditional "women's foods," many women remained undernourished.

That women might not benefit in an equitable manner became clear when Ester Boserup (1970) published overwhelming evidence that women's work burden increased because of development policies. Documenting the extent to which, in the underdeveloped countries, women were active agents in agriculture and the market, Boserup showed that development programs aimed at men had increased women's work burdens as they benefited men and decreased their burdens. She demonstrated that destitution consequent upon development hit women measurably harder than the negatives of development hit men.

Boserup's publications coincided with the rise of the feminist movement in the United States. By 1973, the Percy Amendment to the U. S. Foreign Assistance Act mandated that U. S. assistance help improve women's status. This altered the initial focus of the basic needs approach by mandating that monies be used specifically to provide equity for women. Described as the Women in Development (WID) equity paradigm, this variant of the basic needs approach resulted in the promotion of legal equality for women. However, such legal changes reflected a hierarchical approach in which superior must control inferior for the benefit of the latter.

Percy Amendment constraints required recipient states to create new law that ostensibly promoted the rights of all women, but these laws promoted new forms of externally imposed control that marginalized poor women's concerns. Projects designed by WID administrators brought women "into development" on terms the administrators assigned. Sometimes the goal was simply to increase opportunities by which women might earn additional income without increasing their control over this income or actually decreasing their dependency. In designing projects, administrators tended to discuss benefits as they affected men's interests. Piping water directly to village houses, for example, would be debated by development advisers in terms of the utility to the husband. He would gain utility from the status conferred by an indoor tap, but he would lose utility when his wife no longer exchanged gossip at the well (Sagoff, 1988: 14).

Moreover, the WID projects and the administrators in charge of them were frequently regarded with suspicion as antitraditional influences. Within the development community, information gathered for administrators in charge of WID projects was pigeonholed because the administrators tended to find themselves cut off from communicating with those working on projects regarded as more centrally important. For example, during the 1970s the US AID funded excellent WID studies focused on women, such as one documenting the role of African women in agriculture as primary suppliers of family food. But that information remained at the periphery even of the funding organization's focus. During the 1980s only 4.3 percent of US sAID projects in Africa had a component including women; only four of forty-five agricultural projects designated women as beneficiaries (Stamp 1989: 27–28). The traditions embodying generations of experience in agriculture remained untapped.

Although basic needs development strategies evolved specifically to alleviate poverty, little was known about the concrete conditions of poor women's lives. International studies that began to document the myriad ways in which poor women in developing nations carry what Moser (1991) calls a "triple burden" did not always affect project design. Boserup documented women caring for the family's needs and also producing resources for family use, whether or not they were working in the cash economy. Moser points out that, in societies where public utilities are not easily available, poor women become responsible for obtaining water, fuel, and other items of collective consumption for their households. They are also frequently the rank and file participants in local protests.[1] (The nature of these protests varies widely. In the Himalayas the Chipko movement protesting nonsustainable forestry practices was primarily a movement of indigenous women.) The conflicts that necessarily arise among such disparate responsibilities are deepened when public support (such as desirable day-care facilities) are unavailable. Only a few programs, such as the highly successful Grameen bank,[2] enabled women to design their own income-generating opportunities as they worked together in small mutual, morally binding groups to change their dependency situations.

The basic needs and WID approach emphasized the importance of social justice as well as industrialization. After a first decade aimed at increasing GNP with men as agents of production, theorists of the second decade added two further measurements: the increase of laws promoting development equity; and a strategy that focused planners' attention on providing the poor with increased opportunities.

But in this more complicated definition of development, women continued to be conceived foremost as dependent consumers. Poor women continued to be seen as a (temporary) drain on monies that might otherwise be invested in promoting GNP growth. The needs of women were seen as pitted against the use of resources for industrial development.

The women in development approach also added a second layer of conceptualization: some women were feminists who demanded rights under the claim of equity. Such equity, however, was regarded as a new form of inappropriate interference by the United States. To be required to institute laws protecting women's rights came to be seen as Western cultural imperialism, and feminists in developing countries were frequently labeled elitists and regarded as traitors to their own culture.[3] The needs of women as feminists were pitted against the importance of maintaining cultural integrity. The needs of poor women, however, did not find adequate defense under either heading. Poor women were seen as the passive objects of development rather than participants with their own lives to live.

The basic needs approach concentrated on discovering poverty among such gender-neutral groups as "the urban underemployed," but such language resulted in data that hid the extent to which supposedly gender-neutral categories were filled with women. Moreover, programs that specifically focused on women frequently overlooked the numerous disparate responsibilities of poor women, and offered income-generating programs in ways that exacerbated the situation of impoverished women. For example: when income-generating opportunities are established without day-care provisions, the intended beneficiary may have to leave children unattended while working. In another instance, solar stoves were provided as a means for women to earn additional income by baking goods. Unfortunately, these women worked in the fields during the day and cooked by night. Unless a woman gave up her fieldwork, she owed money for a useless stove. If she gave up the fieldwork, her family's food supply was diminished. In other cases, poor market research sometimes led to the production of goods that could not be sold locally and for which no alternative markets had been developed.

"STRUCTURAL ADJUSTMENT": WOMEN AS A RESOURCE OF LAST RESORT

Before many lessons could be learned about what development policies might do to alleviate poverty, the debt crisis of 1982 forced development planning to adopt another criterion. Under structural adjustment, development is measured by efficient use of resources, with privatization the preferred mode for realizing efficiencies. As a consequence, governments were required by the international lending agencies of last resort to disinvest in welfare provision, which resulted in deep cuts to health, education, and food subsidies.

Under structural adjustment, poor women become the resources of last resort. For example, women may make up for cuts in food subsidies by adding additional hours to their "normal" workload, spending more time obtaining and preparing cheaper foods. When monies available to health clinics are cut, local women voluntarily undertake previously paid work, sweeping the clinic, opening it, and taking training for minor medical procedures so that what little money remains can be used directly for medicines.

Hilary Standing describes Bengali women coping with poverty by working from three in the morning until well after dark (1991: 172). To cope with similar austerities, Nicaraguan women expand their workday to include the predawn in a thirteen-hour round. In Bangladesh, a poor woman may routinely put in sixteen hours a day (Jazairy, Alamgir, and Panuccio, 1992: chap. 1). Despite the obvious increase in their domestic workloads due to structural adjustment, women respond to food shortfalls by exacerbating the tendency of intrafamilial food distributions to short-change young girls and older women.

Increasing the burdens of poor women is not the only way in which countries compelled to improve their balance of payments by lenders of last resort use women's labor as a resource of last resort. Under the impetus of structural adjustment constraints, the femininity of poor women becomes a "natural resource" to be exploited for increasing a country's access to foreign currency. According to Cynthia Enloe, "sex tourism requires Third World women to be economically desperate enough to enter prostitution. . . . [It] requires men from affluent societies to imagine [these women] . . . to be more available and submissive than the women in their own countries. Finally, the industry depends on an alliance between local governments in search of foreign currency and local and foreign businessmen willing to invest in sexualized travel" (1990: 36).

As Siriporn Skrobanek reports, the transaction can be diagrammed: "The Japanese tourist wants a girl for one night. He will pay the hotel $12 . . . [and] the tour operator $50. The tour operator gives the local pimp $20 and the pimp pays the girl . . . $8!" (1987: 212). Skrobanek explains, "The development strategy aiming at integration into the world economic system resulted in . . . peasant women . . . forced by impoverishment to migrate into towns to find jobs . . . based on 'feminine' characteristics" (213).

Structural adjustment stringencies play an obvious part in creating conditions that sustain this equation. Tourism, according to Enloe, "continues to be promoted by bankers and development planners as a means of making the international system less unequal, more financially sound and more politically stable" (1990: 40).

A second way in which the femininity of poor women serves as a resource for earning foreign currency involves large-scale industries more directly. At various points in the process, women's labor is preferred because of the stereotypes that women's handwork is deft and their nature docile, and the expectation that they will be employed for only a few years, before leaving to marry and care for their family. Management is generally male in these corporate environments.

Third, women help a country to earn foreign exchange by going abroad as nannies, domestic servants, entertainers, prostitutes, and mail-order brides. These women are generally afforded fewer legal protections than other immigrants. Their "lives are made precarious not only by the poverty back home but by regulations imposed by home and host governments" (Enloe, 1990: 179).

Women emigrants see the reasons for working abroad as very personal.

They need to earn money to support parents, children, siblings. But international debt politics and distorted development have created the incentives for these women to emigrate. And as Enloe points out, "the politics of international debt is not simply something that has an *impact* on women in indebted countries. [This form of development can only be sustained when] mothers and wives are willing to behave in ways that enable nervous regimes to adopt cost-cutting measures without forfeiting their political legitimacy" (1990: 185).

An unspoken reliance on women makes structural adjustment possible. Governments can keep political legitimacy under the constraints of structural adjustment only because women willingly work those extra hours: to keep their families fed, to keep clinics functioning, to care for their sick if subsidized clinics shut down. But women have to be willing to make even greater sacrifices: to leave children behind with relatives while they migrate to care for some other family's children; to provide the docile, short-term labor force desired by clothing manufacturers, banana exporters, and beach-front hotels; to run the health risks these jobs often involve; to accept prostitution to keep sex tourism attractive, and accept *those* health risks, too, in a world where AIDS is fatal.

Within the paradigm of structural adjustment, women's sacrifices are hidden behind gender-neutral demands that government elites repay loans made by international banking interests. When women are used without specific acknowledgment as a resource of last resort, these are the conceptual consequences: (1) women are expected to be self-sacrificing— good mothers, daughters, and wives whose most important task in life is to give of themselves to benefit others; (2) women who actively protest— for instance, organizing campaigns against sex tourism—are ignored, scolded, or regarded as less fully feminine; (3) development understood primarily in terms of economics mystifies the connection between international economics and the manipulation of femininity; (4) women's status is once again conceptually dependent upon the status of the men in their families, so that women from well-to-do families benefit as consumers from policies that demand unmentioned sacrifice from poor women.

Development policies have dramatically worsened the situations of the poor, and especially of poor women. Decades after Boserup and Percy, "the number of rural women living in absolute poverty rose by about 50 percent—from an estimated 370 million to about 565 million as against an increase of about 30 per cent for rural men" (Jazairy, Alamgir, and Panuccio, 1992: xix). Though development began with the professed intention of diminishing poverty and reducing social inequities, the markedly negative impact of development policies on women's lives shows it to be a failure in its own terms. My analysis suggests strongly that this failure is linked with seriously flawed conceptions of women.

FAILED DEVELOPMENT POLICIES
AS VIOLENCE AGAINST WOMEN

Newton Garver distinguishes four types of violence. In addition to widely recognized forms of overt violence, Garver discusses "quiet forms which do not necessarily involve any overt physical assault on anybody's person or property" (1977: 364). Garver includes within this category psychological violence, in which a person in authority so structures expectations that, whatever the subject individuals do, they will merely confirm the authority's negative expectations. Garver also describes an institutional form of quiet violence: "Any institution which systematically robs certain people of rightful options generally available to others does violence to those people" (369).

Joseph Betz argues that Garver's definition is so broad that "there is simply no extension left for the term 'nonviolent social wrong' in Garver's account" (1977: 341). Thus the question arises whether the myriad social wrongs experienced by poor women during the instantiation of various development paradigms over the last four decades should be regarded as a kind of violence or not.

In various ways, I have argued, the failed development policies of the past three decades have systematically robbed women of rightful options generally available to men. During the first decade, women were reduced to objects of welfare, while men were encouraged to join the cash economy. The later emphasis on equity promoted policies that brought women into development, but frequently this approach was flawed. Opportunities offered to poor women were sometimes structured in ways that increased their unrecognized "triple burden." Women's nurturing behavior was valued so little that the conditions for doing it well were removed, as cash-strapped governments closed prenatal clinics and ended childhood inoculations and preschool programs. As women attempted to keep their children from suffering, they thus involuntarily assumed increased caregiving roles. Robin West (1988) describes this kind of situation as having one's ends displaced before one even formulates them, stifling women's autonomy because the boundaries of the self are involuntarily extended to the dependent other. Again, where WID policies were enacted, women were frequently treated as the subjects to be helped by development agents, rather than as agents with their own purposes. The model was that of the missionary helping the benighted to see the missionary's truth. Women's traditional knowledge was discounted. But other strands of cultural tradition, especially those that protected male privilege, were elevated. Respect for these traditions became reason enough for neglecting the empowerment of women. The resulting inequities of these decades, burdening and impoverishing women, must be seen as social injustices. As such they are wrongs, but are they to be seen as violence?

Betz cautions us that "what affects the psyche directly and not through the body, though it may be wrong, is not violence" (1977: 345). My analysis provides reason for claiming that development policies affected women because of how such policies conceived of them. In development theories, women's very embodiment becomes the ground for reductive practices. First, the pattern of seeing women's reproductive potential as the basis of population explosions depends upon considering women only in their bodily difference from men, and disregarding women above and below the age of fecundity. Development policies that exploit resources and count women's labor among the resources available for exploitation also affect women directly in terms of their bodies, as well as their psyches. In this way, development paradigms that reduce women's life chances categorically because of the fact of embodiment should be seen as a form of violence against women.

There is another and somewhat more disquieting way of understanding the quiet institutional violence that affects 565 million women as a consequence of development projects. In her paper on sexual terrorism, Carole Sheffield postulates that the right of men to control the female body is a cornerstone of patriarchy. In the United States, and in other highly developed modern industrial urban centers of the West—countries that have been taken as the ideal for development projects—"sexual terrorism is a system that functions to maintain male supremacy through actual and implied violence . . . the perpetuation of fear of violence forms the basis of patriarchal power" (1992: 72).

It is a disturbing possibility that authorities in the international development agencies and in the governing bodies of developing nations are themselves deeply imbued with the Western patriarchal presuppositions that continue to characterize many industrialized countries. Without conscious intent, these authorities may export Western patriarchal values together with development. If so, then the project of modernity is so deeply connected with furtherance of violence against women that development in these terms must always fail to alleviate the poverty of poor women.

STRANDS OF HOPE

Since 1989 the International Monetary Fund has introduced the concept of "high quality growth," which pays attention to the plight of the poor and vulnerable and ensures protection of the environment. The UN Development Program has begun to use a human development index that combines life expectancy at birth, literacy, and per capita income.

Perhaps more important, development now seeks to identify power in terms of women's own capacity to increase their self-reliance and make choices in life. Programs like the Grameen Bank seek to empower women who may not want to be integrated into Western-designed development but rather prefer to have choices in defining the kind of society they want.

In practice, an empowerment approach relies on grassroots women's organizations to provide fora in which women become conscious of the need to challenge subordination. Empowerment projects combine traditional tasks (such as tapestry making) and efforts to meet specific practical needs poor women themselves identify (such as homelessness in Bombay) with more strategic discussion of women's legal rights. In the specific case of empowering homeless women in Bombay, participating women became aware of the extent to which their particular problems reflect the patriarchal bias in inheritance legislation and the interpretation of housing rights. (Dandekar, forthcoming)

Although empowerment strategies offer poor women a moral situation in which they can take small incremental steps toward greater justice, the paradigms structuring other policies of international development have made the situations of poor women inequitable. These paradigms and the policies that they promote in effect assumed (1) that in the best of situations women should be connected to the economy as dependents of wage-earning men; (2) that women who themselves earn wages should fit the male model of wage earner, having someone else at home responsible for domestic caring tasks; and (3) that women will self-sacrificingly serve as a resource of last resort to support the continued authority of governments that cut back on welfare provisions in the name of structural adjustment efficiencies. These assumptions, and the development policies built uncritically around them, should be recognized as a form of violence against women, as well as an institutional support of the sexual terrorism more ordinarily seen as violence against women.

CHAPTER THIRTEEN

Resistance to Prevention: Reconsidering Feminist Antiviolence Rhetoric

NADYA BURTON

In this essay I examine some of the "classic" texts on violence against women. These texts, written between 1971 and 1985, were among the first in North America to examine the issues of violence against women, and to do so from an avowedly "feminist" standpoint.[1] A decade later we are well placed to consider how violence against women came to be conceptualized by feminists such as Susan Brownmiller, Andrea Dworkin, Diana Russell, and Susan Griffin, and to understand how much of our thinking and our language was drawn from their work.

I want to look at their approach to four concepts: fear, victimhood, resistance, and prevention. I want to explore the use of these concepts in setting up "commonsense" understandings of violence against women, and to describe the rhetoric of violence being constructed in this literature through the deployment of these terms.

These texts were published after an era of silence, an era in which violence against women did not exist in the public discourse and where all forms of sexual assault were either invisible or collapsed into broader discourses of violence. They brought into the public realm what had previously been invisible or private.

Bringing into language facts and ideas that had previously existed in a less public way can serve as liberating and as a force for social change. On the other hand, as Linda Alcoff and Laura Gray note, "bringing things into the realm of discourse works also to inscribe them into hegemonic struc-

I am grateful to Gordon Thompson and Lisa Weintraub for invaluable insights and critiques that have strengthened and enriched this work.

tures" (1993: 260). Foucault's (1980a: 100–102) conceptualization of both the enabling and limiting workings of discourse helps us avoid the simplistic dichotomy whereby language is defined as either unequivocally liberatory or as wholly repressive. Foucault makes explicit the fact that discourse does not eliminate power, but rather redeploys it, and thus we can see language as a site of struggle where power and resistance are in constant tension.

New discursive worlds were indeed opened up in the feminist antiviolence writings of the decade in question. Much of the rhetoric that came to be solidified by these works arose in opposition to a particular misogynist, patriarchal, and antiwoman set of beliefs and discursive practices now known as "rape myths." There was tremendous need to expose and unsettle these myths as the patriarchal representations they were, uninformed by the lived experiences of many survivors of sexual assault. But the oppositional framework that structured this exposure created deadly traps for the emerging feminist discourse, and feminist antiviolence writers produced a series of simplistic, extreme oppositions. For example, the myth that only certain women could actually be "legitimate" rape victims (white, virgin or married, middle-class, and educated women, for example) was challenged with the new feminist "truth" that *all* women are potential rape victims. The myth that rape occurred only when women resisted was countered with the denial of women's *ability* to resist in the face of the terror. These new "truths" were part of a feminist political strategy to unsettle commonly accepted views of violence against women, yet the result was a new and equally rigid discursive world.

These works simultaneously call for tremendous respect and for serious critique. They served to broaden public understanding of violence against women by making visible a silenced and subjugated world. Yet they are also already outmoded in their stylistic propensity toward totalization and their reductionist attempts to cite sexual violence against women as the single site of women's oppression. Take for instance such sweeping claims as the following by Brownmiller:[2] "Female fear of an open season of rape, and not a natural inclination toward monogamy, motherhood or love, was probably the single causative factor in the original subjugation of woman by man, the most important key to her historic dependence, her domestication by protective mating. . . . Concepts of hierarchy, slavery and private property flowed from, and could only be predicated upon, the initial subjugation of woman" (1975: 6–8). Such a proposition appears obviously problematic to a contemporary reader within an intellectual climate that has been sensitized to reductionist views of history.

FEAR

The following passages illustrate the need felt by early feminist theorists to articulate an essential relationship between womanhood and fear of violence:

> Women and children live in the shadow of terror. Whether it is in the workplace, on the street, or inside the home, the threat of violence stays with us wherever we happen to be. (Guberman and Wolfe, 1985: 9)
>
> I have never been free of the fear of rape. From a very early age I, like most women, have thought of rape as part of my natural environment— something to be feared and prayed against like fire or lightning. (Griffin, 1971: 26)
>
> The fear of rape effects all women. It inhibits their actions and limits their freedom, influencing the way they dress, the hours they keep, and the routes they walk. The fear is well founded, because no woman is immune from rape. (Clark and Lewis, 1977: 23)
>
> From prehistoric times to the present, I believe, rape has played a critical function. It is nothing more or less than a conscious process of intimidation by which *all men* keep *all women* in a state of fear. (Brownmiller, 1975: 5)
>
> We became concerned about sexual assault long before writing this book, for fear of rape lies within the hearts of all women. (Bart and O'Brien, 1985: ix)

It appears to have been almost impossible to write about rape and sexual assault without direct, frequent appeals to fear as the framework within which violence against women operates. Why should this have been so, and what are the consequences of this linkage?

The desire to articulate women's fear so unrelentingly is understandable in the moments immediately following the era of silence. There was a deep need to name and explain the vastly different world women claimed to live in as one dominated by fear and violence.

This "telling" about fear serves quite different functions relative to the audience. On the one hand the revealing of fear as a centerpiece of women's experience speaks in a particular way to a nonfeminist audience, serving as an appeal to the humanity of not only those who may have given it little recognition, but those who may be part of its cause as well. We can assume such an audience, for example, in the case of Susan Griffin's 1971 article in *Ramparts* magazine. However, if we acknowledge that most of these texts were in fact read primarily by women, then the purpose served by talking of fear to those very readers whose lives are apparently imbued with it is very different. According to this rhetoric, women need not be told of the existence of their fear since they are assumed to be intimate with it, but rather that it is a consequence of their gender, and that it unites them with women as a whole. This essentialized link serves a critical function of creating the category of "rape victims"; "you are not alone" was a battle cry of the antirape movement.

The rhetoric of these works serves the dual purpose of deindividualizing rape and placing it firmly in the social and political arena, and of rendering fear an essential part of femaleness. The male rapist is also deindividualized. Brownmiller, for instance, argues that the rapist performs a societal function for men by keeping women in a state of fear. Women need not experience rape to carry that fear with them: "that some men rape provides a sufficient threat to keep all women in a constant state of intimidation" (1975: 229). Rape as a "form of mass terrorism" (Griffin, 1971: 35), as a tool "designed to intimidate and inspire fear" (Brownmiller, 1975: 439), is a consistent theme in these texts and is used to explain the magnitude of rape extending far beyond any individual injury.

This explanation of the relationship between fear and violence connects to a central feminist claim: that rape is not about sex, but is a crime of power and control. The individual rape experience then evaporates under the cloud of a generalized social agenda. Thus fear operates in these texts as a unifier of women. Though it is constructed as specific and extreme in the face of particular violence, it is also seen as ambient and persistent, and simply part of femaleness. Clark and Lewis speak of the "solid empirical basis" for women's fear of men (1977: 139), while Brownmiller writes of the "normal, reactive fear that is produced in women by the presence of an aggressive male intent on violence" (1975: 401).

For the many women who do not feel their experiences to be commensurate with such assertions, the fault then is their own. We cannot explain their lack of fear even by appealing to a notion of "false consciousness," because their failure to fear sufficiently does not serve the dominant interest. In this framing there is no space for those women who do not fear, or for whom fear is only a small part of their being. The universality of fear for women in these texts leaves no space either for the range of other responses that might accompany ideas and experiences of sexual violence (anger, rage, pain, sadness, guilt, power, strength). The construction of fear as hegemonic, while serving to validate the often private, individual feelings of women, simultaneously serves to establish fear as normative and universal.

More problematically, in being understood as the natural response to sexual assault, fear is consistently presumed to imply immobility. In writing of rape that involves minimal physical aggression, Brownmiller insists that "without doubt, any of these circumstances can and does produce immobilizing terror in a victim, terror sufficient to render her incapable of resistance or to make her believe that resistance would be futile" (1975: 42). By insisting that fear and immobility are natural and necessary partners, the rhetoric of these early texts tends to work against a cultivation of resistance by women in violent situations. But I suggest that the connection between fear and immobility is not natural and necessary. Fear might equally operate as an instigation to action and resistance. How women respond depends on the social lessons we have assimilated regarding our own strengths and capacities, and on the skills we have or have not learned.

A curious occlusion in Diana Russell's text illustrates the degree to which resistance has been erased from the profile of the rape victim. In speaking of men's tendency to want to hurt or kill the rapist of a woman close to them, Russell comments that "women rarely express the same sentiment" (1975: 67), but over half the women she interviews in her book speak about wanting to seriously harm or kill their rapists. Presumably because immobility is the primary understandable response of women to their assaults, women's expressed desire to fight back (and their desire for revenge) go unnoticed by Russell.

I have suggested that much of the early feminist antiviolence rhetoric arose in direct opposition to "rape myths." Similarly, the rhetoric that identifies lack of resistance as a natural response to fear arose in part as a strategic response to legal requirements that women needed to prove they had resisted in order for the incident to be seen as actionable sexual assault:

> What makes sexual intercourse rape is not the offender's use of or threat of physical force, but proof that a "rapable" female did not consent to the act in question. . . . If there is no such evidence, then her "consent" will be assumed. Saying "no" is apparently not enough, even in the face of physical violence. . . . Since the victim's consent can be used as a defense to the charge of rape, the victim must resist her attacker to the upmost of her capabilities if her later testimony concerning lack of consent is to appear credible. (Clark and Lewis, 1977: 162)

Susan Brownmiller similarly points out:

> Under the rules of law, victims of robbery and assault are not required to prove they resisted, or that they didn't consent. . . . But victims of rape

and other forms of sexual assault do need to prove these evidentiary requirements—that they resisted, that they didn't consent, that their will was overcome by overwhelming force and fear—because the law has never been able to satisfactorily distinguish an act of mutually desired sexual union from an act of forced, criminal sexual aggression. (1975: 431)

It is not surprising that feminists attempted to name fear as a reason for not resisting, in order to shift the burden of blame for assault to the aggressor, regardless of physical resistance on the part of the woman. In one of the only crimes in which a victim's legal innocence is predicated upon her level of resistance, denying the *necessity* of resistance is an important political goal. Marking fear as a legitimate reason for women's lack of resistance to an assault served to bring many otherwise unacknowledged assault situations into the fold of legally understandable assault.

But this legal strategy slides into the ontological position that something in women's being makes resistance impossible. The notion that "prolonged resistance therefore may invite further abuse, serious injury, or even death," and that "a victim who can remain level-headed during an attack may realize that it is rational to submit to rape in such circumstances" (Clark and Lewis, 1977: 162), comes to serve larger ideological purposes separate from the usefulness of women's resistance. As Pauline Bart and Patricia O'Brien point out, however, most empirical studies in fact affirm the effectiveness of resistance: "When a woman used physical force as a defense technique together with another technique [talking, yelling, fleeing], her chances of avoiding [rape] increased. . . . We are told that if we fight back, if we physically resist, we will pay the price of severe injury or death. Not only is this admonition not supported by our findings, it is also unsupported in the work [of other researchers]" (1985: 34, 40).

In an attempt to eliminate resistance as a definitional requirement for sexual assault, the early feminist anti-violence rhetoric propagated insupportable notions of resistance as ineffective and dangerous (and therefore not advisable). It thus proved itself incapable of juggling the complexities of two discourses which don't map perfectly onto each other: that resistance is not necessary for assault to be assault, but that it does in fact help prevent assault.

We do find occasional accounts of resistance in the early texts, but these are exceedingly rare and often carefully managed. For example, not until late in her book does Brownmiller relay, for the first time, a short list of successful resistance stories. Asking, "do women fight back, and can women fight back successfully?" Brownmiller provides two and a half pages of "testimonies" from women who resisted their aggressors (1975: 397). Furthermore, in posing the question, "is submissive behavior in any way *helpful* to a victim of rape?" (1975: 403), Brownmiller responds with an unequivocal "no."

But it is quite evident that while resistance is an interesting question to be considered in passing, it is in no way a theoretical priority for Brownmiller. The effect is to minimize and render marginal acts of resistance, thus privileging the link between rape and a powerless lack of agency in women, and reinforcing a fear/immobility relationship at the expense of a fear/resistance one.

Brownmiller writes of the genuine and astonished wonderment that she and other women felt in a self-defense class when they came to realize that they could in fact, by way of yells and kicks and punches, instill fear in men (1975: 454). That her own power came as such a shock to Brownmiller confirms that the possibility of women's resistance did not form a significant part of her consciousness.

Brownmiller heads us toward an idea that will be examined more fully in the context of prevention: in choosing to protect ourselves, we appear also to be choosing to take responsibility for the assault visited upon us. Sadly, she seems to deny the possibility that learning to defend oneself might in fact actually work to reduce fear.

On this point Susan Griffin is a notable exception among the writers under review. She demonstrates a nuanced appreciation of how fear can feed on passivity and how a cultivation of strength can work to reduce women's fear: "Much of the study of martial arts . . . is a change in attitude. To work against fear, shock, a feeling of defeat. . . . The body becomes stronger, quicker . . . and the body which feels . . . it can defend itself, affects the mind, cannot be seized in the same way by fear" (1986: 35).

My aim is not to set up a dichotomy: no self-defense and fear versus self-defense and no fear. While learning self-defense may act to reduce fear of violence for some women, it might also serve to make possibilities of assault more real for them, and thus in fact exacerbate their fear (temporarily at least). While one would certainly hope the former to be more likely, the aim of self-defense is primarily to generate strategies and skills to reduce violence (although I would argue that the by-product of this in a good self-defense course is the reduction of fear). The primary issue is to undermine the notion of immobilizing fear and to insist that fear alone in no way precludes resistance.

VICTIMHOOD

The concept of victimhood has recently been the subject of countless polemical denunciations, with the rise of a "new individualism" uniting a range of diverse voices (such as Camille Paglia, Naomi Wolf, and Wendy Kaminer). Feminists seem to want to employ the term "victim" because it connotes blamelessness, helplessness, innocence, and a kind of moral high ground. The "new individualists" invoke instead a world where everyone is responsible for themselves.

In criticizing the use of the term "victim," I make no claims that social power imbalances do not exist (contra the "level playing field" of the new individualists), and none about responsibility. Rather, I am concerned with women's agency as something to be cultivated, not suppressed or denied; and I am concerned with the way feminist discourses have worked against this cultivation.

In most of the texts I examine here, women who have been raped are termed "victims," with rare exceptions (occasionally they are called the "survivor" or simply the "woman who has been raped"). Several of the books are based on interviews with women who have been assaulted, and Diana Russell (1975) provides the starkest contrast between the self-description of the women and the descriptors used by the researcher/theorist. In the twenty-two interviews transcribed in her text, only one woman directly referred to herself as a rape victim (two others spoke of rape victims generally, and the other twenty did not use the word anywhere in their interviews). Russell, on the other hand, consistently uses the word "victim" to describe the women in her study. My particular concern is how the repeated use of the term might in fact come to produce victimhood.

In texts such as the Canadian study of rape by Lorenne Clark and Debra Lewis, the use of the term "victim" appears to reflect the police reports the authors are using as data rather than any particular stance the authors might be taking. However, while we might expect police language to unproblematically use the term "victim," what is intriguing is the way in which "victimhood" is a category claimed rather than eschewed by feminists. Motivating factors behind the fostering of the victim concept are no doubt complex, but legal considerations were particularly important. In this respect, the notion of the "potential victim" has been an important corollary to that of the "actual victim." Clark and Lewis spend a chapter discussing how, in the eyes of the law and of society generally, factors such as appearance, age, marital status, occupation, alcohol use, and mental state function to create a "believable" or "unbelievable" rape victim, a "founded" or "unfounded" complaint, and ultimately a "rapable" or "unrapable" woman: "The one clear and absolutely striking pattern revealed by our research was the extent to which reported rapes were acknowledged to be 'real' only if they involved certain types of victims" (1977: 111).

Feminists claimed potential victimhood on behalf of *all* women. "The point is this: there is no typical 'rape victim'; and conversely, *every* woman and girl is a typical rape victim" (Toronto Rape Crisis Centre, 1985: 62).

It is not a difficult turn from the potential victimization of all women to the notion that it is foolhardy and even dangerous to imagine that one could both be a woman and live outside of the victim construct. Russell writes:

> Some people like to think that a woman who is confident and assertive and who carries around a don't-mess-with-me attitude toward men won't be bothered. While passivity and submissiveness may make women more rapable, *it is a mistake to think that any woman is invulnerable to rape*. Ms. Rawsen [an interviewee] is a very strong woman who earnestly rejects the traditional submissive female role. *But this did not, and does not, make her invulnerable to rape.* (1975: 96; emphasis added)

In this framing, vulnerability is a foregone conclusion. It is generalized as an essential aspect of the "female condition," the implication being that little can be done about it. Is the message in the above passage "don't think it can't happen to you," or is the message, "be afraid because you're destined to be victimized"? Certainly it is both, and this discourse is burdened by its inability to draw a clear distinction between the two messages.

Once the myth that only certain women can be raped is denounced, the question is, how does the statement "all women are vulnerable to rape" come to represent a deep and secret truth about what it is to be a woman? How do we move from: "any woman is a natural target for a would-be rapist" (Brownmiller, 1975: 388), to propositions such as that of Susan Griffin's linking victimization and rape as "central to us—at the core of something which we could not fully explain, perhaps our being" (1986: 28)? Brownmiller's answer is this: "To simply learn the word 'rape' is to take instruction in the power relationship between males and females. To talk about rape, even with nervous laughter, is to acknowledge a woman's special victim status. . . . Even before we learn to read we have become indoctrinated into a victim mentality" (1975: 343).

Brownmiller is aware of the social construction of victimhood perpetuated "by books, movies, popular songs and television serials in which women are most often portrayed as victims, seldom as survivors" (1975:

375). But she overlooks the role her own text plays in that construction. Similarly, the Toronto Rape Crisis Centre on the one hand claims "there is not a girl or woman in this society who is not vulnerable to rape" (1985: 62), and on the other hand criticizes the mental health system's emphasis on individual treatment because it "encourages women to see themselves as helpless victims" (1985: 73). Like Brownmiller the Centre remains unaware of its linking of rape and inevitable victimhood to some universal female status.

The inevitability of women's victimhood also suggests the inevitable failure of resistance.

RESISTANCE

In the violent landscape inhabited by primitive woman and man, some woman somewhere had a prescient vision of her right to her own physical integrity, and in my mind's eye I can picture her fighting like hell to preserve it. After a thunderbolt of recognition that this particular incarnation of hairy, two-legged hominid was not the Homo Sapiens with whom she would like to freely join parts, it might have been she, and not some man, who picked up the first stone and hurled it. How surprised he must have been, and what an unexpected battle must have taken place. Fleet of foot and spirited, she would have kicked, bitten, pushed and run, *but she could not retaliate in kind*. (Brownmiller, 1975: 4–5)

Brownmiller thus inscribes rape as the primordial exigency of life faced by women. While apparently giving us an empowering picture of women's resistance to rape, Brownmiller concludes that in fact this resistance is by definition limited because women cannot do to men exactly what men have done to them. Rape is inescapable, unanswerable, and unsurpassable; women are deficient (that is, penis-less) and are therefore inadequate resisters. "One possibility, and one possibility alone, was available to woman. Those of her own sex whom she might call to her aid were more often than not smaller and weaker than her male attackers. More critical, they lacked the basic physical wherewithal for punitive vengeance; at best they could maintain only a limited defensive action. But among those creatures who were her predators, some might serve as her chosen protectors" (Brownmiller, 1975: 6). Brownmiller's original positing of women's resistance is thus eroded to the point where men must be called upon as protectors. Her book was written at a time when society still operated under the false assumption that rape is predominantly committed by strangers, a result in part of reliance on police records as the primary sources of data; hence there was no contradiction for her in the notion of male protectors.

Brownmiller's construction of women's vulnerability, weakness, and inability to successfully resist is fascinating and troublesome, given its appeal to an inherent biological "incapacity." In appealing to nature and biology as the source of women's inability to resist, Brownmiller contradicts the point, occasionally acknowledged in the early texts, that women's perceived weakness is more likely socially constructed, and grounded partly in a learned devaluation of the female in patriarchal society and a deep training not to fight: "Being able to defend ourselves is only half the battle. Being willing to defend ourselves is the other half. Unlearning to not fight is equally as important as learning to fight" (Russell, 1975: 109).

Women often express disbelief in their ability to break even a nose (which requires very little strength), and yet they almost universally suggest they would kill anyone who threatened their children.[3] The deeply held (and false) belief that women do not have the physical wherewithal to resist male violence is reiterated throughout the pages of most of the texts under study. For all its facetiousness, Andrea Dworkin's "I'm only a woman. There's nothing I can do about it" (1988a: 167) reflects a profound disbelief in women's physical ability to fight. The women interviewed in Diana Russell's study repeatedly say that their lack of strength in relation to their aggressor made resistance impossible: "I was yelling at him at the top of my voice. But he was a lot stronger than me. I realized this when he hit me across the room. There wasn't any way I was going to be able to fight my way out of it" (1975: 60).

The construction of women's physical weakness as the primary reason for their inability to resist is a false one. There is no sex-based deficiency that makes women unable to harm their aggressors. Rather, as two of Diana Russell's interviewees suggest, women are trained not only to disbelieve their strength, but to shy away from physical violence:

He started getting closer and closer to me, and he backed me up against an ironing board. I picked up the iron, and I was holding it in my hand, and I said, "Look," I said, "if you don't let me out that door, I'm going to hit you with this iron." And he said, "Go ahead and hit me." I thought and thought about it, but, I don't know why, I just couldn't do it. So I put it down. (1975: 54)

All I could think of to do to get him away from me was to poke him in the eyes, but I couldn't do it! I just couldn't do that, even if it meant being raped. . . . I'd never done anything as gruesome as poking someone's eyes out before. I just couldn't do it, which in some ways I felt good about at that time because I didn't really want to be able to do that to someone. (1975: 99)

Susan Griffin writes of the more generalized gendered passivity and impotence trained into many females:

To be feminine is to wear shoes which make it difficult to run; skirts which inhibit one's stride; underclothes which inhibit the circulation. Is it not an intriguing observation that those very clothes which are thought to be flattering to the female and attractive to the male are those which make it impossible for a woman to defend herself against aggression? . . . Passivity itself prevents a woman from ever considering her own potential for self-defense and forces her to look to men for protection. . . . Moreover the passive woman is taught to regard herself as impotent, unable to act, unable even to perceive, in no way self-sufficient. (1971: 33)

Clark and Lewis, like Brownmiller, are completely equivocal as to the mythic or real status of women's defenselessness. They point to the "stereotyping of men as strong and dominant and of women as weak and vulnerable" (1977: 139) and in the next paragraph go on to deny the stereotype by positing women's lack of ability to resist as taken-for-granted physical fact: "Men's fear of women, and the misogyny it produces, rests on the awareness that women have good reason to seek revenge, and on the *pure abstract possibility* that women would revenge themselves on men *if they could* (1977: 139; emphasis added).

It is no surprise that examples of resistance are glaringly absent from these texts. Both Diana Russell's and Susan Brownmiller's books present a multitude of horror stories with few examples of resistance. In *No Safe Place*, the Toronto Rape Crisis Centre begins its article on rape with a similar set of disturbing rape situations. It is understandable that feminist writings of this time consciously chose to tell disturbing rape stories and to describe a variety of rape scenarios, intending to unsettle the limited notions of rape in the common consciousness of the era. These texts often successfully worked against the stereotypical picture of rape and broadened notions of sexual violence to more accurately reflect the kinds of sexual assault women actually face. But the absence of women fighting back in these texts makes resistance seem impossible, and leaves the reader disempowered and hopeless.

When resistance is addressed, it is usually presented as ineffective and even dangerous. But Bart and O'Brien and others find otherwise: "We know that women who resisted physically were more likely to avoid rape. But we also know that there was no relationship between the women's use of physical resistance and the rapist's use of additional physical force over and above the rape attempt" (Bart and O'Brien, 1985: 41).

Brownmiller at least suggests that "submissive behavior" is not helpful: "Acquiescent cooperation by *not* screaming or struggling once the intent of the rapist is made manifest gives a victim no guarantee that she will be let off more easily . . . her numb compliance or lack of resistance gave her no blanket insurance against gratuitous physical damage" (1975: 403). Yet the narratives she has selected are mainly stories in which resisters are badly hurt or killed for their efforts. Diana Russell's book also emphasizes the dangers of resistance: "I think the way I handled it this time was about the best. By falling down on the floor and being completely submissive, I didn't get beat up" (1975: 56). The one way in which Russell sees resistance as useful is in the laying of legal charges: "Ms. Fujimoto's advice that rape victims should not physically resist unless they believe they can overcome the rapist is quite widely shared and even more widely followed by rape victims. Unfortunately, passive submission usually makes it much more difficult to press charges, and some rape victims feel very upset with themselves afterward if they reacted submissively" (1975: 43).

But Bart and O'Brien's study of women who attempt to resist rape gives us a very different picture: "The most frequent response [to the question of what women could do to protect themselves], given somewhat more often by avoiders than by raped women, was 'learn self-defense'" (1984: 116). *Stopping Rape* certainly stands out among the feminist antiviolence works of the decade under review for its focus on resistance. Bart and O'Brien are consistently firm in their conclusions that "physical resistance much more frequently resulted in rape avoidance than a beating" (1984: 111). Describing a variety of resistance strategies, their text shows resistance as realistic and empowering, though it does not in all cases guarantee avoidance of rape. Resistance is defined not in terms of success, but rather in terms of women's capacity to act.

In light of the blame women commonly receive for not resisting, the need to refuse that blame made many feminists wary of notions that would imply a degree of participation by women in rape situations. Chief among these notions was the idea of "victim-precipitated rape," in which the woman's role is seen to be causative or in some way at the root of the incident. This notion was considered to be fraught with political dangers because of the perception that it led to victim-blaming.

No thought, however, was given to the manner in which the idea might function proactively in relation to antiviolence strategies. From a Foucaul-

dian perspective, it no longer makes sense to resist seeing rape as an inter-
play between persons or to deny that a woman in some sense is a participant in her rape. And once a woman's participant status is affirmed, the
door is open to understanding that a change in women's behavior from
passivity, pleading, begging, and frozen panic to assertive physical and verbal resistance could help reduce the incidence of sexual assault.

These options were not explored by the authors under study. Instead, in
the effort to avoid victim-blaming, they saw women's behavior as irrelevant. The serious side-effect of this was the all but total effacing of women's
agency in situations of sexual violence, an effect that is profoundly in operation today: resistance is futile, impossible, dangerous, and ultimately
not our responsibility. Such a belief prevents many women from embracing
resistance as at least one part of the solution to the problem of violence
against women.

PREVENTION

The rhetoric emerging from the texts under study worked to marginalize resistance "in the moment" because the individual acts of women
have been deemphasized in the attempt to outline a universal logic of rape,
and to expose and delegitimize that logic. While the individual woman
has been considered powerless in the face of her aggressor, women united
through broad-based political organizing against rape seem more likely to
constitute a force capable of real change. But central to the notion of prevention I want to propose is that it does not operate in the absence of resistance, but in fact works to cultivate the possibility of resistance in the
moment.

The texts analyzed in this essay do make a gesture toward prevention,
yet it is consistently tacked on to the end of each book as a discrete and
poorly integrated appendix.[4] This structuring signals the lack of continuity between strategies of breaking the silence around rape and strategies of
prevention. How do these works conceive of prevention?

The Toronto Rape Crisis Centre suggests that, in addition to their feminist counseling services, they are working toward the eradication of rape
with the following prevention initiatives:

> Rape crisis centres organized Take Back the Night marches as a way of as-
> serting the basic right of women to walk unprotected and free from fear
> on the streets. We began to educate public school children and commu-
> nity groups and labour groups in rape prevention and sexism in an at-

tempt to change attitudes. Many of us started organizing self-help groups for sexual-assault survivors, helping women to see that they are not alone or to blame. . . . Some of us began helping women who wanted alternatives to the legal system to plan confrontations with their rapists. We began acting as a voice of criticism of the systems, particularly the justice system, that work with women who are raped. (1985: 82)

This is an impressive and diverse list of concrete interventions, but we must still ask to what degree it is effective in prevention. Though these strategies empower women, and may eventually help create a more just society where rape will be less acceptable and less frequent, they do little if anything to help women experience less violence here and now. After a Take Back the Night march, after a public education forum on sexual assault, after a self-help group, a confrontation with a rapist, or a rally for legal reform, women still get raped. The strategies do not provide tools and skills to allow women to resist violence in their daily lives.

A very different model of prevention presented in these texts, and found in Russell's work particularly, is that of victim control (Cooper, 1991: 17). Victim control consists of a series of rules, familiar to most women from childhood, which suggest things to do (or more often not to do) in order to avoid threatening or dangerous situations. Russell provides a lengthy list: don't talk to strangers, don't walk alone at night, check the back seat of your car before getting in, don't hitchhike, so on (1975: 284). Such rules are echoed by many "experts" in violence prevention, police and feminists alike. But victim control strategies severely restrict women's freedoms and mobility. By focusing on violence committed by strangers, victim control leaves women unprepared to respond to the kind of violence they are most likely to face, that committed by people they know and often trust. By encouraging the avoidance of potential violence only, they leave women more rather than less fearful, and powerless in the face of violence they have been unable to avoid.

The act of speaking the truth about rape, of breaking the silence, is thought to embody a strong preventive force, driving rape and rapists out of the shadows and into the light of public consciousness. These early texts and many others like them dragged North American society out of the era of silence. As such they served a radical purpose, for without the dismantling of the wall of silence we would be in no position to suggest paths toward prevention. But Susan Griffin has questioned whether the act of naming rape in itself constitutes prevention: "we do not yet have the end of rape. All we have is the feat of naming rape a crime against us" (1986: 33). She insists that she wants "more than the mere unmasking or naming of atrocity." For Griffin, "it is part of human dignity to be able to defend oneself" (1971: 35), and so self-defense is a hopeful path to violence prevention. She opens her book with the following quotation: "Martial arts and self defense study offer a way of self reflection and change. . . . I find that I learned the lessons of patriarchy in my muscles and sinews, as well as in my mind and soul; and this martial arts study is both an UNconditioning process, as well as the condition and creating of a new self" (1986: 1).

Most of the other authors do acknowledge, if only in passing, the potential value of self-defense. They cite several women who consider the possibility of fighting back as a strategy in retrospect: "I think I would be much more tempted to fight [if it happened again]" (Russell, 1975: 197). "When I think about it now, I'm sure I could have fought him off" (Brownmiller, 1975: 402).

In such passages self-defense appears in its straightforward simplicity. But there is a tendency in these texts to complicate strategies of resistance, which, it seems, is related to a tendency to mythologize self-defense, or rather, to mythologize strength. Strength is considered to be the domain of men, to be something that women could possibly attain but do not at present possess. Thus, while one of Diana Russell's interviewees suggests that "the solution is for women to become strong" (1975: 168), the women cited above seemed to sense that the solution is rather to realize the strength they already possess.

Susan Brownmiller presents most clearly the ambivalence that surrounds self-defense and resistance. On the penultimate page of her book, with scores of dead resisters littering the preceding 450 pages, she writes:

> Unthinkingly cruel, because it is deceptive, is the confidential advice given from men to women . . . or even from women to women in some feminist literature, that a sharp kick to the groin or a thumb in the eye will work miracles. Such advice is often accompanied by a diagram in which the vulnerable points of the human anatomy are clearly marked— as if the mere knowledge of these pressure spots can translate into devastating action. It is true that this knowledge has been deliberately obscured or withheld from us in the past, but mere knowledge is not enough. What women need is systematic training in self-defense that begins in childhood, so that the inhibition resulting from the prohibition may be overcome. (1975: 452)

Self-defense is thus constructed by Brownmiller as ineffective and nonviable through her portrayal of it as complex, inaccessible, and necessitating "systematic training from childhood." The claim that "casual" self-defense strategies (what women may learn in a weekend self-defense course) offer a false sense of security is not uncommon among women and feminists. An important reason for this skepticism is that many women equate self-defense with the learning of martial arts techniques, which are skills of great subtlety that many people spend a lifetime perfecting. Indeed, many self-defense courses for women growing out of the martial arts are inadequate: they aim simply to provide a brief introduction to martial arts, and they lack a feminist analysis of empowerment for women.

Good self-defense offers women simple, effective, easy-to-learn strategies that rely neither on physical strength nor extensive training but rather on a realistic belief in one's ability to fight—an ability that we all possess, no matter our strength or stature.[5] Feminist self-defense operates mainly to foster the belief that we are worth fighting for, and that we absolutely have the ability to do so in ways that do not require that we be bigger or stronger than our aggressors.

A more practical path to prevention, which appeals to all of the authors, is legal reform. Clark and Lewis, for example, suggest that "the way to attack sexism [and thus rape] in our society is to undermine and destroy the structures which preserve the unequal legal status of men and women . . . rape would cease to be a problem if persons were sexually and reproductively autonomous, both legally and practically" (1977: 177–82).

Each of these texts, in their concluding pages on prevention, speak to legal reform as a central strategy in the struggle to end violence against women. It is important to note how the construction of legal reform as the solution to rape is grounded, in part, in the construction of the problem. Clark and Lewis say that "the status of women as private, sexual and reproductive property has created the problem of rape as we know it" (1977: 174). According to this construction, changing the law would serve to address certain structural inequalities that render rape a relatively insignificant and "private" crime according to the legal system. Conversely, when the root cause of rape is posited as inherent in men's nature, as Brownmiller suggests ("what it all boils down to is that the human male can rape . . . when men discovered that they could rape, they proceeded to do it"), the solution springs from this construction: men will simply have to choose to stop raping in order for rape to end. Ultimate rape prevention is in the hands of men.

In an effort to coax men toward change, legal reform often takes the form of offender control (Cooper, 1991: 17), the aim being to persuade men, by threat of reprisal, to stop raping. But like victim control, offender control is profoundly limited as effective prevention. In the first place, offender control strategies presuppose already victimized women, and any strategy that requires women to experience violence cannot be properly called prevention.[6] Hand in hand with the after-the-fact nature of offender control is the problem that it does not provide women with tools to deal with and stop violence as they are experiencing it. While laws are being challenged and jail terms toughened, violence in women's lives is not being reduced. Since women are relatively reluctant to bring assault charges against a known aggressor, offender control affects only the kind of violence women are least likely to face, that committed by a stranger.

Several of the authors, despite their call for legal reform, acknowledge the limitations of a toughened legal system to prevent violence: "prevention of rape and far-reaching social changes have never been within the realm of the legal system, and we are calling into the wind if we ask that such change be generated from within the legal system" (Toronto Rape Crisis Centre, 1985: 79).

While legal reform and equality under the law are critical strategies in the struggle to end violence against women, they are long-term and perhaps only utopian solutions. Certainly legal reform serves important purposes, but it does little here and now to allow women to experience less violence.

Despite the systemic change over the past twenty years, we have not witnessed a decrease in the incidence of rape. In light of this experience, the skepticism concerning so-called individual strategies needs to be challenged today more than ever. It is not difficult to imagine that if all, or even most, girls and women were trained in self-defense and assault prevention skills, both completed and attempted rapes would likely decrease drastically.

The texts I have examined here are vitally important. They launched North American feminists and others into an era of antiviolence work that has had significant and far-reaching repercussions for women who experience violence and for society more generally. Their emphasis on "breaking the silence" was crucial, serving to bring violence against women from the domain of the private into the public world where it could be identified, criticized, and confronted. This essay has attempted to address the fact that, while critically challenging traditional and misogynist analyses of violence against women, these texts mobilized a rhetoric which, in attempting to liberate women from violence, actually undermined their agency and capacity for resistance.

While drawing on the valuable legacy of these early texts, our current antiviolence work must no longer marginalize resistance and prevention, but instead must cultivate and nurture women's agency. We need to ask simple questions of all the antiviolence work we do: does it promote women's strengths, reduce our fears, increase our mobility and freedoms, and ultimately does it serve to improve the quality of our lives? If we can answer these questions affirmatively, then we are well on the way to doing antiviolence work differently, and, we can hope, more effectively, than it has been done to date.

Notes on Contributors

Clelia Smyth Anderson is a graduate student of philosophy at the University of Kentucky. She specializes in the phenomenology of the body and in feminist discourse on sexuality. Her main project at the present time is to complete her dissertation entitled "Knowing Desire: Reformulating and Reevaluating the Experience of Desiring."

Semra Asefa works in the areas of public health and health education. She is particularly interested in the impact of cultural traditions, gender roles, and religion on health perceptions and practices. She has worked with Enda Tiers-Monde in Senegal and with the Integrated Holistic Approach–Urban Development Project in Ethiopia. She has published in an anthology entitled *Interpersonal Violence, Health, and Gender Politics* (1994).

Susan J. Brison is Associate Professor of Philosophy at Dartmouth College. She has published articles in social, political, and legal philosophy. She has also held visiting appointments at New York University, Princeton University, and Tufts University. She is coeditor of *Contemporary Perspectives on Constitutional Interpretation* (1993) and her most recent book, *Speech, Harm, and Conflicts of Rights*, is forthcoming from Princeton University Press in 1998.

Nadya Burton is completing her Ph.D. in sociology at the Ontario Institute for Studies in Education, University of Toronto. Her research focuses on women's resistance to violence and the theorization of prevention in the feminist antiviolence movement. She has worked as a counselor and public educator in the antirape movement in Ontario, and currently teaches courses in self-defense and assault prevention.

Natalie Dandekar has taught at the University of Rhode Island, Bentley College, and Reed College. She has published articles in *Philosophical Forum*, *Social Theory and Practice*, and *Business and Professional Ethics Journal*. Currently she is working on a book in which topics of international justice are discussed from a feminist perspective.

Debra A. DeBruin is Assistant Professor of Philosophy at the University of Illinois at Chicago. She has held visiting appointments at Duke University, the University of North Carolina at Chapel Hill, and Pomona College. She has also served as a consultant to the National Academy of Sciences' Institute of Medicine Committee on the Ethical and Legal Issues Relating to the Inclusion of Women in Clinical Studies. In the fall of 1998 she will be Greenwall Postdoctoral Fellow in Bioethics and Health Policy at Johns Hopkins and Georgetown Universities. Her writings include topics in applied ethics, the justification of morality, and the care/justice debate.

Arnold R. Eiser is Professor of Medicine and Chief, Section of General Internal Medicine, at the University of Illinois at Chicago. In addition, he is an Adjunct Associate of the Hastings Center. He is a contributing author of *The Kidney in Collagen Vascular Disease* (1993), and has authored or co-authored articles in *Archives of Internal Medicine*, *New England Journal of Medicine*, and *American Journal of Medicine*.

Yolanda Estes is Visiting Assistant Professor of Philosophy at the University of Colorado, Boulder. Her principal area of interest is the history of philosophy, particularly German Idealism. The title of her dissertation is "The Roles of Intellectual Intuition in Fichte's *Jena Wissenschaftslehre*."

Stanley G. French is Professor of Philosophy at Concordia University in Montreal. He has also taught at the University of Western Ontario and the Université de Nice, France. One of the founders of the Simone de Beauvoir Institute, he served as a fellow for many years. In 1992 French was International Visiting Scholar at the Hastings Center in New York. He is editor of *Philosophers Look at Canadian Confederation / La confédération canadienne: qu'en pensent les philosophes?* (1979) and *Interpersonal Violence, Health, and Gender Politics* (1993, 2d ed. 1994). He has contributed to many anthologies and published articles in *Dialogue*, *The Monist*, *Journal of Philosophy*, and other scholarly journals.

Patricia Kazan is a Social Sciences and Humanities Research Council of Canada (SSHRC) postdoctoral Fellow. She is conducting research in poli-

tical philosophy at Carleton University in Ottawa, examining public policies relating to the accommodation of ethnocultural and gender difference from the perspective of contemporary theories of equality. Kazan has
given numerous public talks and published articles on the following topics: novel defenses in the criminal law (e.g., Battered Woman Syndrome),
difference theory, gender equity, liberalism and group rights, and biotech-
nology and health care needs.

Catharine A. MacKinnon is Professor of Law at the University of Michigan
Law School. She is a lawyer, law educator, and legal scholar. She has held
visiting appointments at the University of Chicago, Harvard University,
Stanford University, Yale University, and at Osgoode Hall of York Univer-
sity, Canada. Her many publications include *Only Words* (1993), *Toward a
Feminist Theory of the State* (1989), *Feminism Unmodified: Discourses on Life and
Law* (1987), and *Sexual Harassment of Working Women* (1979).

Roksana Nazneen is completing her Ph.D. in Concordia University's Humanities interdisciplinary doctoral program. She teaches sociology on a
part-time basis. One of her papers appears in *Interpersonal Violence, Health,
and Gender Politics* (1994) and a second was published in *Canadian Women's
Studies / Les Cahiers de la femme* (Summer 1995). She has written numerous
short stories and novels in Bengali. Eight of her books have been published
in Bangladesh since 1988.

Edith L. Pacillo received her master's degree in social work from Temple
University, and is a graduate of Suffolk University Law School in Boston. The paper that appears in this volume received the 1995 Scribes'
Note and Comment Competition given by the American Society of Writers on Legal Subjects. At the present time she is a judicial clerk for the
Honorable Karen L. Lansing of the State of Idaho Court of Appeals.
Her most recent publication, entitled "Beyond Formal Equality: A Proposal for a New Feminist Analysis of State Regulation of Reproduction,"
appears in the Fall 1997 edition of the *American University Journal of Gender
and the Law*.

Laura M. Purdy is bioethicist at The Toronto Hospital/Princess Margaret
Hospital/Ontario Cancer Institute, and the University of Toronto Joint
Centre for Bioethics. She is also Professor of Philosophy at the University
of Toronto and at Wells College. Her main areas of research are bioethics,
feminism, and family issues. She is the author of *In Their Best Interest? The
Case against Equal Rights for Children* (1992), *Feminist Perspectives in Medical*

Ethics (with Helen B. Holmes; 1992), and *Reproducing Persons: Feminist Issues in Bioethics* (1996).

Wanda Teays is Professor of Philosophy at Mount St. Mary's College in Los Angeles. She has also taught at the University of Massachusetts at Boston and California State University at Northridge. She is the executive secretary of the Pacific Division of the Society for Women in Philosophy. She is the author of *Second Thoughts: Critical Thinking from a Multicultural Perspective* (1996) and has published in the *Journal of Feminist Studies in Religion*. She is currently coediting (with Laura M. Purdy) an anthology on biomedical ethics.

Abby L. Wilkerson, a philosopher, teaches in the Department of English at George Washington University in Washington, D. C. She has published in the *Journal of Homosexuality* and elsewhere. She has done activist and volunteer work on domestic violence, AIDS, and reproductive rights.

Notes

Editors' Introduction

1. *New York Times*, August 25, 1997.
2. Melinda Crane-Engel, "Germany vs. Genocide," *New York Times*, October 30, 1994, p. 59; Dorean Marguerite Koenig, "Women and Rape in Ethnic Conflict and War," *Hastings Women's Law Journal* 5: 2 (Summer 1994): 131; Tracy Wilkinson, "U.S. Official Sees Atrocity Evidence in Bosnia," *Los Angeles Times*, January 22, 1996.
3. See *The Violence against Women Act of 1991*, S. Rep. No. 283, 102 Cong., 1st sess. 34.
4. Lee Romney, "Police Seize Clothes to Collar Prostitution," *Los Angeles Times*, February 20, 1996, p. A3.
5. As noted in Anne M. Coughlin, "Excusing Women," *California Law Review* 82: 1 (January 1994): 15. See Victoria M. Mather, *The Skeleton in the Closet: The Battered Woman Syndrome, Self-Defense, and Expert Testimony*, 39 Mercer L. Rev., 545, 561 (1988).
6. "Development in the Law—Legal Responses to Domestic Violence," *Harvard Law Review* 106 (June 1993): 1588.
7. Quoted in Coughlin, "Excusing Women," 3.
8. As noted by Church, 1997: 97.

1. Surviving Sexual Violence: A Philosophical Perspective

1. Federal Bureau of Investigation, *Uniform Crime Reports for the United States*, 1989, 6.
2. Robin Warshaw (1988) notes that "government estimates find that anywhere from three to ten rapes are committed for every one rape reported. And while rapes by strangers are still underreported, rapes by acquaintances are virtually nonreported. Yet, based on intake observations made by staff at various rape counseling centers (where victims come for treatment, but do not have to file police reports), 70–80 percent of all rape crimes are acquaintance rapes" (12).
3. National Coalition against Domestic Violence, fact sheet, in "Report on Proposed Legislation S.15: The Violence against Women Act," 9. On file with the Senate Judiciary Committee.

4. After I presented this paper at Davidson College in 1992, Iris Young drew my attention to Jeffner Allen's (1986) discussion of her rape. Since that time, I've been pleased to see that more professional philosophers have been giving talks and publishing articles on rape.

5. Another, more perceptive, article is Lois Pineau's (1989) "Date Rape: A Feminist Analysis." In addition, an excellent book on the causes of male violence was written by a scholar trained as a philosopher, Myriam Miedzian (1991). Philosophical discussions of the problem of evil, even recent ones such as that in Nozick, 1989, don't mention the massive problem of sexual violence. Even Nel Noddings's book, *Women and Evil* (1989), which is an "attempt to describe evil from the perspective of women's experience," mentions rape only twice, briefly, and in neither instance from the victim's point of view.

6. See Patricia Williams's discussion of the Ujaama House incident in *The Alchemy of Race and Rights* (1991: 100–116); Mari Matsuda, "Public Response to Racist Speech: Considering the Victim's Story" (1989); and Charles R. Lawrence III, "If He Hollers, Let Him Go: Regulating Racist Speech on Campus" (1990).

7. As the authors of *The Female Fear* note: "The requirement of proof of the victim's nonconsent is unique to the crime of forcible rape. A robbery victim, for example, is usually not considered as having 'consented' to the crime if he or she hands money over to an assailant [especially if there was use of force or threat of force]" (Gordon and Riger, 1991: 59).

8. Quoted in the *New York Times*, September 13, 1991, p. A18. Although Judge Thomas made this statement during his confirmation hearings, his actions while on the Supreme Court have belied his professed empathy with criminal defendants.

9. Barnes, 1984: 2191–92. I thank John Cooper for drawing my attention to this aspect of Aristotle's theory of the emotions.

10. For a clinical description of Post-traumatic Stress Disorder (PTSD), see the *Diagnostic and Statistical Manual,* 3d ed., rev. (American Psychiatric Association, 1987). Excellent discussions of the recovery process undergone by rape survivors can be found in Bard and Sangrey, 1986, Benedict, 1985, Judith Herman, 1992, and Janoff-Bulman, 1992. I have also found it very therapeutic to read first-person accounts by rape survivors such as Estrich, 1987 and Ziegenmeyer, 1992.

11. American Psychiatric Association, 1987: 247.

12. S.15, sponsored by Sen. Joseph Biden (D–Del.), was drafted largely by Victoria Nourse, Special Counsel for Criminal Law, Office of the Senate Judiciary Committee. I am particularly interested in Title III, which would reclassify gender-motivated assaults as bias crimes. From the victim's perspective this reconceptualization is important. What was most difficult for me to recover from was the knowledge that some man wanted to kill me simply because I am a woman. This aspect of the harm inflicted in hate crimes (or bias crimes) is similar to the harm caused by hate speech. One cannot make a sharp distinction between physical and psychological harm in the case of PTSD sufferers. Most of the symptoms are physiological. I find it odd that in philosophy of law, so many theorists are devoted to a kind of Cartesian dualism that most philosophers of mind rejected long ago.

13. *New York Times*, April 19, 1992, p. 36.

14. She characterized a certain theory of equality in this way during the discussion after a Gauss seminar she gave at Princeton University, April 9, 1992.

15. For an illuminating discussion of the ways in which we need to treat people differently in order to achieve genuine equality see Minow, 1990.

16. As recently as 1948, the United States Supreme Court upheld a state law prohibiting the licensing of any woman as a bartender (unless she was the wife or daughter of the bar owner where she was applying to work). *Goesaert v. Cleary*, 335 U.S. 464 (1948).

17. *New York Times*, June 19, 1992, p. 1.

2. Sexual Assault and the Problem of Consent

1. During the early 1980s, many legal theorists opposed this emphasis on consent, favoring laws that emphasized the violent (rather than the sexual) nature of the offence of rape. Their opposition was successful: the offence of rape was remodeled and renamed sexual assault. However, some theorists have since had second thoughts, arguing that this shift in focus has resulted in a greater emphasis on proving evidence of physical violence in the alleged act of rape, prolonging rape trials, and downgrading the perceived seriousness of nonviolent rapes, such as acquaintance or date rape. In the 1990s legal theorists have shifted their attention to two issues: the meaning of consent and the element of fault for sexual assault. See Bronitt, 1994, Henderson, 1992, and MacKinnon, 1989: 174.

Statutes in many U. S. states still emphasize the element of violence in rape. Recently, however, the conception of *force* utilized by state laws has taken on a new meaning. In New Jersey, for instance, courts have interpreted force as inherent in the act of sexual penetration. In *State ex rel. M. T. S.* (609 A.2d 1266 [N.J. 1992]), the Court found that to prove sexual assault, "physical force in excess of that inherent in the act of sexual penetration is not required." Once penetration is established the element of force is satisfied and the proof of rape then turns on the issue of consent. For a discussion of this case, see Trucano, 1993: 203, and Adams et al., 1992–93: 969.

2. Other countries, such as Australia, have invoked statutory provisions governing a much broader range of circumstances and behavior that may vitiate consent. There is also some debate as to whether the existing rules governing the vitiation of consent go far enough. For an argument to extend existing rules governing consent, see Waye, 1992: 94.

3. See sec. 37 of the Crimes Act 1958 (Vic.) which provides jury instructions that specify how the concept of *free agreement* is to be understood, for example: it is not a sign of consent that the complainant did not indicate her lack of consent in words or deeds, or did not physically resist the accused's advances; lack of evidence of physical injuries does not indicate consent; and consent on an earlier occasion cannot be taken as a sign of consent on this occasion.

4. My analysis of the attitudinal model of consent is indebted to Brett, 1994.

5. *Olugboya* Q.B. 320.

6. Brett, of Dalhousie University, has developed his account in two unpublished papers. "Consent and Sexual Assault" was delivered at the Annual Meeting of the Canadian Section of the International Association for the Philosophy of Law and Social Philosophy, June 1982. "Sexual Assault and the Concept of Consent" was presented at the Annual Congress of the Canadian Philosophical Association, June 1994. Brett, 1987 also alludes briefly to this performative account of consent. See Remick, 1993: 1103 and Estrich, 1986: 1087 for discussions of an account of consent that mirrors Brett's.

7. In *How to Do Things with Words*, Austin identifies as performatives those utterances that do not function to describe or report anything at all, that are neither true

nor false, but that when uttered are part of the doing of an action. Austin's examples include uttering the words "I do" in the course of a marriage ceremony, and saying "I name this ship . . ." while smashing a bottle against a ship (1965: 5).

8. In spelling out what an agent must do in order to determine consent, the performative model gives substance to sec. 1 of Bill C-49, now sec. 273.2(b) of the Canadian Criminal Code (amended 1992), which states that in sexual assault cases "It is not a defence to a charge that the accused believed that the complainant consented to the activity that forms the subject-matter of the charge where . . . (b) the accused did not take reasonable steps, in the circumstances known to the accused at the time, to ascertain that the complainant was consenting." Failing to take "reasonable steps" to determine consent indicates that the defendant did not properly attend to his partner's behavior or utterances.

9. This analysis suggests an answer to the question of whether consent is genuine in cases where the act of sexual intercourse is misrepresented as something other than sex, as when unscrupulous individuals misrepresent sexual acts as essential medical procedures. My analysis indicates that fraudulent misrepresentation of the nature and quality of the act to which she has consented negates consent.

10. Brett (1994: 10) is aware of this difficulty, but he does not seem to recognize that its resolution requires that we attend to attitudinal indicators of consent.

11. Brenda Baker makes a similar point about the ambiguity of performances: "although it may be an objective fact about a person's behavior that that person did/did not consent to an action, that fact may occasionally not be discernible by others from that behavior" (1988: 235). However, she does not seem to recognize that this ambiguity presents a problem for the performative account of consent. Against this view, I argue that the ambiguity of performances casts doubt on the claim that we need only attend to performances to discover whether an agent has consented.

12. See the 1992 amendments to sec. 273.2 of the Canadian Criminal Code.

13. *R. v. Sansregret*, 1 S.C.R. 570, 45 C.R. (3d) 193 (S.C.C.) (hereinafter *Sansregret*). In this case the Court did not dispute that the complainant had merely pretended to consent. The issue before the Court was whether the appellant could claim a mistake of fact defense on the basis of his belief that the complainant did in fact consent. The Court upheld the conviction on the grounds that Sansregret had been "wilfully blind" to the true nature of the complainant's consent—Sansregret's coercive conduct made it unreasonable for him to suppose that his victim had granted genuine consent.

14. Boyle, 1984 has referred to this scenario as the "four big men argument" (320).

15. While consideration of the individual's characteristics and the context of the situation may help us settle the matter of consent, they will not by themselves determine who is responsible when an agent's consent is coerced. To settle the issue of responsibility, we need to establish what the person soliciting consent did in fact know and what he should have been expected to know about his partner and her perspective. If, for instance, a man jokingly threatens to lock his partner in a closet if she doesn't acquiesce to his demands for sex, and unbeknownst to him she consents because she is intensely claustrophobic, we might argue that he should not be held accountable for her lack of consent since he was not aware of her claustrophobia. But if he knew she was claustrophobic, and this was in fact the reason he threatened to lock her in a closet, then we might justifiably hold him accountable for coercing consent and convict him of sexual assault.

16. I call this "psychological" duress to distinguish it from duress caused by necessity.

17. For instance, we might consider whether the agent might have been particularly vulnerable to persuasion.

18. See Vandervort, 1990: 492, fn. 8: "behavior is in the realm of empirical fact, consent is in the social realm."

19. For a detailed study of some of the many confusing social conventions governing sexual relations, see Husak and Thomas, 1992.

20. The law has ignored the implicit coercion found in cases where a women is confronted with a demand for sex by a man who has, for instance, beaten her before (e.g., *State v. Alston*, 61 N.C. App. 454, 300 S.E.2d 857 [1983], *rev'd*, 310 N.C. 399, 312 S.E.2d 470 [1984]), taken her car keys and left her stranded in a strange neighborhood (e.g., *State v. Rusk*, 289 Md. 230, 424, A.2d 720 [1981]), or forced his way into her car and demanded she drive to a deserted area (e.g., *Gonzales v. State*, 516, P.2d 592 [Wyo. 1973]).

21. For a discussion of cases that demonstrate a male-biased conception of force, see Estrich's (1987: 63–67) analysis of *State v. Rusk*, 289 Md. 230, 424 A.2d 720 (1981) and *Gonzales v. State*, 516 P.2d 592 (Wyo. 1973).

22. Lynne Henderson (1988) worries that by expanding the conception of force to include nonviolent coercion we will thereby dilute the association of rape with life-threatening "obliteration." She argues that there is an important distinction between rape and undesired sex: "rape denies you are a *person*, that you *exist* . . . [whereas] undesired sex at least does not completely *deny* your personhood . . . women experience total helplessness and obliteration during rape" (1988: 226–27).

23. Consider, for instance, the following cases. In *Commonwealth v. Mlinarich*, 345 Pa. Super. 269, 498 A.2d 395, 397 (1985), a man who abused his position of authority as a foster parent by threatening to return a teenager to a detention home unless she complied with his demands for sex was not convicted of any criminal activity. In *State v. Lester*, 70 N.C. App. 757, 321 S.E.2d 166 (1984), *aff'd*, 313 N.C. 595, 330 S.E.2d 205 (1985), a father who had engaged in sexual activity with all three of his daughters was charged with incest but not rape. In *Commonwealth v. Biggs*, 320 Pa. Super. 265, 267, 467 A.2d 31, 32 (1983), a father who had procured sex from his daughter by claiming a biblical right and threatening to distribute nude photographs of her was acquitted. In *Boro v. Superior Court*, 163 Cal. App. 3d 1224, 210 Cal Rptr. 122 (1985), the defendant procured sex by pretending to be a doctor and convincing the complainant that sexual intercourse was a medically necessary procedure. There are many other cases of nonviolent coercion, in which unscrupulous individuals have lured unsuspecting victims to remote areas by posing as modeling agents (e.g., *Goldberg v. State*, 41 Md. App. 58, 395 A.2d 1213 [Md. Spec. App. 1979]), or as psychologists conducting experiments (e.g., *People v. Evans*, 85 Misc.2d 1088, 379 N.Y.S.2d 912 [N.Y. Sup. Ct. 1975]), and secured their victim's consent through intimidation and fear.

In each of these cases the court refused to recognize the defendant's behavior as coercive. For instance, in *State v. Lester*, at 761, 321 S.E.2d at 168, the court stated that "there is no evidence . . . that the defendant used either actual or constructive force to accomplish the acts with which he is charged. As *Alston* makes clear, the victim's fear of the defendant, however justified by his previous conduct, is insufficient to show that the defendant *forcibly* raped his daughter." In *Commonwealth v. Biggs*, at 268, 467 A.2d at 32, the court stated that "the record clearly shows that the defendant never used or threatened to use force in inducing his daughter to participate in sexual intercourse. Rather, he asserted a biblical basis for the intercourse and assured his daughter's silence by threats, not of force, but of humiliation. Although this conduct is reprehensible, [the court declared] that it [was] not conduct proscribed by section 3121 of the Crimes Code, which forbids intercourse by threat of *forcible compulsion.*" In *Boro v. Superior Court*, the court claimed that the complainant, though misled about the reasons given for why she should participate in sex, knew that she was submitting to sexual intercourse.

24. See Calamari and Perillo, 1977 for a discussion of violent threats (264–65); economic extortion (271); fraud (277); negligent misrepresentation (278–79); and duties to disclose (287–92).

25. Many scholars have commented on the asymmetry between the extensive legal protections against coercion in the commercial sphere and the permissive attitude toward many forms of sexual coercion. See, e.g., Posner, 1992: 392–95; Dripps, 1992: 1802–4; Estrich, 1986: 1115–21; and Schulhofer, 1992: 88–93.

26. Jane Larson refers to this practice as the "sex exception to fraud" (1993: 412). Catharine MacKinnon has commented that the practice of ignoring coercion in sexual relations reflects a culture that approves of male sexual violence toward women (1989: 171–83, 194–214). In her view, what passes for normal sexual relations in our society is overtly coercive. This causes her to question whether a consent standard has a useful role to play in sexual assault law. Consent and free agreement, in her opinion, presuppose a choice that women do not have.

27. See, for instance, the Canadian case of *R. v. Lavallee* (1990) 1 S.C.R. 852, 55 C.C.C. (3d) 97 and the American case of *State v. Wanrow*, 559 P.2d 548 (1977).

28. Theorists have challenged traditional standards of reasonableness regarding self-defense (i.e., the imminence requirement) that are based on a barroom brawl scenario, in which two men of equal size and strength confront each other. They argue that some women, particularly battered women, may be forced to defend themselves in situations that are quite different from that scenario. For instance, they may be physically unable to defend themselves unless they use a weapon. And they may be able to predict impending danger, due to their experience with their batterer's pattern of violence, long before a reasonable man might sense danger. For a detailed discussion of efforts to reconceive the standards of reasonableness in self-defense law, see Schneider, 1980 and Crocker, 1985: 132, 150.

3. Rape, Genocide, and Women's Human Rights

1. Letter from Natalie Nenadic to the author from Zagreb, Croatia, October 13, 1992 (on file with the *Harvard Women's Law Journal*).

2. Ibid.

3. Ibid.

4. See Theodor Meron, *Rape as a Crime under International Humanitarian Law*, 87 AM. J. Int'l. L. 424, 424–28 (1993) (rape as a crime against humanity under international law); Letter from Jordan Paust, 88 AM. J. Int'l. W. 88 (1994) (rape as genocide and other crimes under customary international law).

5. All otherwise unreferenced information on this war is taken directly from first-person accounts by survivors with whom I have worked, other than the information on Hungarians in Vojvodina, which comes from observations by other survivors.

6. Similar experiences are reported in Gutman, 1993: 64–76, 164–67.

7. See *Cora McRae v. Joseph Califano*, 4911: Supp. 630, 759 (E.D.N.Y.), rev'd on other grounds sub nom. *Patricia Harris v. Cora McRae*, 448 U.S. 297 (1980).

8. Nenadic, n. 1.

9. See *Investigation against General McKenzie*, Vercernjy List, Nov. 25, 1992.

10. See generally Louis B. Sohn, *The New International Law: Protection of the Right of Individuals Rather Than States*, 32 Am. U.L. Rev. 1, 9–17 (1982) (outlining the evolution of human rights law after World War II); M. Tardu, 1 Human Rights: The International Petition System 45 (1985) ("The potential of [divisive postwar] debates for conflict escalation was so obvious that all governments became fiercely determined to keep the process under their own control through rejecting individual complaint systems.").

11. This insight was first expressed to me by Asja Armanda of Kareta Feminist Group.

12. For an analysis that "in 1991/1992, Croatia is a woman," see Katja Gattin, Kareta Feminist Group, "Where Have All the Feminists Gone?" (1992) (unpublished paper, Zagreb, on file with the *Harvard Women's Law Journal*).

13. On August 30, 1993, His Excellency Muhamed Sacirbey, ambassador and permanent representative of Bosnia and Herzegovina to the United Nations, brilliantly argued before the UN Security Council that Bosnia and Herzegovina is being gang-raped, forced into submission through the use of violence and aggression, including rape, deprived of means of self-defense, and then treated as if it had been seduced—forced to embrace the consequences and denied legal relief (on file with the *Harvard Women's Law Journal*).

14. Application for the Convention on the Prevention and Punishment of the Crime of Genocide (*Bosnia and Herzegovina v. Yugoslavia* [Serbia and Montenegro]), 1993 I.C.J. 3 (April 8), reprinted in 32 I.L.M. 888 (1993) (order of provisional measures).

15. *K. v. Radovan Karadžic*, 93 Civ. 1163 (S.D.N.Y. 1993).

16. See S.C. Res. 827, U.N. SCOR, 3217th mtg., U.N. Doc. S/RES/827 (May 25, 1993); S.C. Res. 808, U.N. SCOR, 3175th mtg., U.N. Doc. S/RES/808 (Feb. 22, 1993).

5. Violence in Bangladesh

1. The relationship between the wife and the in-laws is more important than the relationship between the wife and the husband. The wife is supposed to serve her in-laws, that is her primary duty.

2. *Weekly Chitrabangla*, September 30, 1993, p. 23. All quotations from this publication have been translated by the author of this paper.

3. Girls with fair skin are considered more beautiful. When the bride has fair skin, sometimes the demand for dowry decreases. I did not realize that I had dark skin until I got married.

4. Taslima Nasrin's *Nirbachita Column* (1993) is the only book ever published in Bangladesh which expresses a feminist point of view. She writes about her experiences as a woman in Bangladeshi society. Her book has been banned by the government, and an Islamic fundamentalist group has offered a reward of 50,000 taka for her dead body. Nasrin is currently in hiding, running for her life.

5. Quotations from Nasrin have been translated by the author of this paper.

7. Identifying Sexual Harassment: The Reasonable Woman Standard

1. I address only the gender specificity of the standard in this paper. However, women are not a homogenous group (nor are men). Thus, our standard should require

that we judge alleged causes of sexual harassment from the perspective of a reasonable person of the same gender, but also the same race, class, and perhaps other characteristics as the alleged victim. The argument for this expanded claim is a project for another paper.

2. In 1980 the Equal Employment Opportunity Commission (EEOC) adopted guidelines ruling that quid pro quo sexual harassment is a form of sex discrimination. But note that EEOC guidelines are not binding on the courts. See *Meritor Savings Bank v. Vinson*, 58.

3. In 1985 the EEOC issued guidelines specifying that behavior creating such a hostile environment constitutes prohibited sexual harassment. But note, again, that EEOC guidelines are not binding upon the courts. In 1986 the U. S. Supreme Court ruled that hostile environment sexual harassment is, indeed, a form of sex discrimination. See *Meritor Savings Bank v. Vinson* and Abrams, 1989.

4. Other objections have been raised to the gender specificity of the reasonable woman standard. For example, in *Radtke v. Everett*, the Supreme Court of Michigan argues that at the time of the adoption of its state Civil Rights Act, "standards of conduct were only defined by the reasonable person" (*Radtke v. Everett*, 165). Thus, the court reasons, since the legislature must have intended that a gender-neutral standard be employed, we should not now adopt a gender-specific one (*Radtke v. Everett*, 165–66).

5. See *Radtke v. Everett*; see also *Rabidue v. Osceola Refining Co.* and the dissenting opinion in *Ellison v. Brady*.

6. The subset of the community comprises persons of the same gender as the alleged victim; in most cases, this would mean women.

7. The general characterization of this aspect of oppression (which I provide in this sentence) owes much to Young, 1990a: 58–61. The fuller account of this aspect of oppression (in what follows here) is my own.

8. The one apparent exception is "male nurse." One might contend that if it were false universalism that prompted us to specify gender, we would never specify male gender as we do in "male nurse." Thus, one might suggest, what accounts for our specification of gender is not false universalism, but simply the fact that certain fields have traditionally been dominated by one gender, thus making it noteworthy when someone of the opposite gender works in such a field. I have two responses to this argument: (1) Even on this view, our linguistic practices are linked to the oppression of women, since the sexual division of labor in our society is an aspect of women's oppression, and (2) we should reject this view. If it were correct, we would specify gender *whenever* someone works in a field that traditionally has been dominated by the other gender. But we do not say "male flight attendant" or "male secretary" or "male grade-school teacher," for example. Unlike most occupations, "nurse" is not a truly gender-neutral term, but is gender-specific (female), as is "mother." (The link between "nurse" and breast-feeding supports this hypothesis.)

9. Things are even more complicated than this example suggests. See DeBruin, 1994a and 1994b.

10. Here Gilligan discusses not only Lawrence Kohlberg, her usual opponent, but a number of major figures in the psychology of human development.

11. Assuming that the alleged victim is female, as is almost always the case.

12. Those who are not convinced of the truth of this claim on the basis of their social observations alone will find a discussion of corroborating research in Abrams, 1989: 1203–6.

13. Cf. *Rabidue v. Osceola Refining Co.*, in which the court ruled that the display of pornography, even in conjunction with other conduct, had a negligible effect and so could not constitute sexual harassment.

8. "Her Body Her Own Worst Enemy":
The Medicalization of Violence against Women

1. Philosopher Susan Sherwin (1992) presents a sustained and convincing argument that women's interests in the area of medicine and health are likely to be undermined without a feminist analysis in bioethics, because of sexism in the health care system as well as androcentric and other biases in mainstream bioethics.

2. See *The Journal of Medicine and Philosophy* (1982) special issue on "Women and Medicine," edited by Caroline Whitbeck. Several authors in this volume, particularly Mary C. Rawlinson, address the pathologization of femaleness.

3. Anthropologist Brigitte Jordan treats childbirth "within a biosocial framework, that is to say, as a phenomenon that is produced jointly and reflexively by (universal) biology and (particular) society. The distinction between what is biological and what is social is, in many ways, merely analytic. It has no ontological status" (1983: 1). Clearly, rape and battery are unlike childbirth in the sense that they are fully conscious and deliberate acts by men, for which women cannot bear responsibility. They are like childbirth, however, in having physiological consequences that may require medical treatment, and as examples of the medicalization of life experiences of women.

4. Bill Moyers's interviews (1993) with medical researchers and clinicians attest to a growing body of research that demonstrates the importance of humanistic concerns in diagnosis, treatment, and prognosis. See also Goleman and Gurin, 1993, Pennebaker, 1990, and Peterson and Bossio, 1991.

5. Mary Daly's *Gyn/Ecology* critiques "the Gynecological Culture" and its "imposed totalitarian heterosexism" (1978: 264) and misogyny, identifying medicine as an aspect of patriarchal culture that destroys women's selfhood. Like many feminists, I am deeply indebted to Daly's work. My approach differs from hers, however, in at least two significant ways. First, Daly posits an inherent or essential "Female Self " alienated and undermined by the external forces of patriarchy; and while I too am concerned with the erosion of women's selfhood, I do not identify femaleness as the core of women's identities. Second, although Daly critiques medicine as a patriarchal institution, her purpose is to offer a vision of feminism as radical lesbian separatism, rather to work toward the transformation of medicine, as I am attempting to do.

6. See Bannister, 1993 and Walker, 1979 for analyses of the disadvantages battered women face in attempting to voice their concerns in the legal system.

7. At least this textbook includes a chapter on the topic, unlike others such as Danforth and Scott, 1986 and Rosenwaks, Benjamin, and Stone, 1987.

8. See Nagel, 1986 and Bordo, 1990.

9. Iris Young (1990a) argues that mainstream liberal philosophy is based on a "distributive paradigm" that frames the relation between health and justice in terms of access to health care. She calls for a broader approach focusing on oppression (which takes many forms beyond economic, distributive concerns) as a central aspect of injustice. For important treatments of access to health care, see Daniels, 1985 and Gauthier, 1983, whose views I critique in my forthcoming book *Diagnosis: Difference: The Moral Authority of Medicine* (Cornell).

10. See, for example, the May–June 1994 issue of the *Hastings Center Report* on these topics, as well as Dula and Goering, 1994.

11. See M. Heldke and Stephen H. Kellert, "Objectivity as Responsibility," *Metaphilosophy* 26: 4 (October 1995), 360–78.

12. See, for example, Ivan Illich (1977).

9. Media Liability for Personal Injury Caused by Pornography

1. State v. Herberg, 324 N.W.2d at 347 (Minn. 1982). The pornographic books seized from David Herberg included: VIOLENT STORIES OF KINKY HUMILIATION; VIOLENT STORIES OF DOMINANCE AND SUBMISSION; BIZARRE SEX CRIMES: SHAMED VICTIMS; and WATERSPORTS FETISH: ENEMAS AND GOLDEN SHOWERS.

2. *See generally* JOAN HOFF, LAW, GENDER, AND INJUSTICE, 331–49 (1991); DEBORAH L. RHODE, JUSTICE AND GENDER, 269–73 (1991 ed.); Ann Russo, *Pornography's Active Subordination of Women: Radical Feminists Reclaim Speech Rights, in* WOMEN MAKING MEANING at 144 (Lana F. Rakow ed., 1992); Martha Middleton, *Anti-porn Legal Theorists Gather in Chicago,* NAT'L L.J. Mar. 22, 1993, at 7; Robin West, *The Feminist-conservative Anti-pornography Alliance and the 1986 Attorney General's Commission on Pornography Report,* 1986 AM. B.F. RES. J. at 682; David T. Friendly, *The War against Pornography,* NEWSWEEK, Mar. 18, 1985, at 58; *Where Do We Stand on Pornography?,* MS. Jan.–Feb., 1994, at 3345.

3. *See* RUTHANN ROBSON, LESBIAN (OUT)LAW: SURVIVAL UNDER THE RULE OF LAW 68–69 (1992); Nan D. Hunter and Sylvia A. Law, *Brief Amici Curiae of Feminist Anti-censorship Task Force, et al., in* American Booksellers Association v. Hudnut, 21: 1 & 2 MICH. J.L. REFORM 69, 118–22 (Fall 1987–Winter 1988) [hereinafter FACT *Brief*] (opposing anti-pornography stance on grounds that censorship harms women more than it helps). At least one scholar, however, points out that these advocates do not seek to protect violent pornography from "censorship," but rather nonviolent, non-sexist erotica produced by and for women. *See* Note, *Pornography, Equality and a Discrimination-free Workplace: A Comparative Perspective,* 106 HARV. L. REV. at 1077 (1993).

4. *See* CATHARINE A. MACKINNON, *The Sexual Politics of the First Amendment, in* FEMINISM UNMODIFIED: DISCOURSES ON LIFE AND LAW 291 n. 107 (1984) [hereinafter FEMINISM UNMODIFIED]; Mimi H. Silbert and Ayala M. Pines, *Pornography and Sexual Abuse of Women, in* MAKING VIOLENCE SEXY: FEMINIST VIEWS ON PORNOGRAPHY at 115 (Diana E.H. Russell ed., 1993) [hereinafter MAKING VIOLENCE SEXY] (stating 24% of rape survivors in study reported perpetrator mentioned pornography during attack); Cheryl A. Champion, *Clinical Perspectives on the Relationship between Pornography and Sexual Violence,* 4 LAW & INEQ.J., 22–27 (1986); *see also* Barnes v. Glen Theatre, Inc., 111 5. Ct. 2456, 2469 (1991) (Souter, J., concurring) (asserting state's interest in preventing sexual assault sufficient grounds for regulating nude dancer business); ATTORNEY GENERAL'S COMMISSION ON PORNOGRAPHY, U.S. DEPARTMENT OF JUSTICE, FINAL REPORT 392, 773–80 (1986) [hereinafter A.G. REPORT]; *see generally* ANDREA DWORKIN & CATHARINE A. MACKINNON, PORNOGRAPHY AND CIVIL RIGHTS: A NEW DAY FOR WOMEN'S EQUALITY 24–30 (1988); Diana E.H. Russell, *Pornography and Rape: A Causal Model, in* MAKING VIOLENCE SEXY, 120–50 (Diana E.H. Russell ed. 1993); Russo, at 146.

5. *See* Edward Donnerstein, *Pornography and the First Amendment: What Does the Re-*

search Say?, 4 LAW & INEQ.J. at 18 (1986). Donnerstein cites research indicating that viewing pornography increases men's self-reported likelihood to rape women. *Id.* at 19. Additionally, the author performed a scientific experiment in which men who viewed pornography subsequently witnessed what they believed was a real rape trial. *Id.* at 21. Compared to a control group, the subjects found the rape survivor less credible, less injured, more worthless, and more responsible for the rape. *Id.* at 22. Donnerstein states that images of violence against women are also present in mainstream media. *Id.* at 18. For example, the author describes a magazine advertisement for a television movie which states, "he raped her . . . but she loved him." *Id.*, *see also* Friendly, at 61.

6. *See, e.g.*, MACKINNON, *Francis Biddle's Sister: Pornography, Civil Rights, and Speech, in* FEMINISM UNMODIFIED, at 175; and HOFF, at 336.

7. *See, e.g.*, Herceg v. Hustler Magazine, 814 F.2d at 1018 (5th Cir. 1987) (involving magazine description of autoerotic asphyxiation allegedly leading to young boy's death), *cert. denied*, 485 U.S. 959 (1988); Olivia N. v. National Broadcasting Co., 126 Cal. App. 3d at 495, 178 Cal. Rptr. at 893 (dismissing claim that television broadcast negligently caused rape of young girl), *cert. denied*, 458 U.S. 1108 (1982); Weirum v. RKO Gen., Inc., 15 Cal. 3d at 49, 539 P.2d at 41, 123 Cal. Rptr. at 473 (1975) (holding radio station liable for motorist's death caused by negligent broadcast). The First Amendment states, in pertinent part: "Congress shall make no law . . . abridging the freedom of speech." U.S. CONST. amend. I. The First Amendment applies to the states through the Fourteenth Amendment. U.S. CONST. amend. XIV, §1; *see* Richmond Newspapers, Inc. v. Virginia, 448 U.S. at 575 (1980) (recognizing First Amendment applicable to states through Fourteenth Amendment).

8. *Compare Weirum* 15 Cal. 3d at 48, 539 P.2d at 472 (holding First Amendment does not bar negligence liability for physical injury caused by words) *with Olivia N.*, 126 Cal. App. 3d at 494, 178 Cal. Rptr. at 892 (holding negligence liability for physical injury impermissibly chills free speech).

9. *See, e.g.*, Jonathan M. Hoffman, *From Random House to Mickey Mouse: Liability for Negligent Publishing and Broadcasting*, 21 TORT & INS. L.J. at 65–66 (1985); Andrew B. Sims, *Tort Liability for Physical Injuries Allegedly Resulting from Media Speech: A Comprehensive First Amendment Approach*, 34 ARIZ. L.REV. at 233 (1992); Gerald R. Smith, Note, *Media Liability for Physical Injury Resulting from the Negligent Use of Words*, 72 MINN. L.REV. at 1195 (1988).

10. *Compare* New York v. Ferber, 458 U.S. at 758 (1982) (holding states may prohibit child pornography because it causes children psychological and emotional harm) *with* American Booksellers Ass'n v. Hudnut, 771 F.2d at 329 (1985) (asserting pornography causes employment discrimination, rape, and battery against women but receives First Amendment protection), *aff'd mem.*, 475 U.S. 1001 (986). Moreover, feminists argue, the patriarchal legal system perpetuates itself by calling itself "objective," thereby making women's perspective "subjective" and, therefore, legally irrelevant. *See, e.g.*, Frances Olsen, *The Sex of Law*, in THE POLITICS OF LAW: A PROGRESSIVE CRITIQUE 453–55 (David Kairys ed., 1990) [hereinafter THE POLITICS OF LAW]; Leslie Bender, *A Lawyer's Primer on Feminist Theory and Tort*, 38 J. LEGAL EDUC. 3, 8–9 (1989); Catharine A. MacKinnon, *Feminism, Marxism, Method and the State: Toward Feminist Jurisprudence*, SIGNS, 635–36 (Summer 1983) [hereinafter MacKinnon, *Toward Feminist Jurisprudence*] *See also* Hoyt v. Florida, 368 U.S. at 61–62 (1961) (holding exclusion of women from jury duty reasonable because women are "center of home and family life"); Bradwell v. Illinois, 83 U.S. (16 Wall.) at 141 (1872) (discussing women's inherent inability to practice law because of their natural timidity).

Additionally, courts have held that discrimination on the basis of pregnancy is not gender discrimination. *See* General Electric v. Gilbert Co., 429 U.S. at 145–46 (1976). Currently, the law prohibits women from participating in military combat. *See* Rostker v. Goldberg, 453 U.S. at 78 (1981). In addition, under current constitutional doctrine, gender discrimination receives an intermediate scrutiny standard of review, whereas racial discrimination receives the higher standard of strict scrutiny. *Compare* Craig v. Boren, 429 U.S. at 197 (1976) *with* City of Richmond v. J.A. Croson Co., 488 U.S. at 493 (1989).

Feminist legal scholars have set forth a variety of historical critiques of women's legal status, ranging from liberal to radical theoretical approaches. Martha Siegel, *A Practitioner's Guide to Feminist Jurisprudence*, BOSTON BAR J., Sept.–Oct. 1993 at 6. *See* Jo Freeman, *The Legal Revolution, in* WOMEN: A FEMINIST PERSPECTIVE, 371–94 (Jo Freeman ed., 1989); HOFF, at 1; Olsen, at 453–67; Nadine Taub & Elizabeth M. Schneider, *Women's Subordination and the Role of Law, in* THE POLITICS OF LAW, 151–76 (David Kairys ed., 1990). Although liberal and radical feminist legal scholars agree on the dangers of patriarchy, one commentator described their differing prescriptive philosophies as "a fight between those who wish to end male supremacy and those who wish to do better under it." Tamar Lewin, *Furor on Exhibit at Law School Splits Feminists*, N.Y. TIMES, Nov. 13, 1992, at B9. Radical feminists argue for an altogether new jurisprudence, rather than incorporating women's views into the existing patriarchal structure. *See* MacKinnon, *Toward Feminist Jurisprudence*, at 65. According to the radical view, until women are truly "free," as opposed to just "equal to men," their perspective is that of a victim, and incorporating their perspective into the law remains a hollow victory. *See* MACKINNON, FEMINISM UNMODIFIED, at 166–71. These scholars argue that feminist jurisprudence must focus on obliterating male oppression of women. MACKINNON, FEMINISM UNMODIFIED, at 166–71.

11. *See* Bender, at 8–9; MacKinnon, *Toward Feminist Jurisprudence*, at 638, 658.

12. *See infra* notes 20–52 and accompanying text.

13. *See infra* notes 53–134.

14. *See infra* notes 135–40. This Note uses the term "pornographer" to refer to commercial and private producers and distributors of pornography.

15. For convenience, this Note uses the term "publication" to refer to all forms of pornography including homemade and commercially produced films and videotapes, books, magazines, still photographs, cable television networks, telephone pornography, and computer software. For example, the computer game MacPlaymat [sic] allows the user to insert objects into the vagina of an anatomically correct woman and shackle and gag her while she makes noises indicating pleasure. *See* MAKING VIOLENCE SEXY, at 15–16. A Native American woman described being raped by white men who were apparently reenacting a video game entitled "Custer's Revenge." *See* MAKING VIOLENCE SEXY, at 55–56 (discussing implication of pornographic video in rape). The rapists told the woman, "a squaw out alone deserves to be raped." MAKING VIOLENCE SEXY, at 55–56. One pornographic telephone recording depicted, among other things, fathers having sex with their daughters and a baby sucking on a bottle of her father's semen. *See* Brian T. v. Pacific Bell, 210 Cal. App. 3d at 898, 258 Cal. Rptr. at 708 (1989) (describing contents of pornographic telephone messages). After listening to the message, a twelve-year-old boy coerced a four-year-old girl to perform oral sex on him. *Id.*

16. *See infra* notes 53–103 and accompanying text.

17. *See infra* notes 116–34 and accompanying text.

18. In addition to bodily injury caused by acts such as vaginal, anal, and oral rape, incest, child abuse, bestiality, autoerotic asphyxiation, and bondage, studies show por-

nography causes mental harm to female pornographic "actors," including suicidal thoughts and behavior, lowered self-esteem, and sexual dysfunction. *See* A.G. REPORT, at 280, 767–835 (discussing findings of harm to women); Laura Lederer, *Then and Now: An Interview with a Former Pornography Model, in* TAKE BACK THE NIGHT: WOMEN ON PORNOGRAPHY, at 67–68 (Laura Lederer ed., 1980) [hereinafter TAKE BACK THE NIGHT]. One commentator argues further that pornography is what pornography depicts: sexual abuse of women. *See* CATHARINE A. MACKINNON, ONLY WORDS 27, 29, 40 (1993) [hereinafter ONLY WORDS]. Scholars assert that pornography causes women economic harm through forced participation, prostitution, and pornography-induced sex discrimination. *See* Catharine A. MacKinnon, *Pornography, Civil Rights and Speech,* 20 HARV. C.R.C.L. L. REV. 1, 46–50 (1985) [hereinafter *Civil Rights and Speech*]. Pornography also frequently includes racist themes. *See* Alice Mayall & Diana E.H. Russell, *Racism in Pornography, in* MAKING VIOLENCE SEXY, at 167–68; Tracey A. Gardner, *Racism in Pornography and the Women's Movement, in* TAKE BACK THE NIGHT, at 113. Additionally, some scholars assert that pornography perpetuates homophobic stereotypes. *See* John Stoltenberg, *Pornography and Freedom, in* MAKING VIOLENCE SEXY, at 70–72; Charlotte Bunch, *Lesbianism and Erotica in Pornographic America, in* TAKE BACK THE NIGHT, at 91–94. Women who repeatedly view pornography become desensitized to its effects, although they still have negative perceptions of the material. *See* Charlene Y. Senn, *The Research on Women and Pornography: The Many Faces of Harm, in* MAKING VIOLENCE SEXY, at 189. The author also found that women who became desensitized to pornography experienced more difficulty in voicing their anger at the depictions, possibly leading to greater emotional harm from repression, decreased potential for political/social action against pornography, and acceptance of male domination as inevitable. *See id.* at 189–90. Additionally, the women in the study did not experience emotional harm as a result of viewing non-sexist, non-violent erotica. *See id.* at 181, 193.

19. *See* Gertz v. Robert Welch, Inc., 418 U.S. at 347 (1974) (holding states may impose liability for defamation caused by negligent publication). In addition to injury to reputation, negligent speech may cause economic injury. *See* Steven J. Weingarten, *Note, Tort Liability for Nonlibelous Negligent Statements: First Amendment Considerations,* 93 YALE L.J. 744, 744 n. 9 (1984) (stating negligent speech such as misrepresentation may cause economic harm). Additionally, the author asserts that courts currently lack adequate standards for addressing physical harm caused by negligent publications. *See id.*

20. *See* RESTATEMENT (SECOND) OF TORTS §282 (1963) (hereinafter RE-STATEMENT] (stating purpose of negligence tort to protect others against unreasonable risk of harm).

21. *See id.* §281 cmts.a-h (discussing elements of negligence cause of action).

22. *See id.* §281 (defining negligence as conduct which creates unreasonable risk); W. PAGE KEETON ET AL., PROSSER & KEETON ON THE LAW OF TORTS §30, at 164, §34, at 208 (5th ed. 1984 & Supp. 1988) [hereinafter PROSSER & KEETON]. As a threshold matter, courts must decide whether a duty exists as a matter of law. *See id.* §37 at 236. Specifically, courts measure a defendant's conduct against that of a "reasonably prudent *man* under like circumstances." RESTATEMENT §283 (emphasis added). Some scholars criticize the reasonable man standard as not only sexist, but ethnocentric as well. *See* Bender, at 20–24.

23. *See* RESTATEMENT §291; *see also* PROSSER & KEETON §31, at 169. Courts determine the magnitude of the risk by considering the value of the interest invaded, the likelihood of invasion, the degree of harm, and the number of people whose interests

the invasion harms. RESTATEMENT §293. The utility of the conduct depends on its legally cognizable social value and the burden of implementing less dangerous alternatives or precautions. RESTATEMENT §292 at 56–57. Judge Learned Hand expressed in algebraic terms the concept of liability as whether the burden of adequate precaution (B) is less than the probability of harm (P) multiplied by the gravity of resulting injury (L), or if B is less than PL. United States v. Carroll Towing Co., 159 F.2d at 173 (2d Cir. 1947). One liberal feminist legal scholar criticizes this formulation for placing emphasis on economic efficiency at the expense of caring social relations. *See* Bender, at 30 n. 113.

24. *See* PROSSER & KEETON §4, at 20; PROSSER & KEETON §4, at 25; PROSSER & KEETON §2, at 10.

25. *See* Palsgraf v. Long Island R.R. Co., 248 N.Y. at 345, 162 N.E. at 101 (1928) (stating defendant's conduct must create risk to plaintiff to justify liability); PROSSER & KEETON §30, at 164. Breach of duty represents a factual determination for the jury. *See* PROSSER & KEETON §37, at 237.

26. *See* PROSSER & KEETON §30, at 165.

27. *See* PROSSER & KEETON §30, at 165. Depending on the facts of a case, a jury may determine cause-in-fact either by the "but for" test or the "substantial factor" test. *See* PROSSER & KEETON §41, at 267–68. When two or more factors contributed to a plaintiff's injuries, or when a defendant's conduct had inconsequential effects, juries may apply the substantial factor test; when no competing causes exist, juries need only find that the plaintiff's injury would not have occurred but for the defendant's negligence. *See* PROSSER & KEETON §41, at 267–68.

28. *See* Palsgraf, 248 N.Y. at 355, 162 N.E. at 100 (limiting liability by ceasing to trace events past reasonable point); PROSSER & KEETON §41, at 264.

29. *See, e.g.*, Herceg v. Hustler Magazine Inc., 814 F.2d at 1024 (5th Cir. 1987), *cert. denied*, 485 U.S. 959 (1988); Olivia N. v. National Broadcasting Co., 126 Cal. App. 3d at 495, 178 Cal. Rptr. 888, 892 *cert. denied*, 458 U.S. 1108 (1982); Walt Disney Prods., Inc. v. Shannon, 247 Ga. at 405, 276 S.E.2d at 583 (1981) (holding negligence claim barred on First Amendment grounds). *But see* Braun v. Soldier of Fortune Magazine, Inc., 968 F.2d 1110, 1119 (11th Cir. 1992) (concluding First Amendment allows liability for facially dangerous commercial advertisement), *cert. denied*, 113 S. Ct. 1028 (1993). *See generally* Sims, at 269; Weingarten, at 747.

30. *See generally* Thomas C. Kates, Note, *Publisher Liability for "Gun for Hire" Advertisements: Responsible Exercise of Free Speech or Self Censorship?*, 35 WAYNE L. REV. at 1206 (1989).

31. *See* New York Times Co. v. Sullivan, 376 U.S. 254, 265 (1964) (holding common-law tort liability constitutes state action).

32. *See, e.g., Herceg*, 814 F.2d at 1022–23; *Olivia N*, 126 Cal. App. 3d at 496, 178 Cal. Rptr. at 893; *Walt Disney Prods., Inc.*, 247 Ga. at 405, 276 S.E.2d at 583.

33. *See* Kates, at 1206.

34. *See* Gertz v. Robert Welch, Inc., 418 U.S. at 343–44 (1974) (discouraging case-by-case balancing in favor of categorization approach); Cass R. Sunstein, *Pornography and the First Amendment*, 1986 DUKE L.J., 602–605; *infra* notes 36–52 and accompanying text. Nonetheless, in certain types of cases involving injury from speech, the Supreme Court of the United States does engage in ad hoc balancing of competing interests to determine liability. *See* Gertz, 418 U.S. at 347–48 (balancing interests in defamation case). In *Gertz*, the Court balanced the competing interests of public debate and private reputational injury because of the "*strong and legitimate state interest in com-*

pensating private individuals for injury to reputation." Id. at 348–49 (emphasis added). In distinguishing between public and private plaintiffs' interests, the Court recognized that private individuals do not voluntarily expose themselves to public scrutiny in the same manner as public officials. *See id.* at 344; *see also* Dun & Bradstreet, Inc. v. Greenmoss Builders, Inc., 472 U.S. at 762 (1985) (balancing private interests against interests in constitutional protection of speech). In *Dun & Bradstreet,* which involved an erroneous credit report, the Court found legitimate concern that imposing liability would inhibit core speech. *See id.* (distinguishing speech requiring First Amendment protection from speech which courts may limit). *See generally* Smith, at 1204–07.

35. *See* Kates, at 1206–07 (varying degrees of First Amendment protection dependent upon category of speech in question).

36. *See, e.g.,* NAACP v. Claiborne Hardware Co., 458 U.S. 886, 913, 915 (1982) (holding states may not prohibit peaceful political activity which comprises "the core" of First Amendment (quoting Henry v. First Nat'l Bank, 595 F.2d at 303 (5th Cir. 1979))); Carey v. Brown, 447 U.S. at 466–67 (1980) (holding expression on public issues rests on "highest rung" of the First Amendment hierarchy); New York Times v. Sullivan, 376 U.S. at 266 (1964) (holding expressing and communicating information of public interest entitled to First Amendment protection); *see also* Kates, at 1205 (asserting First Amendment only prohibits proscription of speech which framers intended to protect).

37. *See* Red Lion Broadcasting Co. v. FCC, 395 U.S. at 390 (1969) (opining free speech fundamental to self-government). In 1919, Justice Holmes espoused his now famous "marketplace of ideas" theory, advocating extreme judicial restraint in free-speech cases. Abrams v. United States, 250 U.S. at 630 (1919) (Holmes, J., dissenting).

38. *See* United States v. O'Brien, 391 U.S. at 379 (1987) (holding states must narrowly tailor regulation of speech to important governmental interest); Sunstein, at 602 (stating regulation of high-value speech requires powerful showing of governmental interest).

39. *See, e.g.,* Gannett Co. v. DePasquale, 443 U.S. 368, 393 n. 25 (1979) (emphasizing chief purpose of First Amendment remains avoiding prior restrains) (quoting Near v. Minnesota, 283 U.S. at 713 (1931)); Bantam Books Inc. v. Sullivan, 372 U.S. at 70 (1963) (asserting proponent of prior restraint bears heavy presumption against its validity); Kingsley Books, Inc. v. Brown, 354 U.S. at 443 (1957) (arguing prior restraint and subsequent punishment pose equal threat of impermissibly chilling speech). The Court shows particular concern with avoiding prior restraints on speech that criticizes public officials acting in their public capacity, because this political speech lies at the core of the First Amendment. *See New York Times,* 376 U.S. at 279 (asserting law that inhibits public debate inconsistent with First Amendment).

40. *See* Miller v. California, 413 U.S. 15, 23 (noting First Amendment never treated as absolute right) (quoting Breard v. Alexandra, 341 U.S. 622, 642 (1951). A minority of Supreme Court Justices have advocated the absolutist view. *See generally* Kates, at 1205 n. 11. "Absolutists" argue that the strict language of the First Amendment, requiring Congress to make "no law" abridging freedom of speech, compared to more lenient language such as the Fourteenth Amendment prohibition against "unreasonable searches and seizures," evidences the framer's intent to give citizens an unregulated right of free speech. *See generally* Kates, at 1205 n. 10.

41. *See* O'Brien, 391 U.S. at 379 (allowing restraints which do not suppress speech).

42. *See* Central Hudson Gas & Elec. Corp. v. Public Serv. Comm'n, 447 U.S. at 562–63 (1980) (holding commercial speech receives intermediate level of protec-

tion); *see also* David W. Kantaros, Comment, *Striking an Appropriate Balance between Negligence and Freedom of the Press for Publishers*, 27 SUFFOLK U.L. REV. at 246–47 (1993); Kates, at 1207–09.

43. *See Central Hudson*, 447 U.S. at 566 (setting forth restrictions on state regulations of commercial speech); Young v. American Mini Theatres, 427 U.S. at 69–73 (1976) (discussing limited protection afforded commercial speech).

44. *See Central Hudson*, 447 U.S. at 561–64 (defining commercial speech and constitutional means of regulation).

45. *See*, e.g., New York v. Ferber, 458 U.S. at 764–75 (1982) (holding First Amendment does not protect child pornography from properly tailored state action); Miller v. California, 413 U.S. at 23 (1973) (stating First Amendment does not protect obscene material describing "patently offensive sexual conduct"); Brandenburg v. Ohio, 395 U.S. at 447 (1969) (holding state may proscribe speech likely to incite "imminent lawless action").

46. *See* Chaplinsky v. New Hampshire, 315 U.S. at 572 (1942) (words which inflict injury or tend to incite breach of peace receive no First Amendment protection).

47. *See* Beauharnais v. Illinois, 343 U.S. at 266 (1952) (libelous statements not within constitutional protection). Although defamation receives no First Amendment protection, to determine liability, the Court does apply a balancing test which considers whether the published information is of public concern and whether the injured person is a public figure. *See* Gertz v. Robert Welch, Inc., 418 U.S. at 341–48 (1974) (explaining rationale for balancing competing interests of state and injured party); *see also supra* note 34.

48. *See Brandenburg*, 395 U.S. at 447 (words that incite violence not protected under First Amendment).

49. *See Miller*, 413 U.S. at 25 (patently offensive obscenity not protected by First Amendment). In *Miller*, the Supreme Court of the United States held that when defining obscenity, triers of fact must consider the following factors: whether an average person, applying contemporary community standards, would find that the work, taken as a whole, appeals to prurient interests; whether the work depicts, in a patently offensive manner, sexual conduct defined by a closely tailored applicable state law; and whether the work, taken as a whole, lacks serious literacy, artistic, political, or scientific value. *Id.* at 24. The *Miller* test represents the culmination of American obscenity laws that began in the early Colonial period. *See* Martin Karo and Marcia McBrian, *The Lessons of Miller and Hudnut: On Proposing a Pornography Ordinance that Passes Constitutional Muster*, 23: 1 MICH. J.L. REFORM 179, 182–85 (1989). In Roth v. United States, the Court held that legally obscene material, defined as sexual material "utterly without redeeming social importance," receives no constitutional protection. Roth v. United States, 354 U.S. at 484–85 (1957). For the next 16 years, however, the Court's definition proved troublesome, prompting Justice Stewart's assertion that although he could not define obscenity, "I know it when I see it." Jacobellis v. Ohio, 378 U.S. at 197 (1964) (Stewart, J., concurring).

Subsequent cases attempted to resolve ambiguities in the *Miller* test. *See* Caryn Jacobs, *Patterns of Violence: A Feminist Perspective on the Regulation of Pornography*, 7 HARV. WOMEN'S L.J. 5, 26 (1984). Feminist legal scholars, however, criticize the *Miller* definition as both underinclusive and overinclusive because it might include slightly erotic material, while excluding material so violent that its sexual undertones become obscured. *See* RHODE, at 265. Moreover, commentators argue that the Court's requirement that the work be considered as a whole may provide protection to "soft core" pornographic magazines, such as Playboy, which include serious articles along with violent and violative pictures of women. *See* Andrea Dworkin & Catharine MacKinnon, *Questions and Answers, in* MAKING VIOLENCE SEXY, at 78. In contrast to the Supreme Court, Dworkin asserts that obscenity and pornography are not synonymous, and defines pornography, using its Greek roots, as the graphic (*graphos*) depiction of whores (*pornos*). ANDREA DWORKIN, PORNOGRAPHY, MEN POSSESSING WOMEN (1981) [hereinafter MEN POSSESSING WOMEN; *see also* Herceg v. Hustler Magazine, 814 F.2d at 1026–27 (5th Cir. 1987) (Jones, J., dissenting) (asserting that Hustler magazine emphasizes connection between sex and violence even if not technically obscene), *cert. denied*, 108 5. Ct. 1219 (1988). Additionally, feminist legal scholars question the "neutrality" of the "average person" standard in *Miller*. MACKINNON, FEMINISM UNMODIFIED, at 174. MacKinnon refers to this problem as "point-of-viewlessness" because the historical exclusion of women from the definition and design of the legal system makes women's viewpoint invisible in the law. *See* MacKinnon, *Toward Feminist Jurisprudence*, at 638–39. Therefore, the assertedly objective "average person" standard is inherently biased. *See* MACKINNON, FEMINISM UNMODIFIED, at 167. MacKinnon rhetorically states, "When is a viewpoint not a viewpoint? When it's yours." MACKINNON, FEMINISM UNMODIFIED, at 212. Finally, scholars assert that the Miller test appears more concerned with morality (specifically, male arousal) than the subordination of women perpetuated by pornographic materials. *See* MACKINNON, FEMINISM UNMODIFIED, at 175. *But see* Karo & McBrian, at 182 (advocating use of the *Miller* test in proposed anti-pornography ordinances). In response to these perceived inadequacies of the *Miller* definition, MacKinnon and Dworkin define pornography as graphic, sexually explicit words or pictures that subordinate women and also include women in one of eight enumerated acts which typify pornography. *See* DWORKIN & MACKINNON, at 101. The United States Court of Appeals for the Seventh Circuit found this definition unconstitutional. *See* American Booksellers Ass'n, Inc. v. Hudnut, 771 F.2d at 332 (7th Cir. 1985), *aff'd mem.*, 475 U.S. 1001 (1986); *see infra* notes 139–43 and accompanying text.

50. *See* New York v. Ferber, 458 U.S. at 765 (1982) (holding states may prohibit child pornography). The Supreme Court of the United States altered the *Miller* test in cases involving child pornography so that the trier of fact need not find the materials appeal to the prurient interest of the average person, the conduct portrayed need not be patently offensive, and the material need not be considered as a whole. *See id.* at 764–65. The Court reasoned that while *Miller* serves to protect the interests of unwilling community members from exposure to pornography, the purpose of child pornography laws includes the compelling state interest in protecting the psychological and physical well-being of children. *Id.* at 756. More important, the Court recognized that the production and distribution of child pornography is causally related to the sexual abuse of children. *See id.* at 785 n. 9 (finding pornography harms children).

51. *See* Kates, at 1206–1207.

52. *See* Smith, at 1201; *supra* note 39 and accompanying text.

53. *See* Herceg, 814 F.2d at 1019 (stating *Hustler* invoked First Amendment defense in wrongful death action); DeFilippo v. National Broadcasting Co., 446 A.2d at 1038 (R.I. 1982) (stating broadcasting company asserted First Amendment defense).

54. *See* Herceg v. Hustler Magazine, Inc., 814 F.2d at 1019 (5th Cir. 1987) (plaintiff's amended complaint included incitement allegation), *cert. denied*, 108 5. Ct. 1219 (1988); *DeFilippo*, 446 A.2d at 1040 (asserting incitement only proscribed class of speech which plaintiffs could allege).

55. *See* Schenck v. United States, 249 U.S. at 52 (1919) (holding Congress may prohibit speech which creates "clear and present danger").

56. 395 U.S. 444 (1969).

57. *Id.* at 447. Although the *Brandenburg* test replaced the "clear and present danger" test, one court recently used the clear and present danger test in a case involving bodily injury allegedly resulting from a television broadcast. *See* Walt Disney Prods., Inc. v. Shannon, 247 Ga. at 405, 276 S.E.2d at 583 (1981).

58. *See* Hess v. Indiana, 414 U.S. at 108–109 (1973) (refining incitement test to require intent). This intent element of the incitement test remains a continual source of confusion for courts and commentators. *See* United States v. Kelner, 534 F.2d at 1027 (2d Cir. 1976) (opining imminence element equivalent to specific intent because threat must express speaker's intent); Gerald Gunther, *Learned Hand and the Origins of Modern First Amendment Doctrine: Some Fragments of History*, 27 STAN. L. REV. at 737 (1975). One commentator argues that neither the "directed to inciting" prong, nor the "likely to produce" prong require actual intent. *See* Anne K. Hilker, Note, *Tort Liability of the Media for Audience Acts of Violence: A Constitutional Analysis*, 52 5. CAL. L. REV. at 561–63 (1979). Consequently, the author concludes that courts may impose liability for negligent incitement. *Id.* at 570. On the other hand, another commentator argues that negligence and incitement are mutually exclusive. *See* Weingarten, at 749.

59. *See Brandenburg*, 395 U.S. at 454–55 (Douglas, J., concurring) (asserting incitement test allows states to punish speech based on content).

60. *See,* e.g., Herceg v. Hustler Magazine, Inc. 814 F.2d at 1022–23 (5th Cir. 1987) (holding magazine article not incitement), *cert. denied*, 485 U.S. 959 (1988); Olivia N. v. National Broadcasting Co., 126 Cal. App. 3d at 496, 178 Cal. Rptr. at 893 (barring plaintiff's recovery), *cert. denied*, 458 U.S. 1108 (1982); Walt Disney Prods., Inc. v. Shannon, 247 Ga. at 405, 276 S.E.2d at 583 (holding plaintiff unable to prove television broadcast constituted incitement).

61. 126 Cal. App. 3d 488, 178 Cal. Rptr 888 *cert. denied*, 458 U.S. 1108 (1982).

62. 814 F.2d 1017 (5th Cir. 1987), *cert. denied*, 485 U.S. 959 (1988).

63. *See infra* notes 64–83 and accompanying text; *see also* Zamora v. CBS, Inc., 480 F. Supp. 199, 206 (S.D. Fla. 1979) (imposing civil liability restrains broadcaster's First Amendment rights because plaintiff unable to show incitement); McCollum v. CBS, Inc., 202 Ca. App. 3d at 1003, 249 Cal. Rptr. at 195 (1988) (ruling plaintiff unable to prove incitement and civil liability would lead to self-censorship); *Walt Disney*, 247 Ga. at 404, 276 S.E.2d at 582 (applying analogous "clear and present danger test," court found defendant not liable); DeFilippo v. National Broadcasting Co., 446 A.2d at 1042 (R.I. 1982) (holding First Amendment bars recovery because plaintiff unable to prove incitement).

64. *Olivia N.*, 126 Cal. App. 3d at 493, 178 Cal. Rptr. at 891.

65. Olivia N. v. National Broadcasting Co., 126 Cal. App. 3d at 493, 178 Cal. Rptr. at 81, *cert. denied*, 458 U.S. 1108 (1982). The *Olivia N.* court referred to the rape with a bottle as "artificial rape." *Id.* One commentator criticized the court's use of the word "artificial," tying this characterization of pornography induced rape to the societal defense of pornography as "simulated," rather than actual, violence against women. *See* MACKINNON, ONLY WORDS, at 27, 122 n. 37.

66. *See Olivia N.*, 126 Cal. App. 3d at 490, 178 Cal. Rptr. at 890.

67. *See id.*

68. *See id.* at 491 n. 1, 178 Cal. Rptr. at 891 n. 1. In his opening statement, *Olivia N.*'s

attorney told the jury that he would prove negligence, not incitement, by the broadcaster. *Id.*

69. *Id.* The court also distinguished the instant case from Weirum v. RKO Gen., Inc., 15 Cal. 3d 40, 123 Cal. Rptr. 468, 539 P.2d 36 (1975), because in that case the defendants actively encouraged the reckless conduct that caused the fatal accident. *See Olivia N.,* 126 Cal. App. 3d at 497, 178 Cal. Rptr. at 893–94 (distinguishing *Weirum* as basis for imposing liability); *see also infra* text accompanying notes 94–98.

70. *See Olivia N.,* 126 Cal. App. 3d at 496, 178 Cal. Rptr. at 893 (finding television broadcast in protected category of speech).

71. *See id.* at 494, 178 Cal. Rptr. at 892 (citing New York Times v. Sullivan, 376 U.S. 254 (1964)). In reaching its conclusion, the court relied on *Times v. Sullivan,* although that case involved defamation of a public official and its holding focused on prior restraint of political speech, not physical injury resulting from speech. *See Olivia N.,* 126 Cal. App. 3d at 495, 178 Cal. Rptr. at 892 (applying *Times v. Sullivan* reasoning to personal injury case); *supra* note 39 and accompanying text.

72. *See Olivia N.,* 126 Cal App. 3d at 497, 178 Cal. Rptr. at 894 (holding plaintiff barred from recovering damages).

73. *See* 814 F.2d at 1022–23 (5th Cir. 1987) (holding magazine article did not reach level of encouragement necessary to constitute incitement), *cert. denied,* 108 S. Ct. 1219 (1988).

74. *See Herceg,* 814 F.2d at 1018 (explaining practice of autoerotic asphyxia); *see also* Kennedy v. Washington Nat'l Ins. Co., 401 N.W.2d 842 (Wis. 1987) (holding death from autoerotic asphyxiation accidental for insurance purposes, notwithstanding decedent's voluntary risk of death). Prior to the *Herceg* case, Playboy magazine also described the practice in detail, and warned of the serious danger of doing it alone. *See* Jane E. Brody, *'Autoerotic Death' of Youths Causes Widening Concern,* N.Y. TIMES, March 27, 1984, at C1. The Federal Bureau of Investigation estimates that autoerotic asphyxiation results in 500 to 1,000 deaths per year, the majority of which are teenage males. *Id.* at C1. Researchers indicate that counting the actual number of accidental deaths resulting from autoerotic asphyxiation is difficult because many are misdiagnosed as homicide or suicide, or covered up by the victims' families. *Id. See generally Thrills That Kill,* A.B.A. J., July 1, 1987, at 80.

75. *Herceg,* 814 F.2d at 1018. The article also contained a recommendation that readers not attempt autoerotic asphyxia and a statement that the description was solely for educational purposes. *Id.*

76. *Id.* at 1019.

77. *Id.*

78. Herceg v. Hustler Magazine, Inc., 814 F.2d at 1019 (5th Cir. 1987), *cert. denied,* 485 U.S. 959 (1988).

79. *Herceg,* 814 F.2d at 1024. The court opined that categorizing protected speech as the appellants proposed would create a threat of censorship to all speech. *Id.*

80. *See Herceg,* 814 F.2d at 1022 (determining whether article constituted incitement).

81. *See id.* at 1022–23 (holding article did not constitute incitement). The court also noted that the plaintiffs' reliance on Weirum v. RKO Gen. was not sustainable because *Weirum* involved active encouragement of reckless conduct. *See Herceg,* 814 F.2d at 1023–24 (distinguishing Weirum); *see also infra* text accompanying notes 94–98.

82. *See Herceg,* 814 F.2d at 1023 (discussing negligence claim). The court also stated

that because the trial proceeded on an incitement theory, the jury did not return findings on the negligence issue, thus the court decided whether Texas tort law would have supported a negligence claim. *See id.* at 1025 (concluding no factual basis for determining negligence issue). *But see* Hilker, at 570. The *Herceg* court also relied on *Times v. Sullivan* for its assertion that civil liability for protected speech violates the First Amendment. *See Herceg*, 814 F.2d at 1023 (quoting New York Times Co. v. Sullivan, 376 U.S. 254 (1964)). *Times v. Sullivan*, however, involved defamation of a public official and the Court's concern with large damage awards leading to prior restraints on public debate, not personal injury caused by speech. *See Times*, 376 U.S. at 278 (recognizing multiple damage awards against newspapers may cause publisher to limit publication of public criticism).

83. Herceg v. Hustler Magazine, Inc., 814 F.2d at 1023 (5th Cir. 1987), *cert. denied*, 485 U.S. 959 (1988).

84. *See id.* at 1025 (Jones, J., concurring in part and dissenting in part). Judge Jones concurred in part because the plaintiff did not cross appeal the dismissal of the negligence claim, thus limiting the court to a consideration of whether the article constituted incitement. *Id.*

85. *See Herceg* at 1026 (Jones J. concurring in part and dissenting in part) (reasoning pornography not equivalent of core speech).

86. *Herceg* at 1027; *see supra* notes 33–39 and accompanying text. MacKinnon similarly asserts that the Court developed the free speech doctrine to protect communists, a political minority, from majoritarian political suppression. *See* MACKINNON, ONLY WORDS, at 38–39.

87. See *Herceg* at 1028 (Jones, J. concurring in part and dissenting in part) (discussing values underlying First Amendment protection); *see also supra* note 49 and accompanying text. Commentators similarly argue that pornography's sole purpose is to create the physical effect of sexual arousal and gratification, rather than to communicate an idea. *See* Frederick Schauer, *Speech and "Speech"—Obscenity and "Obscenity": An Exercise in the Interpretation of Constitutional Language*, 67 GEO. L.J. at 922–25 (1979). Bob Guccione, publisher of *Penthouse*, said the purpose of pornography was: "When a guy's peeping at a girl through a little hole in the wall, he doesn't give a shit what her interests are, what her background is, what her profession is. When she's taking off her clothes, that's what he's interested in. That's all he's going to react to . . . [T]he more realistic we can show these girls . . . the more successful we're going to be." EDWARD DE GRAZIA, GIRLS LEAN BACK EVERYWHERE: THE LAW OF OBSCENITY AND THE ASSAULT ON GENIUS 578 (1992).

88. See *Herceg* at 1026–27 (Jones, J. concurring in part and dissenting in part). For example, the New York City Police Department seized pornographic films, known as "snuff" films, which depicted actual murders of women. See Beverly LaBelle, *Snuff—The Ultimate in Woman-Hating*, in TAKE BACK THE NIGHT at 272–73 (discussing seizure of "snuff" films). After the seizure, a New York pornographic movie theatre featured the movie "snuff," advertised as depicting a real murder, although producers claimed no actual murder occurred in the film. Beverly LaBelle, *Snuff—The Ultimate in Woman-Hating*, in TAKE BACK THE NIGHT, at 272–73. In the film, the protagonist, named Satan, stabs a pregnant woman and dismembers and disembowels another woman for sexual pleasure. *Id.* at 273.

89. See *Herceg* at 1027–28 (analogizing to defamation law). While the dissenting opinion analogized to the defamation law balancing test, the majority's approach applied defamation law as controlling, and accordingly barred the action. *See id.* at 1023

(relying on defamation law to bar action); *see also* Olivia N. v. National Broadcasting Co., 126 Cal. App. 3d at 495, 178 Cal. Rptr. at 892 (relying on defamation law to bar recovery), *cert. denied* 458 U.S. 1108 (1982); and accompanying text.

90. *See Herceg*, 814 F.2d at 1026 (Jones, J., concurring and dissenting); *Id.* at 1024.

91. *See Id.* at 1029 (Jones, J. concurring in part and dissenting in part).

92. *See supra* notes 64–83 and accompanying text.

93. *See* Hyde v. City of Colombia, 637 S.W.2d at 273 (Mo. Ct. App. 1982) (allowing recovery in negligent publication case); *cert. denied,* 459 U.S. 1226 (1983); Weirum v. RKO Gen., Inc., 15 Cal. 3d at 49, 539 P.2d 36, 41, 123 Cal. Rptr. at 473 (1975) (allowing recovery in wrongful death case); *infra* notes 95–102 and accompanying text. One commentator criticized these two cases as using a "harm oriented" approach in which the courts focused on the plaintiffs' interest in compensation to the exclusion of free-speech concerns. *See* Smith, at 1211.

94. 15 Cal. 3d 40, 539 P.2d 36, 123 Cal. Rptr. 468 (1975).

95. *Id.* at 43, 539 P.2d at 37, 123 Cal. Rptr. at 470.

96. *Id.* at 45, 539 P.2d at 39, 123 Cal. Rptr. at 471.

97. *Id.* at 46, 539 P.2d at 39, 123 Cal. Rptr. at 472.

98. *See id.* at 48, 539 P.2d at 40, 123 Cal. Rptr. at 472 (stating "First Amendment does not sanction the infliction of harm merely because achieved by word, rather than act").

99. 637 S.W.2d 251 (Mo. Ct. App. 1982), *cert. denied,* 459 U.S. 1226 (1983).

100. *Id.* at 253.

101. *Id.* at 273. Subsequently, Hyde also observed the kidnapper in the vicinity of her home several times after the newspaper published her name and address. *Id.* at 254 n. 2.

102. *See id.* at 264–65 (asserting defendant's free speech adequately protected in negligence action).

103. *See* Braun v. Soldier of Fortune Magazine, Inc., 968 F.2d at 1122 (11th Cir. 1992) (affirming district court's holding that First Amendment does not shield publisher from liability), *cert. denied,* 113 5. Ct. 1028 (1993); Carter v. Rand McNally & Co., No. 76-1864-F (D. Mass. Sept. 25, 1980). In *Rand McNally,* a jury awarded the plaintiffs a total of $100,000 for injuries sustained while following defendant's textbook instructions for a laboratory experiment involving extremely flammable methyl alcohol. *Id.*; *see* Herceg v. Hustler Magazine, 814 F.2d at 1029 (5th Cir. 1987) (Jones, J., concurring in part and dissenting in part) (reasoning that tort remedy in pornography case appropriately balances harms), *cert. denied,* 485 U.S. 959 (1988); *see also* E. Patrick McQuaid, *Publisher of Science Text Held Liable for Inadequate Laboratory Instructions,* CHRON. HIGHER EDUC., July 27, 1981, at 13.

104. *See* Eimann v. Soldier of Fortune Magazine, Inc., 880 F.2d at 836 (5th Cir. 1989) (recognizing commercial speech, such as classified advertisements, receives limited First Amendment protection), *cert. denied,* 493 U.S. 1024 (1990); Norwood v. Soldier of Fortune Magazine, Inc., 651 F. Supp. at 1400 (W.D. Ark. 1987) (recognizing First Amendment not absolute bar to publisher liability); Felix H. Kent, *Magazine Liable for Ad Negligence,* 199 N.Y.L.J., Mar. 25, 1988, at 2.

105. 651 F. Supp. 1397 (W.D. Ark 1987).

106. *Id.* at 1398. One advertisement read, in part, "GUN FOR HIRE. . . . Discreet and very private. . . . All jobs considered." The other read, in part, "GUN FOR HIRE. . . . All jobs considered. . . . Privacy guaranteed." *Id.*

107. *Id.* at 1403.

108. *Id.*

109. *Id.* at 1402.

110. Norwood v. Soldier of Fortune Magazine, Inc., 651 F. Supp. at 1400–02 (W.D. Ark 1987). *See generally* Kates, at 1210–12. Following the court's ruling, the parties settled out of court for an undisclosed sum of money. *See* Debbie Lee, Note, *"Gun for Hire" Advertisement That Backfired and Hit the Publisher in the Pocketbook*, 8 Loy. ENT. L.J. 439, 439 n. 2 (1988).

111. 880 F.2d 830 (5th Cir. 1989), *cert. denied*, 493 U.S. 1024 (1990).

112. *See id.* at 834 n. 1; *see also supra* notes 21–28 and accompanying text.

113. *Eimann*, 880 F.2d at 831.

114. *Id.* at 832.

115. *Id.*

116. *See* Eimann v. Soldier of Fortune Magazine, Inc., 880 F.2d at 834 (5th Cir. 1989) (discussing application of risk-utility balancing test); *cert. denied*, 493 U.S. 1024 (1990). Justice Learned Hand first articulated the risk-utility test in United States v. Carroll Towing Co., 159 F.2d 169 (2d Cir. 1947).

117. *See Eimann*, 880 F.2d at 834.

118. *Id.*

119. *Id.* at 835.

120. *Id. See supra* notes 43–44 and accompanying text.

121. *See* Eimann v. Soldier of Fortune Magazine, Inc., 880 F.2d at 835–36 (5th Cir. 1989) (holding liability for unreasonable risk not unconstitutional), *cert. denied*, 493 U.S. 1024 (1990).

122. *See* 968 F.2d at 1122 (11th Cir. 1992) (holding magazine liable for publishing unambiguous advertisement that posed unreasonable risk of harm), *cert. denied*, 113 S. Ct. 1028 (1993); Mae Charles Babb, Comment, *Braun v. Soldier of Fortune Magazine Inc.: Advertisement for Hit Man Brings Four Million Dollar Hit to Publisher*, 44 MERCER L. REV. at 1350–53 (1993); *infra* notes 126–34 and accompanying text.

123. *Braun*, 968 F.2d at 1112.

124. *Id.*

125. *Id.*

126. *Id.* at 1116. The court also distinguished the unambiguous wording of Savage's advertisement from the advertisement in *Eimann*, and held that Savage's ad should have alerted a reasonable publisher to a clearly identifiable unreasonable risk of harm. *Id.* at 1116 n. 3.

127. *See* Braun v. Soldier of Fortune Magazine, Inc., 968 F.2d at 1116 (11th Cir. 1992) (modifying negligence standard to include facially unambiguous threat of harm in publication), *cert. denied*, 113 S. Ct. 1028 (1993).

128. *See Braun*, 968 F.2d at 1117.

129. *See id.* at 1118.

130. *See id.*

131. 418 U.S. 323 (1974); *see supra* note 34.

132. *See* Braun v. Soldier of Fortune Magazine, Inc., 968 F.2d at 1118 (11th Cir. 1992) (quoting Gertz v. Robert Welch, Inc., 418 U.S. at 346 (1974)), *cert. denied*, 113 5. Ct. 1028 (1993). The *Braun* court's argument by analogy to defamation law resembles the argument in the *Herceg* dissent. *See* Herceg v. Hustler Magazine, 814 F.2d, 1028 (5th Cir. 1987) (Jones, J., dissenting in part and concurring in part), *cert. denied*, 485 U.S. 959 (1988); *supra* text accompanying note 84.

133. *See Braun*, 968 F.2d at 1118 (finding no constitutional prohibition against holding publishers liable for negligent advertising).

134. *See id.* at 1122.

135. *See* MACKINNON, FEMINISM UNMODIFIED, at 175–76.

136. *See* Catharine A. MacKinnon, *Pornography as Defamation and Discrimination*, 71 B.U. L. REV. at 801–802 (1991).

137. *Id.* at 801.

138. *See* Penelope Seator, *Judicial Indifference to Pornography's Harm: American Booksellers v Hudnut*, 17 GOLDEN GATE U.L. REV. at 299 n. 9 (1987) (providing legislative history of Minneapolis Ordinance and related testimony); Morrison Torrey, *The Resurrection of the Anti-pornography Ordinance*, 2 TEX. J. WOMEN & L. at 114 (1993). MAKING VIOLENCE SEXY presents the testimony in edited form. *See* MAKING VIOLENCE SEXY at 48–62. The city's mayor vetoed the Minneapolis Ordinance twice. *See* Seator, at 299 n. 8. City governments in Los Angeles, California, and Cambridge, Massachusetts, also introduced similar ordinances. *See id.* Voters defeated the Cambridge ordinance by fewer than 4,000 votes. *See* N.Y. TIMES, Nov. 12, 1985, at A16, col. 6 (proposed Human Rights Ordinance defeated by vote of 13,031 to 9,419).

139. 598 F. Supp. 1316 (S.D. Ind.), *aff'd*, 771 F.2d 323 (7th Cir. 1985), *aff'd mem.*, 475 U.S. 1001 (1986).

140. *See Hudnut*, 771 F.2d at 332 (holding ordinance's definition of pornography unconstitutional). In 1989, a voter referendum also passed a version of the Model Ordinance in Bellingham, Washington, which a trial court later declared unconstitutional. *See* Village Books v. City of Bellingham, No. 88-1470 (W.D. Wash. Feb. 9, 1989); *see also* Margaret A. Baldwin, *Pornography and the Traffic in Women: Brief on Behalf of Trudee Able-Peterson, et al., Amici Curiae in Support of Defendant and Intervenor-defendants, Village Books v. City of Bellingham*, 1 YALE J.L. & FEMINISM at 112–13 (1989). The defendant, the City of Bellingham, declined to defend the suit. *Id.* at 113.

The proposed Federal Pornography Victim's Compensation Act of 1991 also would have created a cause of action against pornographers for victims who could show that the pornography that substantially caused their injuries had a reasonably foreseeable connection with their injuries. *See* Pornography Victim's Compensation Act, S. 983, 102d Cong., 1st Sess. §3(a) (1991); *see also* Torrey, at 116–17 (describing proposed federal legislation in detail). The Act, however, never reached a vote in Congress. *See* Stephanie B. Goldberg, *1st Amendment Wrongs: A New Approach to Fighting Pornography Says Free Speech Has Nothing to Do with It*, CHICAGO TRIBUNE, Mar. 17, 1993 (Tempo), at 1. *See generally* Charley Roberts, *Senators Debate Porn Bill*, THE LOS ANGELES DAILY J., Mar. 13, 1992, at 5; the Committee on Federal Legislation and the Committee on Communications and Media Law, Pornography Victims Compensation Act, Apr., 1992, THE RECORD OF THE ASSOCIATION OF THE BAR OF THE CITY OF NEW YORK 326; Henry J. Reske, *Feminists Back Anti-porn Bill*, A.B.A. J. June, 1992, at 32.

In 1992, the Massachusetts Joint Committee on the Judiciary began hearings on an anti-pornography bill similar to the Model Ordinance. *See* An Act to Protect the Civil Rights of Women and Children, Mass. H.B. 5194, 1992 Reg. Sess., 177th Gen. Ct. §2(c); *see also* Tamar Lewin, *Pornography Foes Push for Right to Sue*, N.Y. TIMES, Mar. 15, 1992, §1 Part 1), at 16; Thomas C. Palmer, Jr., *A Bill of Divorcement; Women Are Split on Anti-pornography Law*, BOSTON GLOBE, Mar. 29, 1992 (Focus), at 69.

141. *See Hudnut*, 771 F.2d at 332 (stating pornography threatens women's safety and chances for legal equality).

142. *Id.* at 329. The majority opinion stated that other "unhappy effects" of pornography include rape, battery, domestic violence, and employment and wage discrimination. *Id.* Commentators have offered detailed explanations of the complex legal issues

raised in defense of and in opposition to the Model Ordinance and the Hudnut decisions; *see* DWORKIN AND MACKINNON; Karo and McBrian; Andrea Dworkin, *Pornography is a Civil Rights Issue for Women*, 21 MICH. J.L. REFORM 55 (Fall 1987–Winter 1988); MACKINNON, FEMINISM UNMODIFIED, at 163–97, 206–13; Seator, *supra* note 138; FACT *Brief, supra* note 3; Randall D.B. Tigue, *Civil Rights and Censorship—Incompatible Bedfellows*, 11 WM. MITCHELL L. REV. 81 (1985).

143. *See* HOFF, at 345. Hoff asserts that the heart of the dilemma courts face lies in "liberal legalism's" inability to withstand the anti-pornography challenge to male dominated legal principles. *See* HOFF, 345–46.

144. *E.g.*, Herceg v. Hustler Magazine, Inc., 814 F.2d 1017 (5th Cir. 1987), *cert. denied*, 485 U.S. 959 (1988); Olivia N. v. National Broadcasting Co., 126 Cal. App. 3d 488, 178 Cal. Rptr. 888, *cert. denied*, 458 U.S. 1108 (1982); Weirum v. RKO Gen., 15 Cal. 3d 40, 539 P.2d 36, 123 Cal. Rptr. 468 (1975); *see supra* notes 55–60 and accompanying text.

145. *See Herceg*, 814 F.2d at 1023 (stating incitement test applies to unlawful crowd behavior); *supra* notes 55–58 and accompanying text.

146. *See Herceg*, 814 F.2d at 1023 (opining incitement theory does not fit facts of wrongful death case); Sims, at 256; Sunstein, at 602; Weingarten, at 744; *supra* notes 61–103 and accompanying text.

147. *See* Hess v. Indiana, 414 U.S. at 108–109 (1973) (requiring plaintiff to show speaker intended to incite); *supra* note 58 and accompanying text.

148. *See supra* note 58 and accompanying text.

149. *See supra* note 146 and accompanying text.

150. *See* Smith, at 1214, 1228.

151. *See* Brandenburg v. Ohio, 395 U.S. 444, 450, 454–55 (1969) (Douglas, J., concurring) (opining that incitement test allows states to impose prior restraints on speech); *supra* notes 37–39 and accompanying text; *supra* note 59 and accompanying text.

152. *See* Weirum v. RKO Gen., Inc., 15 Cal. 3d at 48, 539 P.2d 36, 40, 123 Cal. Rptr. at 472 (1975) (reasoning liability based on creation of unreasonable risk protects free speech interests); Hyde v. City of Columbia, 637 S.W.2d at 264–65 (Mo. Ct. App. 1982) (asserting First Amendment accommodates balance between free press and law of torts), *cert. denied*, 459 U.S. 1226 (1983); *see supra* notes 94–102.

153. *See* Olivia N. v. National Broadcasting Co., 126 Cal. App. 3d at 496, 178 Cal. Rptr. at 893 (stressing danger of self-censorship as prior restraint on expression), *cert. denied*, 458 U.S. 1108 (1982); Smith, at 1229.

154. *See* Gertz v. Robert Welch, Inc., 418 U.S. 323, 348 (1974) (recognizing state interest in compensating individuals for reputational injury); *supra* note 34.

155. *See, e.g.*, Herceg v. Hustler Magazine, Inc., 814 F.2d at 1022–23 (5th Cir. 1987) (holding wrongful death action barred because plaintiff unable to prove incitement), *cert. denied*, 485 U.S. 959 (1988); Olivia N. v. National Broadcasting Co., 126 Cal. App. 3d at 496, 178 Cal. Rptr. at 893 (barring plaintiffs recovery notwithstanding negligence allegation), *cert. denied*, 458 U.S. 1108 (1982); Walt Disney Prods., Inc. v. Shannon, 247 Ga. at 405, 276 S.E.2d at 583 (1981) (barring recovery because plaintiff unable to prove television broadcast constituted incitement); *see also* Smith, at 1217–18.

156. *See Herceg*, 814 F.2d at 1022–23 (holding pornographic instruction in protected category of expression); *Olivia N.*, 126 Cal. App. 3d at 498, 178 Cal. Rptr. at 893 (holding First Amendment shields broadcaster from civil liability for personal injury claim).

157. *See Herceg*, 814 F.2d at 1023 (holding fear of civil liberty "'markedly more inhibiting that the fear of prosecution under a criminal statute'") (quoting New York Times Co. v. Sullivan, 376 U.S. 254 (1964); *Olivia N.*, 126 Cal. App. 3d at 495, 178 Cal. Rptr. at 892 (relying on defamation case law as controlling in personal injury case); Smith, at 1214–15; *supra* note 71 and accompanying text; *see also supra* note 82 and accompanying text; *supra* note 89 and accompanying text.

158. *See Herceg*, 814 F.2d at 1025 (Jones, J., concurring in part and dissenting in part) (questioning inequitable result of majority's reasoning); Smith, at 1217–18; *supra* notes 33–52 and accompanying text.

159. *See* Sunstein, at 591; *supra* note 49 and accompanying text. *Compare* Miller v. California, 413 U.S. 14, 18 n. 2 (describing pornography as subset of proscribable obscenity) *with Herceg*, 814 F.2d at 1024 (refusing to place pornographic magazine in less-protected category of speech).

160. *See* Herceg v. Hustler Magazine, Inc., 814 F.2d at 1027 (5th Cir. 1987) (criticizing majority for equating pornography with core speech), *cert. denied*, 485 U.S. 959 (1988). The efficacy of the judicial definition of pornography depends on adequately defining the harm that state regulations should seek to avoid. *See* Sunstein, at 594–95. The feminist approach focuses on pornography's harm to women, not on moral or aesthetic offensiveness. Sunstein, at 594–95.

161. *See Miller*, 413 U.S. 35; *supra* note 87 and accompanying text.

162. *See Herceg*, 814 F.2d at 1024 (holding First Amendment shields magazine from liability); American Booksellers Ass'n, Inc. v. Hudnut, 598 F. Supp. 1316 (S.D. md.) (holding anti-pornography ordinance violates pornographers' free speech rights), *aff'd*, 771 F.2d 323 (7th Cir. 1985), *aff'd mem.*, 475 U.S. 1001 (1986); *supra* notes 74–83 and accompanying text; Palmer, at 69 (stating pornography seven- to ten-billion dollar per year industry).

163. *See* MACKINNON, ONLY WORDS, at 16–17; Sunstein, at 606; *supra* note 87 and accompanying text.

164. *See* MACKINNON, FEMINISM UNMODIFIED, at 172; Sunstein, *supra* note 34, at 597; *see also supra* note 5 and accompanying text; *supra* notes 15 and 88; *supra* note 4 and accompanying text.

165. *See* MACKINNON, FEMINISM UNMODIFIED, at 175.

166. 968 F.2d 1110 (11th Cir. 1992), *cert. denied*, 113 S. Ct. 1028 (1993).

167. *See id.* at 1118 (applying risk-utility test to protect both parties' interests); *supra* notes 126–34 (discussing *Braun* court's reasoning and holding). MacKinnon similarly argues that because women are harmed in the making of pornography, it is therefore foreseeable that men who attempt to reenact what they see in pornography will also harm women. *See* MACKINNON, ONLY WORDS, at 20–21, 120 n. 30.

168. *Compare* Herceg v. Hustler Magazine, Inc., 814 F.2d at 1022–23 (5th Cir. 1987) (holding plaintiff barred from recovery because unable to prove incitement), *cert. denied*, 485 U.S. 959 (1988) *with Braun*, 968 F.2d at 1118 (holding First Amendment not absolute bar to recovery). *See also supra* notes 126–34 (discussing *Braun* balancing test).

169. *See Braun*, 968 F.2d at 1118 (holding risk-utility test adequately protects First Amendment concerns); Eimann v. Soldier of Fortune Magazine, Inc., 880 F.2d at 836 (5th Cir. 1989) (recognizing social utility of commercial speech in discussion of risk-utility test), *cert. denied*, 493 U.S. 1024 (1990).

170. *See Braun*, 968 F.2d at 1118 (applying balancing test to protect injured parties' interests); *supra* notes 116–29 and accompanying text.

171. *See* Babb, at 1355–56; Kantaros, at 249–50; *see also* Smith, at 1223–24.

172. *See Braun*, 968 F.2d at 1119 (analyzing advertisement to determine whether risk of harm unreasonable).

173. *See* Herceg v. Hustler Magazine, Inc., 814 F.2d 1029 (5th Cir. 1987) (Jones, J., concurring in part and dissenting in part) (stating liability for most harmful pornography unlikely to impermissibly chill pornography industry), *cert. denied*, 485 U.S. 959 (1988).

174. *See* PROSSER & KEETON §37 at 237.

175. *See Braun*, 968 F.2d at 1119–20 (requiring clearly identifiable risk of harm to impose liability).

176. *See* RESTATEMENT §281 at 4; *supra* note 21 and accompanying text; *supra* notes 55–59 and accompanying text.

177. *See* HOFF, at 3; *supra* note 10 and accompanying text.

178. *See* American Booksellers Ass'n, Inc., v. Hudnut, 771 F.2d at 332 (7th Cir. 1985) (striking down anti-pornography ordinance), *aff'd mem.*, 475 U.S. 1001 (1986), *reh'g denied*, 475 U.S. 1132 (1986); Village Books v. City of Bellingham, No. 88-1470 (W.D. Wash. Feb. 9, 1989) (rejecting anti-pornography ordinance); *supra* notes 138–40 and accompanying text.

179. *See* MACKINNON, FEMINISM UNMODIFIED, at 283 n. 52. As the Soldier of Fortune cases proved, publishers do not continue to publish unprofitable material. *See* Kent, at 1. *But see* Sunstein, at 596 n. 52.

180. *See* RESTATEMENT §282 at 9; PROSSER & KEETON §4 at 25; *supra* note 20 and accompanying text.

181. *See supra* note 18 and accompanying text.

182. *See* Russo, at 162; *supra* note 21 and accompanying text.

183. *See* MACKINNON, FEMINISM UNMODIFIED, at 175. MacKinnon argues that because women have begun to talk openly about the violence in their lives, the judiciary should recognize that protecting pornography as speech is equivalent to protecting sexual abuse of women. *See* MACKINNON, ONLY WORDS, at 8–9. Interestingly, the Supreme Court of the United States relied on this argument when it upheld a ban on child pornography, but rejected the argument when it applied to pornography involving abuse of adult women. *Compare* New York v. Ferber, 458 U.S. at 758 n. 9 (1982) (finding production and distribution of child pornography harms children) *with* American Booksellers Ass'n, Inc., v. Hudnut, 771 F.2d at 329 (7th Cir. 1985) (holding pornography's harm to women contributes to its status as protected speech), *aff'd mem.*, 475 U.S. 1001 (1986), *reh'g denied*, 475 U.S. 1132 (1986). Some commentators argue that the rationale applied in *Ferber* also applies to adult female pornography participants and women who have been injured by pornography. *See* Karo and McBrian, at 198–200; Jacobs, at 36–41; *supra* note 50 and accompanying text.

184. *See supra* notes 2–5 and accompanying text.

185. *See* RHODE, at 272–73.

186. *See* Braun v. Soldier of Fortune Magazine, Inc., 968 F.2d at 1116 (11th Cir. 1992) (requiring facially unreasonable risk of harm), *cert. denied* 113 S. Ct. 1028 (1993); RESTATEMENT §291 at 54 (stating risk unreasonable when magnitude outweighs social utility of conduct); *supra* note 3.

187. *See Braun*, 968 F.2d at 1119–20 (stating publication negligent if poses unreasonable risk of harm to public); *supra* note 3 and accompanying text.

188. *See* Russo, at 145.

189. *See* RESTATEMENT §281 at 4–9 (stating injured party must prove actual injury in negligence claim); Russo, at 159–62.

190. *See supra* notes 138–40 and accompanying text.
191. *See* Middleton, at 7.

10. The Myth of the Happy Hooker:
Kantian Moral Reflections on a Phenomenology of Prostitution

1. We do not discuss the present legal status of prostitution, since the problematic aspects of prostitution do not depend on its criminality. In fact, strong argument could be offered in defense of decriminalizing prostitution, but we do not offer it here. If prostitution were decriminalized, then at least some threats to the lives and health of prostitutes might be mitigated: they might have legal recourse when they became victims of coercion, theft, and assault.

On the origins of prostitution and the need for a theory of prostitution see Jaggar, 1980: 348–68. For a comparison of prostitution in different societies see Shrage, 1994. For a discussion on the role of prostitution and marriage in patriarchal, capitalist society see Pateman, 1988. For a discussion of the need for prostitutes to assume a subject position in philosophical discourse on prostitution see Bell, 1994.

2. Although not an empirical investigation, this essay depends on empirical observation. It is informed by the art, literature, and self-descriptions of prostitutes. In order to protect the privacy of these women, specific details of these conversations and the identities of the women themselves will remain confidential. We hope to convey a sense of the pain and struggle that traditional modes of empirical investigation often fail to capture.

3. Our moral reflections are "Kantian" insofar as we presuppose basic Kantian notions of human dignity and morality, as well as particular views about freedom, recognition, subjectivity, and objectification that are rooted in German Idealism. Although we assume a Kantian approach to morality, we do not mean to imply that this essay represents Kant's account of women, sexuality, or prostitution.

4. The phenomenological portion of this paper should not be confused with a phenomenology in the traditional Husserlian sense. "Phenomenology" in this context refers to a descriptive account of an individual's, or individuals', experience rather than a generalized account of experience. Such an account is perspectival by definition.

5. Potential forms of prostitution falling under this definition include kissing booths, pornography, some marriage relationships, some dating relationships, many labor relationships, and so on. We do not argue that these diverse activities constitute prostitution.

6. Many feminists, for instance Alison Jaggar, Catharine MacKinnon, Carole Pateman, and Sarah Wynter, argue that prostitution exists solely in a context of sexual oppression and misogyny. Jaggar suggests that even male prostitution reflects the fundamental misogynist character of society, that male prostitutes are feminized to the extent that they are prostituted. We agree that prostitution involves misogynist, sexist elements and serves as an instrument of domination, but we would maintain that it reflects a larger problem of oppression of which sexism and misogyny represent a subset.

7. Kant's "principle of humanity," a formulation of the Categorical Imperative, states: "Act in such a way that you always treat humanity, whether in your own person or in the person of any other, never simply as a means, but always at the same time as an end" (1964: 96). Actions should not merely consider humanity as an end in itself but should promote this end. To be sure, promoting the moral perfection of oneself and

others is a "meritorious" rather than a "strict" duty, but it is not for that reason "optional" (ibid.: 96–97).

8. This concept of human subjectivity originates with Kant and is perpetuated throughout German Idealism. Fichte begins with Kant's notion of an intelligible subject or "transcendental I" and argues that it appears in consciousness through the empirically determined, limited, embodied individual members of a social whole. According to both the Kantian and Fichtean theories of morality, rational beings such as ourselves possess dignity because they are "ends in themselves."

9. In expanding on the views of Hegel, Freud, Sartre, and de Beauvoir, feminists such as Judith Butler, Iris M. Young, and Sandra Bartky have greatly enriched our understanding of the integral relationship between subjectivity and sexuality.

10. If Linda Lemoncheck's clarifying variety of observations in "What's Wrong with Being a Sex Object?" indicate the diversity of public opinion, then "objectification" has been defined in many different ways; the apparent diversity of opinion on this topic may be an indication of miscommunication rather than disparate values (1994: 199–205). Sandra Bartky clearly states what we mean by objectification in a sexual context: "A person is sexually objectified when her sexual parts or sexual functions are separated out from the rest of her personality and reduced to the status of mere instruments or else regarded as if they were capable of representing her. On this definition then the prostitute would be a victim of sexual objectification, as would the Playboy bunny, the female breeder, and the bathing beauty" (1990: 26).

11. It should be self-explanatory that we violate a person's freedom when we involve them in activities without their obvious agreement. For this reason, consent is a necessary condition of sexual relations according to the implications of most classical moral theories. To assume that consent is a sufficient condition for morally acceptable sexual relations, however, seems a reckless moral attitude.

12. We suffer when we must engage in undesired activities, and we suffer when our desires are ignored or unfulfilled. Most moral theories, including the Kantian, admit that we are allowed to act according to some desires and that we ought to take others' desires into consideration as well.

13. In this context, "concern" does not mean a type of emotional sympathy, but simply a moral regard for the integrity of others' interests, which include their needs, desires, and projects as well as their moral well-being.

14. Many sexual abusers attempt to justify their actions by claiming that their victims "really" wanted, needed, or enjoyed the sexual encounter. Some claim to feel genuine concern and affection for their victims, which reveals that even the abuser recognizes the significance of concern and desire within sexual relations.

15. A recent article in *Playboy* concurs with this analysis. In "The Rules of the Game," James R. Peterson cites Al Goldstein's explanation of why men seek the services of prostitutes:

Of all the commentators, *Screw* publisher Al Goldstein was most honest, reporting a story about the night he spent $1000 on an escort. "It was splendid, rollicking sex. When it was over I felt like willing my body to science. And then she left. She left. As the supreme final act in our opera of fucking, her leaving was like a cherry on a sundae, a sumptuous dessert after a seven course meal, a plunge into cool water after running a marathon. That's when I had my glistening realization. I realized I wasn't paying this woman for sex. I was paying her for the luxury of her leaving after sex." (1995: 52)

16. The issue is that their fiduciary agreement is intended to excuse him from any obligation. If in fact he assumes some responsibility, it is viewed as an act of generosity rather than as a duty.

12. International Development Paradigms and Violence against Women

1. Poor women protest different issues in different countries. In the foothills of the Himalayas, the protest movement engaging poor women began as a political protest against the sale of alcohol, and actually succeeded in imposing prohibition for a time. The movement evolved into ecological protests known as Chipko. Although Chipko has been described as an ecofeminist protest movement, the leadership was Gandhian. Publicity was generated primarily by men, but the rank and file of the movement were almost entirely hill women of the Garwal region.

In South Africa, women sustained local political protest against apartheid practices. In eastern Canada, poor women engage in protest activity designed to promote fair pricing practices by a grocery chain. Prior to the protest, suburban stores that were inaccessible without an automobile offered cheaper prices to consumers than did the inner city shops which these women, who lacked automobiles, were accustomed to patronize.

Moser's point about poor women engaging in protest movements generalizes the nature of the time allotment involved as a part of the triple burden shared by poor women around the globe.

2. The Grameen Bank began as a nongovernmental organization in Bangladesh. Over 90 percent of the borrowers are women who, before borrowing, establish groups of five willing to cosign loans for each other. These mutual, morally binding group guarantees take the place of collateral. Once the group is established, two of the five are allowed to apply for a loan. Depending on the repayment success established by these first two loan recipients, the next two borrowers can apply. Subsequently the fifth can also. Individual borrowers identify their own viable income-generating activities. The loans are authorized by "bicycle bankers" (someone who brings banking services to the poor by bicycle, rather than operating out of a building), who also maintain records. Repayment stretches over fifty weeks. A small percentage of the group's loans are credited to a group fund, earning interest and serving as insurance in cases of emergency default. All five members must also save a very tiny sum each week.

During more than thirteen years of operation, Grameen Bank loans enabled the poor to enter remunerative occupations, and to repay their debts at an astonishing 97 percent. Average household income of members is 25 to 50 percent higher than comparable non-Grameen Bank users. In a country where 56 percent of non-Grameen Bank users fall below the poverty line, only 20 percent of those who use the bank are still below poverty. The landless have benefited most.

The International Fund for Agricultural Development and other NGOs have adapted the Grameen Bank approach of replacing collateral with group guarantees, utilizing large numbers of "bicycle bankers" to supervise and support small-scale entrepreneurial loans made available to women in at least six other countries.

3. In addition to the case of Taslima Nasrin, currently in exile in Stockholm (Mary Ann Weaver, 1994: 48), the profiles in Mahnaz Afkhami (1994) provide case studies of women from Malawi, Iran, Afghanistan, Argentina, Chile, and other countries whose activities on behalf of women's rights as human rights has earned them the enmity of their own governments and forced them to leave their own countries.

13. Resistance and Prevention: Reconsidering Feminist Antiviolence Rhetoric

1. The particular texts I am looking at are as follows: "Rape: The All-American Crime" (Griffin, 1971); *Against Our Will: Men, Women, and Rape* (Brownmiller, 1975); *The Politics of Rape: The Victim's Perspective* (Russell, 1975); *Rape: The Price of Coercive Sexuality* (Clark and Lewis, 1977); *Stopping Rape: Successful Survival Strategies* (Bart and O'Brien, 1985); *No Safe Place: Violence against Women and Children* (Guberman and Wolfe, 1985); "Rape" (Toronto Rape Crisis Centre, 1985); *Rape: The Politics of Consciousness* (Griffin, 1986 [originally published in 1979]); "I Want a Twenty-four-hour Truce During Which There is No Rape" (Dworkin, 1988c [originally published in 1983]); "Violence Against Women: It Breaks the Heart, Also the Bones" (Dworkin, 1988d [originally published in 1984]).

I am aware that there are a number of other texts that belong alongside the ones I have chosen. I have selected those texts and authors whose names resounded in the halls of the small-town Ontario grassroots rape crisis center where I worked between 1984 and 1989. The one exception to this criterion of choice is Bart and O'Brien's *Stopping Rape*, the only text among those examined which is primarily about resistance and prevention.

2. Of the texts reviewed, Brownmiller's chiefly historical analysis most often tends toward an extreme "grand narrative."

3. This has been repeatedly demonstrated in the assault prevention course that I teach.

4. Some authors present these sections as "conclusions," but the term "appendix" is more appropriately descriptive of their supplementary nature. In Diana Russell's and Susan Griffin's works these sections do appear as actual appendices.

5. Good and empowering self-defense teaches a wide array of physical and verbal techniques that can be used in different ways by women (and children) of very differing strengths and abilities. Size, shape, strength, and ability may condition which strategies are most effective and useful for a particular woman, but almost all women are capable of resisting violence in one way or another. The self-defense course that I teach grew out of the Child Assault Prevention Project (Cooper, 1991), an effective, empowering program that provides children skills and strategies to resist and prevent violence and abuse, and has been adapted to provide prevention training for both the elderly and for women with differing abilities.

6. To the best of my knowledge, no studies have conclusively proven that increased legal sanctions significantly deter sexual violence.

Bibliography

Abdalla, Raqiya H. D. (1982). *Sisters In Affliction: Circumcision and Infibulation of Women in Africa*. London: Zed Books.

Abrams, Kathryn. (1989). "Gender Discrimination and the Transformation of Workplace Norms." *Vanderbilt Law Review* 42 (May): 1183–1248.

Adams, Rhonda, et al. (1992–93). "Rape Law—Lack of Affirmative Action and Freely Given Permission—New Jersey Supreme Court Holds that Lack of Consent Constitutes 'Physical Force.'" *Harvard Law Review* 106(4): 969–74.

Addelson, Kathryn Pyne. (1993). "Knower/Doers and Their Moral Problems." In *Feminist Epistemologies*. Linda Alcoff and Elizabeth Potter, eds. New York: Routledge.

———. (1983). "The Man of Professional Wisdom." In *Discovering Reality: Feminist Perspectives in Epistemology, Metaphysics, Methodology, and Philosophy of Science*. S. Harding and M. Hintikka, eds. Dordrecht: D. Reidel.

Addelson, Kathryn Pyne, and Elizabeth Potter. (1991). "Making Knowledge." In *(En)gendering Knowledge: Feminists in Academe*. Joan Hartman and Ellen Messer-Davidow, eds. Knoxville: University of Tennessee Press.

Afkhami, Mahnaz. (1994). *Women in Exile*. Charlottesville: University Press of Virginia.

A'Haleem, Asma M. (1992). "Claiming Our Bodies and Our Rights: Exploring Female Circumcision as an Act of Violence." In *Freedom from Violence*. Margaret Schuler, ed. New York: OEF International. (Available from United Nations/UNIFEM)

Aidoo, Ama Ata. (1993). *Changes, A Love Story*. New York: Feminist Press at CUNY.

Alcoff, Linda. (1996). "Philosophy and Racial Identity." *Radical Philosophy* 75 (January/February): 5–14.

Alcoff, Linda, and Laura Gray. (1993). "Survivor Discourse: Transgression or Recuperation?" *Signs* 18(2): 260–90.

Alcoff, Linda, and Elizabeth Potter, eds. (1993). *Feminist Epistemologies*. New York: Routledge.

Allard, Sharon Angella. (1991). "Rethinking the Battered Woman Syndrome: A Black Feminist Perspective." *UCLA Women's Law Journal* 1(1): 191–208.

Allen, Jeffner. (1986). *Lesbian Philosophy: Explorations.* Palo Alto, Calif.: Institute of Lesbian Studies.

Altekar, A. S. (1973). *The Position of Women in Hindu Civilization: From Prehistoric Times to the Present Day.* Delhi: Motilal Banarsidass.

American Association of University Women Educational Foundation. (1992). *How Schools Shortchange Girls: The AAUW Report.* New York: Marlowe.

American Psychiatric Association. (1987). *Diagnostic and Statistical Manual of Mental Disorders.* 3d ed., rev. Washington: American Psychiatric Press.

American Psychological Association. (1987). "If Sex Enters into the Psychotherapy Relationship." Washington: American Psychological Association.

Andersen, Erich D., and Anne Read-Andersen. (1992). "Constitutional Dimensions of the Battered Woman Syndrome." *Ohio State Law Journal* 53(2): 366.

Anzovin, Steven, ed. (1986). *Terrorism.* New York: H. W. Wilson.

Arthur, John A. (1992). "Social Change and Crime Rates in Puerto Rico." *International Journal of Offender Therapy and Comparative Criminology.* 36(2): 103–119.

——. (1991). "Development and Crime in Africa: A Test of Modernization Theory." *Journal of Criminal Justice.* 19(6): 499–513.

Austin, J. L. (1965). *How to Do Things with Words.* New York: Oxford University Press.

Baier, Annette. (1994). "Sustaining Trust," "Trust and Antitrust," "Trust and its Vulnerabilities," "Trusting People," and "Unsafe Loves." In *Moral Prejudices: Essays on Ethics.* Cambridge, Mass.: Harvard University Press.

——. (1989). "Trusting Ex-intimates." In *Person To Person.* George Graham and Hugh Lafollette, eds. Philadelphia: Temple University Press.

Baker, Brenda. (1988). "Consent, Assault, and Sexual Assault." In *Legal Theory Meets Legal Practice.* A. Bayefsky, ed. Edmonton: Academic Printers & Publishing.

Baker, Robert, and Frederick Elliston, eds. (1994). *Philosophy and Sex.* 2d ed. Buffalo, N.Y.: Prometheus.

Bannerji, Himani. (1995). "In the Matter of 'X': Building 'Race' into Sexual Harassment" and "RE: Turning the Gaze." In *Thinking Through: Essays on Feminism, Marxism, and Anti-racism.* Toronto: Women's Press.

Bannister, Shelley A. (1993). "Battered Women Who Kill Their Abusers: Their Courtroom Battles." In *It's A Crime: Women and Justice.* Roslyn Muraskin and Ted Alleman, eds. Englewood Cliffs, N.J.: Regents/Prentice Hall.

Barash, D. (1979). *The Whisperings Within.* New York: Harper and Row.

Bard, Morton, and Dawn Sangrey. (1986). *The Crime Victim's Book.* New York: Brunner/Masel.

Barnes, Jonathan, ed. (1984). *The Complete Works of Aristotle.* Vol. 2. Princeton: Princeton University Press.

Bar On, Bat-Ami. (1993). "Marginality and Epistemic Privilege." In *Feminist Epistemologies.* Linda Alcoff and Elizabeth Potter, eds. New York: Routledge.

Barry, Kathleen. (1979). *Female Sexual Slavery.* Englewood Cliffs, N.J.: Prentice Hall.

Bart, Pauline B., and Patricia H. O'Brien. (1984). *Stopping Rape: Successful Survival Strategies.* New York: Pergamon Press.

Bartky, Sandra. (1990). *Femininity and Domination.* New York: Routledge.

Beauchamp, Tom, and Lawrence B. McCullough. (1984). *Medical Ethics: The Moral Responsibilities of Physicians.* Englewood Cliffs, N.J.: Prentice Hall.

Beauchamp, Tom, and LeRoy Walters, eds. (1989). *Contemporary Issues in Bioethics.* 3d ed. Belmont, Calif.: Wadsworth.

Beauvoir, Simone de. (1952). *The Second Sex.* Trans. H. M. S. Parshley. New York: Knopf.

Bell, Linda A. (1993). *Rethinking Ethics in the Midst of Violence: A Feminist Approach to Freedom.* Lanham, Md.: Rowman & Littlefield.

Bell, Shannon. (1994). *Reading, Writing, and Rewriting the Prostitute Body.* Bloomington: Indiana University Press.

Bem, Sandra Lipsitz. (1993). *The Lenses of Gender: Transforming the Debate on Sexual Inequality.* New Haven: Yale University Press.

Benedict, Helen. (1985). *Recovery: How to Survive Sexual Assault—for Women, Men, Teenagers, Their Friends and Families.* Garden City, N.Y.: Doubleday.

Bennett, M. B. (1987). "Afro-American Women, Poverty, and Mental Health: A Social Essay." *Women and Health* 12(3–4): 213–18.

Bernstein, Barbara, and Robert Kane. (1981). "Physicians' Attitudes toward Female Patients." *Medical Care* 19(6): 600–608.

Betz, Joseph. (1977)."Violence: Garver's Definition and a Deweyan Correction." *Ethics* 87 (4): 339–51.

Birke, Lynda. (1986). *Women, Feminism and Biology: The Feminist Challenge.* New York: Metheun.

Bleier, Ruth. (1984). *Science and Gender: A Critique of Biology and Its Theories on Women.* New York: Pergamon Press.

Blodgett-Ford, Sayoko. (1993). "Do Battered Women Have a Right to Bear Arms?" *Yale Law and Policy Review* 11: 509–60.

Blum, L., M. Homiak, J. Housman, and N. Scheman. (1976). "Altruism and Women's Oppression." In *Women and Philosophy: Toward a Theory of Liberation.* C. C. Gould and M. W. Wartofsky, eds. New York: Putnam.

Bochnak, Elizabeth, ed. (1981). *Women's Self-defense Cases: Theory and Practice.* Charlottesville, Va.: Michie.

Bok, Sissela. (1978). *Lying: Moral Choice in Public and Private Life.* New York: Pantheon.

Boldt, Richard C. (1992). "The Construction of Responsibility in the Criminal Law." *University of Pennsylvania Law Review* 140: 2245–2332.

Bordo, Susan R. (1990). "Feminism, Postmodernism, and Gender-scepticism." In *Feminism/Postmodernism.* Linda J. Nicholson, ed. New York: Routledge.

——. (1988). "Anorexia Nervosa: Psychopathology as the Crystallization of Culture." In *Feminism and Foucault: Reflections on Resistance.* I. Diamond and L. Quinby, eds. Boston: Northeastern University Press.

Boserup, Ester. (1970). *Woman's Role in Economic Development.* London: Allen and Unwin.

Boston Women's Health Book Collective. (1992). *The New Our Bodies, Ourselves.* New York: Simon & Schuster.

Bouhoutsos, Jacqueline C. (1985), "Therapist-client Sexual Involvement: A Challenge for Mental Health Professionals and Educators." *American Journal of Orthopsychiatry* 55(2): 177–82.

Bouhoutsos, J., J. C. Holroyd, H. Lerman, et al. (1983). "Sexual Intimacy between Psychotherapists and Patients." *Professional Psychologist: Research and Practice* 14(2): 185–96.
Boyle, Christine. (1984). *Sexual Assault*. Toronto: Carswell.
Braidotti, Rosi. (1994). *Nomadic Subjects: Embodiment and Sexual Difference in Contemporary Feminist Theory*. New York: Columbia University Press.
———. (1993). "Embodiment, Sexual Difference, and the Nomadic Subject." *Hypatia* 8(1): 1–13.
Brett, Nathan. (1994). "Sexual Assault and the Concept of Consent." Unpublished paper presented at the Annual Congress of the Canadian Philosophical Association, Calgary.
———. (1987). "Commentary." In *Legal Theory Meets Legal Practice*. Anne Bayefsky, ed. Edmonton: Academic Printers and Publishing.
———. (1982). "Consent and Sexual Assault." Unpublished paper presented at the Annual Meeting of the Canadian Section of the International Association for Philosophy of Law and Social Philosophy, Ottawa.
Brison, Susan J. (1995). "On the Personal as Philosophical." *American Philosophical Association Newsletter on Feminism and Philosophy* 95(1): 37–40.
Bronitt, Simon. (1994). "The Direction of Rape Law in Australia: Toward a Positive Consent Standard." *Criminal Law Journal* 18: 249–53.
Brown, L. S. (1988). "Harmful Effects of Post-termination Sexual and Romantic Relationships between Therapists and Their Former Clients." *Psychotherapy* 25(2): 249–55.
Brownmiller, Susan. (1994). "Making Female Bodies the Battlefield." In *Mass Rape: The War against Women in Bosnia-Herzegovina*. Alexandra Stiglmayer, ed. Lincoln: University of Nebraska Press.
———. (1975). *Against Our Will: Men, Women and Rape*. New York: Simon and Schuster.
Bryant, Alan W. (1989). "The Issue of Consent in the Crime of Sexual Assault." *The Canadian Bar Review* 68 (March): 94–154.
Burgess, Ann W., and Carol R. Hartman, eds. (1986). *Sexual Exploitation of Patients by Health Professionals*. New York: Praeger.
Burkhart, Barry, and Mary Ellen Fromuth. (1991). "Individual Psychological and Social Psychological Understandings of Sexual Coercion." In *Sexual Coercion: A Sourcebook on Its Nature, Causes, and Prevention*. E. Grauerholz and M. Koralewski, eds. Lexington, Mass.: Lexington Books.
Burleigh, Nina. (1990). "Swaying in the Wind." *Chicago Tribune*, March 18.
Butler, Judith. (1990). *Gender Trouble: Feminism and the Subversion of Identity*. New York: Routledge.
———. (1989). "Sexual Ideology and Phenomenological Description: A Feminist Critique of Merleau-Ponty's *Phenomenology of Perception*." In *The Thinking Muse: Feminism and Modern French Philosophy*. Jeffner Allen and Iris Marion Young, eds. Bloomington: Indiana University Press.
———. (1987). *Subjects of Desire: Hegelian Reflections in Twentieth Century France*. New York: Columbia University Press.
Calamari, John D., and Joseph M. Perillo. (1977). *The Law of Contracts*. 2d ed. St. Paul: West.

Caldwell, J. C. (1980). "The Wealth Flows Theory of Fertility Decline." In *Determinants of Fertility Trends: Theories Re-examined*. C. Hohn & R. Mackensen, eds. Liege: Ordina.

——. (1978). "A Theory of Fertility: From High Plateau to Destabilization." *Population and Development Review* 4(4): 553–77.

——. (1976). "Toward a Restatement of Demographic Transition Theory." *Population Development Review* 2(3–4): 321–66.

Caplan, Paula. (1995). *They Say You're Crazy! How the World's Most Powerful Psychiatrists Decide Who's Normal*. Reading, Mass.: Addison-Wesley.

——. (1993). *The Myth of Women's Masochism*. 2d ed. Toronto: University of Toronto Press.

Carr, M., and G. E. Robinson. (1990). "Fatal Attraction: The Ethical and Clinical Dilemma of Patient-therapist Sex." *Canadian Journal of Psychiatry* 35(2): 122–27.

Carr, M., G. Robinson, D. Stewart, and D. Kussin. (1991). "A Survey of Canadian Psychiatric Residents Regarding Resident-educator Sexual Contact." *American Journal of Psychiatry* 148(2): 216–20.

Carter, Sunny. (1994). "A Most Useful Tool." In *Living with Contradictions: Controversies in Feminist Social Ethics*. Alison M. Jaggar, ed. Boulder, Colo.: Westview.

Cartledge, Sue. (1983). "Duty and Desire: Creating a Feminist Morality." In *Sex and Love: New Thoughts on Old Contradictions*. S. Cartledge and J. Ryan, eds. London: Women's Press.

Cartledge, Sue, and Joanna Ryan, eds. (1983). *Sex and Love: New Thoughts on Old Contradictions*. London: Women's Press.

Cartwright, Peter S. (1988). "Sexual Violence." In *Novak's Textbook of Gynecology*. 11th ed. Howard W. Jones, III, Anne Colston Wentz, Lonnie S. Burnett, and Edmund R. Novak, eds. Baltimore: Williams & Wilkins.

Chang, D. (1976). *Criminology: A Cross Cultural Perspective*. Durham: North Carolina Academic Press.

Childress, James. (1982). *Who Should Decide: Paternalism in Health Care*. New York: Oxford University Press.

Chomsky, Noam. (1965). *Aspects of the Theory of Syntax*. Cambridge, Mass: MIT Press.

Christman, John. (1988). "Constructing the Inner Citadel: Recent Work on the Concept of Autonomy." *Ethics* 99(1): 109–24.

Church, Jennifer. (1997). "Ownership and the Body." In *Feminists Rethink the Self*. Diana Tietjens Meyers, ed. Boulder, Colo.: Westview.

Clark, Lorenne, and Debra Lewis, eds. (1977). *Rape: The Price of Coercive Sexuality*. Toronto: Women's Educational Press.

Clinard, M., and D. Abbott. (1973). *Crime in Developing Countries: A Comparative Perspective*. New York: John Wiley.

Code, Lorraine. (1991). *What Can She Know? Feminist Theory and the Construction of Knowledge*. Ithaca: Cornell University Press.

College of Physicians and Surgeons of Ontario. (1992). "CPSO Sexual Abuse Recommendations." Toronto: The College of Physicians and Surgeons of Ontario.

Collins, Patricia Hill. (1990). *Black Feminist Thought: Knowledge, Consciousness, and the Politics of Empowerment*. Boston: Unwin Hyman.

Connell, R. W. (1987). "Sexual Politics." In *Gender and Power: Society, the Person, and Sexual Politics*. Stanford, Calif.: Stanford University Press.

Conrad, Peter. (1992). "Medicalization and Social Control." *Annual Reviews in Sociology* 18: 209–32.

Conrad, Peter, and Joseph W. Schneider. (1980). "Looking at Levels of Medicalization: A Comment on Strong's Critique of the Thesis of Medical Imperialism." *Social Sciences and Medicine* 14 A(1): 75–79.

Cooper, Sally. (1991). *Strategies for Free Children: Child Abuse Prevention for Elementary School Children*. Columbus, Oh.: National Assault Prevention Center.

Corea, Gena. (1985). *The Hidden Malpractice: How American Medicine Mistreats Women*. New York: Harper and Row.

Coughlin, Anne M. (1994). "Excusing Women." *California Law Review* 82(1): 1–93.

Creach, Donald L. (1982). "Partially Determined Imperfect Self-Defense: The Battered Wife Kills and Tells Why." *Stanford Law Review* 34 (February): 615–38.

Creedence Clearwater Revival. (1972). "Someday Never Comes." *Mardi Gras* (recording).

Crocker, Phyllis. (1985). "The Meaning of Equality for Battered Women Who Kill Men in Self-defense." *Harvard Women's Law Journal* 8 (Spring): 121–53.

Culver, Charles, and Bernard Gert. (1982). "Valid Consent." In *Philosophy in Medicine: Conceptual and Ethical Problems in Medicine and Psychiatry*. New York: Oxford University Press.

Cutler, Jeffrey M. (1989). "Criminal Law—Battered Woman Syndrome: The Killing of a Passive Victim—A Perfect Defense or a Perfect Crime?—State v. Norman." *Campbell Law Review* 11 (Spring): 263–78.

Dalmiya, Vrinda, and Linda Alcoff. (1993). "Are 'Old Wives' Tales' Justified?" In *Feminist Epistemologies*. Linda Alcoff and Elizabeth Potter, eds. New York: Routledge.

Daly, Mary. (1978). *Gyn/Ecology: The Metaethics of Radical Feminism*. Boston: Beacon Press.

Dandekar, Natalie. (forthcoming). "International Justice—A Feminist Issue." In *A Companion to Feminist Philosophy*. Alison Jaggar and Iris Marion Young, eds. Oxford: Basil Blackwell.

Danforth, David N., and James R. Scott, eds. (1986). *Obstetrics and Gynecology*. 5th ed. Philadelphia: Lippincott.

Daniels, Norman. (1985). *Just Health Care*. Cambridge: Cambridge University Press.

Davis, Angela. (1990). *Women, Culture, and Politics*. New York: Vintage Books.

———. (1981). *Women, Race, and Class*. New York: Vintage Books.

Davis, Kathy. (1988). "Paternalism under the Microscope." In *Gender and Discourse: The Power of Talk*. Alexandra Todd and Sue Fisher, eds. Norwood, N.J.: Ablex.

Day, Dian. (1990). "Survey of 1600 Adolescent Girls in Nova Scotia." Halifax, N.S.: Nova Scotia Advisory Council on the Status of Women.

DeBruin, Debra A. (1994a). "Justice and the Inclusion of Women in Clinical Studies: A Conceptual Framework." In *Women and Health Research: Ethical and Legal Issues of Including Women in Clinical Studies*. Vol. 2. A. Mastroianni, R. Faden, and D. Federman, eds. Washington: National Academy Press.

——. (1994b). "Justice and the Inclusion of Women in Health Research: An Argument for Further Reform." *Kennedy Institute of Ethics Journal* 4(2): 117–46.

De Grazia, Edward. (1992). *Girls Lean Back Everywhere: The Law of Obscenity and the Assault on Genius.* London: Constable.

Delacoste, Frederique, and Priscilla Alexander, eds. (1987). *Sex Work: Writings by Women in the Sex Industry.* Pittsburgh: Cleis Press.

De Sousa, Ronald. (1987). *The Rationality of Emotion.* Cambridge, Mass.: MIT Press.

Dewey, John. (1960). *Theory of the Moral Life.* New York: Holt, Rinehart & Winston.

Diamond, I., and L. Quinby, eds. (1988). *Feminism and Foucault: Reflections on Resistance.* Boston: Northeastern University Press.

Dickens, Bernard M. (1990). "Legal Analysis: Sexual Impropriety in Psychotherapy." Presented to the College of Physicians and Surgeons of Ontario. Commissioned through the Joint Centre for Bioethics, University of Toronto.

Dickson, Anne. (1985). *The Mirror Within: A New Look at Sexuality.* London: Quartet Books.

Diprose, Rosalyn. (1995). "The Body Biomedical Ethics Forgets." In *Troubled Bodies: Critical Perspectives on Postmodernism, Medical Ethics, and the Body.* Paul A. Komesaroff, ed. Durham: Duke University Press.

Dowd, Michael. (1992). "Dispelling the Myths about the 'Battered Woman's Defense': Towards a New Understanding." *Fordham Urban Law Journal* 19 (Spring): 567–83.

Downs, Laura Lee, and Joan W. Scott. (1993). "If 'Woman' Is Just an Empty Category, Then Why Am I Afraid to Walk Alone at Night? Identity Politics Meets the Postmodern Subject." *Comparative Studies in Society and History* 35(2): 414–37.

Dreifus, Claudia, ed. (1977). *Seizing Our Bodies: The Politics of Women's Health.* New York: Vintage Books.

Dripps, Donald. (1992). "Beyond Rape: An Essay on the Difference between the Presence of Force and the Absence of Consent." *Columbia Law Review* 92 (November): 1780–1809.

Dula, Annette, and Sara Goering, eds. (1994). *It Just Ain't Fair: The Ethics of Health Care for African Americans.* Westport, Conn.: Praeger.

Dworkin, Andrea. (1988a). *Pornography and Civil Rights.* Recording. Iowa State University.

——. (1988b). *Letters from a War Zone: Writings 1976–1987.* New York: E. P. Dutton. London: Secker and Warburg.

Džombic, S. (1992). "Go and Give Birth to Chetniks." *Vercernjy List*, November 25.

Easlea, Brian. (1981). *Science and Sexual Oppression: Patriarchy's Confrontation with Woman and Nature.* London: Weidenfeld and Nicolson.

Edelstein, Ludwig. (1989). "The Hippocratic Oath: Text, Translation, and Interpretation." In *Cross-Cultural Perspectives in Medical Ethics: Readings.* R. Veatch. ed. Boston: Jones and Bartlett.

Editorial Board. (1952). "Forcible and Statutory Rape: An Exploration of the Operation and Objectives of the Consent Standard." *Yale Law Journal* 62(1): 55–83.

Ehrenreich, Barbara, and John Ehrenreich. (1970). *The American Health Empire: Power, Profits, and Politics*. New York: Random House.

Eichler, Margrit. (1988). *Non-sexist Research Methods: A Practical Guide*. Boston: Allen and Unwin.

Eichler, Margrit, Anna Lisa Reisman, and Elaine Borins. (1992). "Gender Bias in Medical Research." *Women and Therapy* 12(4): 61–70.

El Dareer, Asma. (1982). *Woman, Why Do You Weep?* London: Zed Press.

Enloe, Cynthia. (1990). *Bananas, Beaches, and Bases*. Berkeley: University of California Press.

Estrich, Susan. (1987). *Real Rape*. Cambridge, Mass: Harvard University Press.

———. (1986). "Rape." *Yale Law Journal* 95 (May): 1087–1184.

Faden, Ruth, and Tom Beauchamp. (1986). *A History and Theory of Informed Consent*. New York: Oxford University Press.

Fausto-Sterling, Anne. (1992). *Myths of Gender: Biological Theories about Women and Men*. 2d ed. New York: Basic Books.

Fee, Elizabeth, ed. (1983). *Women and Health: The Politics of Sex in Medicine*. Farmingdale, N.Y.: Baywood.

Fee, Elizabeth, and Nancy Krieger, eds. (1994). *Women's Health, Politics, and Power: Essays on Sex/Gender, Medicine, and Public Health*. Amityville, N.Y.: Baywood.

Fidell, L. (1980). "Sex Role Stereotypes and the American Physician." *Psychology of Women Quarterly* 4(3): 313–30.

Fischer, Karla, Neil Vidmar, and Rene Ellis. (1993). "The Culture of Battering and the Role of Mediation in Domestic Violence Cases." *SMU Law Review* 46 (Summer): 2117–74.

Fisher, Helen. (1992). *The Anatomy of Love: The Natural History of Monogamy, Adultery, and Divorce*. New York: Norton.

———. (1991). "Monogamy, Adultery, and Divorce in Cross-species Perspective." In *Man and Beast Revisited*. Michael Robinson and Lionel Tiger, eds. Washington: Smithsonian Institution Press.

Foucault, Michel. (1980a). *The History of Sexuality Volume I: An Introduction*. Trans. Robert Hurley. New York: Vintage Books.

———. (1980b). *Power/Knowledge: Selected Interviews and Other Writings, 1972–1977*. C. Gordon, ed. Brighton: Harvester Press.

———. (1975a). *Discipline and Punish: The Birth of the Prison*. Trans. A. Sheridan. Harmondsworth: Penguin.

———. (1975b). *The Birth of the Clinic*. Trans. A. M. Sheridan Smith. New York: Vintage Books.

Fox, Renée C. (1977). "The Medicalization and Demedicalization of American Society." *Daedalus* 106(1): 9–22.

Frankenberg, Ruth. (1993). *White Women, Race Matters: The Social Construction of Whiteness*. Minneapolis: University of Minnesota Press.

French, Stanley G. (1996). "The Causes of Violence against Women." *Zonta International Summit on Violence against Women*. Chicago: Zonta International.

———. (1994). "Interpersonal Violence: Power Relationships and Their Effects on Health." In *Interpersonal Violence, Health, and Gender Politics*. S. G. French, ed. 2d ed. Dubuque, Iowa: Brown & Benchmark.

———. (1990). "Aspects moraux et cécité morale." In *La Formation fondamentale.* Christiane Gohier, ed. Montreal: Logiques.

———, ed. (1993). *Interpersonal Violence, Health, and Gender Politics.* Dubuque, Iowa: Brown & Benchmark.

Freud, Sigmund. (1924). "The Economic Problems of Masochism." In *Collected Papers 2.* Trans. J. Rivière. New York: Basic Books.

Friedman, Robert I. (1996). "India's Shame: Sexual Slavery and Political Corruption are Leading to an AIDS Catastrophe." *The Nation,* April 8.

Frye, Marilyn. (1984). "Critique." In *Philosophy and Sex.* 2d ed. Robert Baker and Frederick Elliston, eds. Buffalo, N.Y.: Prometheus Books.

———. (1975). "Male Chauvinism: A Conceptual Analysis." In *Philosophy and Sex.* Robert Baker and Frederick Elliston, eds. Buffalo, N.Y.: Prometheus Books.

Gabbard, Glen O., ed. (1989). *Sexual Exploitation in Professional Relationships.* Washington: American Psychiatric Press.

Gallagher, Winifred. (1988). "Sex and Hormones." *The Atlantic Monthly,* March, 77–82.

Gambetta, Diego, ed. (1988). *Trust: Making and Breaking Cooperative Relations.* New York: Basil Blackwell.

Gans, J., and D. Blyth. (1990). *America's Adolescents: How Healthy Are They?* Chicago: American Medical Association.

Garver, Newton. (1977). "What Violence Is." In *Philosophy for a New Generation.* A. K. Bierman and James A. Gould, eds. New York: Macmillan.

Gattin, Katja. (1992). "Where Have All the Feminists Gone?" Unpublished paper on file with the *Harvard Women's Law Journal.*

Gauthier, David. (1983). "Unequal Need: A Problem of Equity in Access to Health Care." In *Securing Access to Health Care: The Ethics Implications of Differences in the Availability of Health Services.* Vol. 2. Washington: President's Commission for the Study of Ethical Problems in Medicine and Biomedical and Behavioral Research.

Gelles, Richard J., and Murray A. Straus. (1978). "Determinants of Violence in the Family: Toward a Theoretical Integration." In *Contemporary Theories about the Family.* W. R. Burr et al., eds. New York: Free Press.

Genet, Jean. (1964). *The Thief's Journal.* Trans. Bernard Frechtman. New York: Grove Press.

Gilligan, Carol. (1982). *In a Different Voice: Psychological Theory and Women's Development.* Cambridge, Mass.: Harvard University Press.

———. (1977). "In a Different Voice: Women's Conceptions of Self and Morality." *Harvard Educational Review* 47(4): 481–517.

Giobbe, Evelina. (1994). "Confronting the Liberal Lies about Prostitution." In *Living with Contradictions: Controversies in Feminist Social Ethics.* Alison M. Jaggar, ed. Boulder, Colo.: Westview.

Goldberg, Steven. (1973). *The Inevitability of Patriarchy.* New York: William Morrow.

Goleman, Daniel. (1995). "Her Fantasies Link Sex; His Are More Action Oriented." *Chicago Tribune Womanews,* June 25, 8.

Goleman, Daniel, and Joel Gurin, eds. (1993). *Mind/Body Medicine.* Yonkers, N.Y.: Consumer Reports.

Gordon, Margaret T., and Stephanie Riger. (1991). *The Female Fear: The Social Cost of Rape*. Urbana: University of Illinois Press.

Govier, Trudy. (1993). "Self-Trust, Autonomy, and Self-Esteem." *Hypatia* 8(1): 99–120.

———. (1992). "Trust, Distrust, and Feminist Theory." *Hypatia* 7(1): 16–33.

Grant, Toni. (1988). "Sweet Surrender, Body and Soul." In *Being a Woman: Fulfilling Your Femininity and Finding Love*. New York: Random House.

Grauerholz, Elizabeth, and Mary A. Koralewski, eds. (1991). *Sexual Coercion: A Sourcebook on Its Nature, Causes, and Prevention*. Lexington, Mass.: Lexington Books.

Griffin, Susan. (1986). *Rape: The Politics of Consciousness*. San Francisco: Harper and Row.

———. (1971). "Rape: The All-American Crime." *Ramparts* 10(3): 26–35.

Grosz, Elizabeth. (1995a). "Animal Sex: Death and Desire." In *Sexy Bodies: The Strange Carnalities of Feminism*. Elizabeth Grosz and Elspeth Probyn, eds. London: Routledge.

———. (1995b). "Refiguring Lesbian Desire." In *Space, Time, and Perversion*. London: Routledge.

Grundy, K. W., and M. A. Weinstein. (1974). *The Ideologies of Violence*. Columbus, Ohio: Merrill.

Guberman, Connie, and Margie Wolfe. (1985). "Introduction." In *No Safe Place: Violence against Women and Children*. Connie Guberman and Margie Wolfe, eds. Toronto: Women's Press.

Gutman, Roy. (1993). *A Witness to Genocide: The 1993 Pulitzer Prize–Winning Dispatches on the "Ethnic Cleansing" of Bosnia*. New York: Lisa Drew Books.

Haidt, J., S. H. Koller, and M. G. Dias. (1993). "Affect, Culture, and Morality, or Is It Wrong to Eat Your Dog?" *Journal of Personality and Social Psychology* 65(4): 613–28.

Hanson, David W. (1993). "Battered Women: Society's Obligation to the Abused." *Akron Law Review* 27 (Summer): 19–56.

Haraway, Donna. (1991). *Simians, Cyborgs, and Women: The Reinvention of the Future*. New York: Routledge.

———. (1989). *Primate Visions: Gender, Race, and Nature in the World of Modern Science*. New York: Routledge.

Harding, Sandra. (1991). "Thinking from the Perspective of Lesbian Lives." In *Whose Science? Whose Knowledge? Thinking from Women's Lives*. Ithaca: Cornell University Press.

———, ed. (1993). *The "Racial" Economy of Science: Toward a Democratic Future*. Bloomington: University of Indiana Press.

Hare, R. M. (1981). *Moral Thinking: Its Levels, Method, and Point*. New York: Oxford University Press.

Harris, Lynn. (1996). "Dating Violence: The Problem Teenage Girls Are Afraid to Talk About." *Parade Magazine, Milwaukee Journal Sentinel*, September 22, 4–7.

Harrison, Ross. (1986). "Rape: A Case Study in Political Philosophy." In *Rape: An Historical and Cultural Enquiry*. Sylvana Tomaselli and Roy Porter, eds. New York: Basil Blackwell.

Hart, H. L. A. (1968). *Punishment and Responsibility*. Oxford: Clarendon Press.

Hart, Mechthilde U. (1992). *Working and Educating for Life: Feminist and International Perspectives on Adult Education.* New York: Routledge.

Harvard Law Review. (1993). "Developments in the Law: Legal Responses to Domestic Violence." Vol. 106 (May): 1498–1620.

Hatfield, E. (1983). "What Do Women and Men Want from Love and Sex." In *Changing Boundaries: Gender Roles and Sexual Behavior.* E. R. Allegier and N. B. McCormick, eds. Palo Alto, Calif.: Mayfield.

Heinrich, Larry, Hon. Michael S. Jordan, and Marijane Hemza-Placek. (1994). "Perspectives on the Battered Woman Syndrome: It's Time to Modify Illinois Law." *Illinois Bar Journal* 82 (February): 84–85.

Heise, Lori L. (1994). "Gender-based Abuse: The Global Epidemic." In *Reframing Women's Health: Multidisciplinary Research and Practice.* Alice J. Dan, ed. Thousand Oaks, Calif.: Sage.

Held, Virginia. (1987). "Non-contractual Society: A Feminist View." In *Science, Morality, and Feminist Theory.* M. Hanen and K. Nielsen, eds. Calgary: University of Calgary Press.

Heldke, Lisa M., and Stephen H. Kellert. (1995). "Objectivity as Responsibility." *Metaphilosophy* 26(4): 360–78.

Henderson, Lynne. (1992). "Rape and Responsibility." *Law and Philosophy* 11: 127–78.

———. (1988). "What Makes Rape a Crime?" *Berkeley Women's Law Journal* 3: 193–229.

Herman, Judith Lewis. (1992). *Trauma and Recovery.* New York: Basic Books.

Herman, Robin. (1992). "What Doctors Don't Know about Women." *Washington Post* Health Section. December 8, 10–16.

Hill, Thomas. (1973). "Servility and Self-respect." *The Monist* 57.

Hoagland, Sarah. (1988). *Lesbian Ethics: Toward New Value.* Palo Alto, Calif.: Institute for Lesbian Studies.

Hoff, Joan. (1991). *Law, Gender, and Injustice: A Legal History of U. S. Women.* New York: New York University Press.

hooks, bell. (1994). *Teaching to Transgress: Education As the Practice of Freedom.* New York: Routledge.

———. (1989). *Talking Back: Thinking Feminist, Thinking Black.* Boston: South End Press.

Hosken, Fran. (1982). *The Hosken Report: Genital and Sexual Mutilation of Females.* 3d. ed. Lexington, Mass.: Women's International Network News.

Hotaling, Gerald T., and Murray A. Straus. (1980). "Culture, Social Organization, and Irony in the Study of Family Violence." In *The Social Causes of Husband-wife Violence.* M. A. Straus and Gerald T. Hotaling, eds. Minneapolis: University of Minnesota Press.

Hubbard, Ruth, and Marion Lowe. (1981). *Woman's Nature: Rationalizations of Inequality.* New York: Pergamon Press.

Hunter, Anne E., ed. 1991. *Genes and Gender, I–VI.* New York: Feminist Press.

———, ed. (1991). *Genes and Gender, VI: On Peace, War, and Gender. A Challenge to Genetic Explanations.* New York: Feminist Press.

Husak, Douglas, and George C. Thomas III. (1992). "Date Rape, Social Conventions, and Reasonable Mistakes." *Law and Philosophy* 11: 95–126.

Illich, Ivan. (1977). *Medical Nemesis: The Expropriation of Health*. New York: Bantam Books.

Illingworth, Patricia M. L. (1988). "The Friendship Model of Physician/Patient Relationship and Patient Autonomy." *Bioethics* 2(1): 23–36.

Irvine, Janice. (1990). *Disorders of Desire: Sex and Gender in Modern American Sexology*. Philadelphia: Temple University Press.

Jackson, Margaret. (1987). "'Facts of Life' or the Eroticization of Women's Oppression? Sexology and the Social Construction of Heterosexuality." In *The Cultural Construction of Sexuality*. P. Caplan, ed. New York: Tavistock.

Jacobus, Mary, Evelyn Fox Keller, and Sally Shuttleworth, eds. (1990). *Body/Politics: Women and the Discourses of Science*. New York: Routledge.

Jaggar, Alison M. (1994a). "Prostitution." In *Living with Contradictions: Controversies in Feminist Social Ethics*. Alison M. Jaggar, ed. Boulder, Colo.: Westview.

———. (1994b). *Living with Contradictions: Controversies in Feminist Social Ethics*. Boulder, Colo.: Westview.

———. (1980). "Prostitution." In *The Philosophy of Sex*. Alan Soble, ed. Totowa, N.J.: Rowman & Littlefield.

James, S. A. (1994). "Reconciling Human Rights and Cultural Relativism: The Case of Female Circumcision." *Bioethics* 8(1): 1–26.

Janoff-Bulman, Ronnie. (1992). *Shattered Assumptions: Toward a New Psychology of Trauma*. New York: Free Press.

Jazairy, Idriss, Mohiuddin Alamgir, and Theresa Panuccio. (1992). *The State of World Rural Poverty: An Inquiry into Its Causes and Consequences*. New York: New York University Press.

Jeffcoate, T. (1967). *Principles of Gynaecology*. London: Butterworth.

Jones, Kathleen B. (1988). "On Authority, or, Why Women Are not Entitled to Speak." In *Feminism and Foucault: Reflections on Resistance*. I. Diamond and L. Quinby, eds. Boston: Northeastern University Press.

Jordan, Brigitte. (1983). *Birth in Four Cultures*. Montreal: Eden.

Jordanova, Ludmilla. (1989). *Sexual Visions: Images of Gender in Science and Medicine between the Eighteenth and Twentieth Centuries*. New York: Harvester Wheatsheaf.

Journal of Medicine and Philosophy. (1982). 7(2), special issue: Women and Medicine.

Julty, Sam. (1979). *Men's Bodies, Men's Selves*. New York: Dell Books.

Kant, Immanuel. (1964). *Groundwork on the Metaphysics of Morals*. Scranton, Pa.: HarperCollins.

———. (1956). *Critique of Practical Reason*. Trans. Lewis White Beck. Indianapolis: Bobbs Merrill.

Katz, Jay. (1984). *The Silent World of Doctor and Patient*. New York: Free Press.

———. (1977). "Informed Consent—a Fairy Tale?" *University of Pittsburgh Law Review* 39(2): 137–74.

Kaufman, Michael. (1987). "The Construction of Masculinity and the Triad of Men's Violence." In *Beyond Patriarchy: Essays by Men on Pleasure, Power, and Change*. M. Kaufman, ed. New York: Oxford University Press.

Keeton, W. Page. (1984). *Prosser and Keeton on the Law of Torts*. 5th ed. St. Paul, Minn.: West.

Keller, Evelyn Fox. (1985). *Reflections on Gender and Science*. New Haven: Yale University Press.

Kemper, Theodore. (1990). *Social Structure and Testosterone*. New Brunswick, N.J.: Rutgers University Press.

Kimmel, Michael S., and Michael Messner. (1992). "Introduction." In *Men's Lives*. 2d ed. M. S. Kimmel and M. Messner, eds. New York: Macmillan.

Kimura, Doreen. (1992). "Sex Differences in the Brain." *Scientific American*, 267 (September): 118–25.

Kitzinger, Sheila. (1983). *Woman's Experience of Sex*. New York: Putnam.

Kochan, Deborah. (1989). "Beyond the Battered Woman Syndrome: An Argument for the Development of New Standards and the Incorporation of a Feminine Approach to Ethics." *Hastings Women's Law Journal* 1: 89.

Koenig, Dorean Marguerite. (1994). "Women and Rape in Ethnic Conflict and War." In *Hastings Women's Law Journal* 5(2): 129–41.

Kohlberg, Lawrence (1981). *The Philosophy of Moral Development: Moral Stages and the Idea of Justice*. San Francisco: Harper and Row.

Kolb, Trudy M., and Murray A. Straus. (1974). "Marital Power and Marital Happiness in Relation to Problem-solving Ability." *Journal of Marriage and the Family* 36 (November): 756–66.

Komesaroff, Paul A. (1995a). "Introduction: Postmodern Medical Ethics?" In *Troubled Bodies: Critical Perspectives on Postmodernism, Medical Ethics, and the Body*. Paul A. Komesaroff, ed. Durham: Duke University Press.

——. (1995b). "From Bioethics to Microethics; Ethical Debate and Clinical Medicine." In *Troubled Bodies: Critical Perspectives on Postmodernism, Medical Ethics, and the Body*. Paul A. Komesaroff, ed. Durham: Duke University Press.

Koso-Thomas, Olayinka. (1992). *The Circumcision of Women: A Strategy for Eradication*. London: Zed Books.

Krieger, Nancy, and Elizabeth Fee. (1994). "Man-made Medicine and Women's Health: The BioPolitics of Sex/Gender and Race/Ethnicity." In *Women's Health, Politics, and Power: Essays on Sex/Gender, Medicine, and Public Health*. E. Fee and N. Krieger, eds. Amityville, N.Y.: Baywood.

Krieger, Nancy, Elizabeth Fee, et al. (1993). "Racism, Sexism, and Social Class: Implications for Studies of Health, Disease, and Well-being." *American Journal of Preventive Medicine* 9(2): 82–122.

Krieger, Nancy, Elizabeth Fee, and Mary Bassett. (1986). "The Health of Black Folk: Disease, Class, and Ideology in Science." *Monthly Review* 38 (July–August): 74–85.

La Ganga, Maria L. (1994). "Battered Women Discover Leaving Is No Simple Task." *Los Angeles Times*, July 4.

Larkin, June. (1994). *Sexual Harassment: High School Girls Speak Out*. Toronto: Second Story Press.

Larson, Jane. (1993). "Women Understand So Little, They Call My Good Nature 'Deceit': A Feminist Rethinking of Seduction." *Columbia Law Review* 93 (March): 374–472.

Lawrence, Charles R., III. (1990). "If He Hollers Let Him Go: Regulating Racist Speech on Campus." *Duke Law Journal* 3: 431–83.

Leacock, E. (1978). "Women's Status in Egalitarian Society: Implications for Social Evolution." *Current Anthropology* 33 (February): 247–74.

Lederer, Laura, ed. (1980). *Take Back the Night: Women on Pornography*. New York: Morrow.

Leeder, D. (1989). "Medicine and Paradigms of Embodiment." *Journal of Medicine and Philosophy* 9 (February): 29–43.

Lemoncheck, Linda. (1994). "What's Wrong with Being a Sex Object?" In *Living with Contradictions: Controversies in Feminist Social Ethics*. Alison M. Jaggar, ed. Boulder, Colo.: Westview.

Lengyel, Linda B. (1990). "Survey of State Domestic Violence Legislations." *Legal Reference Services Quarterly* 10(1–2): 59–82.

Levine, Robert J. (1986). *Ethics and Regulation of Clinical Research*. 2d ed. Baltimore: Urban and Schwarzenberg.

Lingis, Alphonso. (1987). "The Libidinal Origin of Meaning and the Value of the I." *enclitic* 1–2(17–18): 80–94.

——. (1985). *Libido*. Albany: State University of New York Press.

Litewka, Jack. (1977). "The Socialized Penis." In *For Men Against Sexism*. J. Snodgrass, ed. Albion, Calif.: Times Change Press.

Lock, Margaret (1994). *Encounters with Aging: Mythologies of Menopause in Japan and North America*. Berkeley: University of California Press.

Longino, Helen, and Ruth Doell. (1983). "Body, Bias, and Behavior: A Comparative Analysis of Reasoning in Two Areas of Biological Science." *Signs* 9(2): 206–27.

Lowell, Robert. (1977). *Selected Poems*. New York: Farrar, Straus and Giroux.

Maart, Rozena. (1993). "Consciousness, Knowledge, and Morality: The Absence of Knowledge of White Consciousness in Contemporary Feminist Theory." In *A Reader in Feminist Ethics*. Debra Shogun, ed. Toronto: Canadian Scholars' Press.

Mabogunje, Akin L. (1981). *The Development Process: A Spatial Perspective*. New York: Holmes and Meier.

MacIntyre, Alasdair. (1982). "Risk, Harm, and Benefit Assessments as Instruments of Moral Evaluation." In *Ethical Issues in Social Science Research*. T. Beauchamp, R. Faden, R. J. Wallace and L. Walters, eds. Baltimore: Johns Hopkins University Press.

Mackey, J. (1979). "The Politics of Adultery." In *The Women Say, The Men Say*. E. B. Shapiro, ed. New York: Dell Books.

MacKinnon, Catharine A. (1993a). *Only Words*. Cambridge: Harvard University Press.

——. (1993b). "Turning Rape into Pornography: Postmodern Genocide." *Ms.*, July–August, 24–30.

——. (1989). *Toward a Feminist Theory of the State*. Cambridge: Harvard University Press.

——. (1987). *Feminism Unmodified: Discourses on Life and Law*. Cambridge: Harvard University Press.

——. (1982). "Feminism, Marxism, Method, and the State: An Agenda for Theory." *Signs* 7(3): 515–44.

——. (1979). *Sexual Harassment of Working Women*. New Haven: Yale University Press.

Madden, Alison M. (1993). "Clemency for Battered Women Who Kill Their Abusers: Finding a Just Forum." *Hastings Women's Law Journal* 4(1): 1–86.

Mamdini, M. (1972). *The Myth of Population Control: Family, Caste, and Class in an Indian Village.* New York: Monthly Review Press.

Marolla, Joseph, and Diana Scully. (1979). "Rape and Psychiatric Vocabularies of Motive." In *Gender and Disordered Behavior.* E. S. Gomberg and V. Franks, eds. New York: Brunner/Mazel.

Martin, Emily. (1987). *The Woman in the Body: A Cultural Analysis of Reproduction.* Boston: Beacon Press.

Marx, Karl. (1972). Preface to the first German edition of *Capital and Selections.* In *Marx/Engels Reader.* Robert C. Tucker, ed. New York: W. W. Norton.

Massumi, Brian, ed. (1993). *The Politics of Everyday Fear.* Minneapolis: University of Minnesota Press.

Mather, Victoria M. (1988). "The Skeleton in the Closet: The Battered Woman Syndrome, Self-Defense and Expert Testimony." *Mercer Law Review* 39 (Winter): 545–89.

Matsuda, Mari. (1989). "Public Response to Racist Speech: Considering the Victim's Story." *Michigan Law Review* 87(8): 2320–81.

May, William F. (1975). "Code, Covenant, Contract, or Philanthropy." *Hastings Center Report* 6(5): 29–38.

McPhedran, Marilou. (1991). *Task Force on Sexual Abuse of Patients: The Final Report.* Toronto: College of Physicians and Surgeons of Ontario.

Menkel-Meadow, Carrie, Martha Minow, and David Vernon. (1988). *Journal of Legal Education.* Special issue: Women in Legal Education—Pedagogy, Law, Theory, and Practice, 39(1–2).

Merleau-Ponty, Maurice. (1962). *The Phenomenology of Perception.* Trans. Colin Smith. New York: Humanities Press.

Mernissi, F. (1975). *Beyond the Veil: Male-female Dynamics in a Modern Muslim Society.* New York: John Wiley.

Metcalf, A., and M. Humphries, eds. (1990). *The Sexuality of Men.* London: Pluto Press.

Miedzian, Myriam. (1991). *Boys Will Be Boys: Breaking the Link between Masculinity and Violence.* New York: Doubleday.

Mill, John Stuart. (1970). "The Subjection of Women." In *Essays on Sex Equality.* A. S. Rossi, ed. Chicago: University of Chicago Press.

Minow, Martha. (1990). *Making All the Difference: Inclusion, Exclusion, and American Law.* Ithaca: Cornell University Press.

Mohanty, Chandra Talpade. (1991). "Under Western Eyes: Feminist Scholarship and Colonial Discourses." In *Third World Women and the Politics of Feminism.* Chandra Mohanty, Ann Russo, and Lourdes Torres, eds. Bloomington: Indiana University Press.

Moir, Anne, and David Jessel. (1989). *Brain Sex: The Real Difference between Men and Women.* London: Joseph.

Morgan, Marabel. (1973). *The Total Woman.* Markham, Ont.: Simon and Schuster.

Moscarello, R. J., J. Katalin, J. Margittai, and M. Rossi. (1994). "Differences in Abuse Reported by Female and Male Canadian Medical Students." *Canadian Medical Association Journal* 150(3): 357–63.

Moser, Caroline O. N. (1991). "Gender Planning in the Third World." In *Gender and International Relations*. Rebecca Grant and Kathleen Newland, eds. Bloomington: Indiana University Press.

Moyers, Bill. (1993). *Healing and the Mind*. New York: Doubleday.

Murphy, Hon. Sheila M. (1992). "Orders of Protection and the Battered Woman Syndrome." *Loyola University Law Journal* 23(3): 397–406.

Nagel, Thomas. (1986). *The View from Nowhere*. New York: Oxford University Press.

Nasrin, Taslima. (1993). *Nirbachita Column*. Dhaka: Gyankosh.

Nelson, Lynn Hankinson. (1993). "Epistemological Communities." In *Feminist Epistemologies*. Linda Alcoff and Elizabeth Potter, eds. New York: Routledge.

——. (1990). *Who Knows: From Quine to a Feminist Empiricism*. Philadelphia: Temple University Press.

Nicholi, B. (1978). "The Therapist-patient Relationship." In *The Harvard Guide to Modern Psychiatry*. A. M. Nicholi, Jr., ed. Cambridge: Harvard University Press.

Nisbett, R. E. (1993). "Violence and U. S. Regional Culture." *American Psychologist* 48(4): 441–49.

Noddings, Nel. (1989). *Women and Evil*. Berkeley: University of California Press.

——. (1984). *Caring: A Feminine Approach to Ethics and Education*. Berkeley: University of California Press.

Novak, E. R., G. S. Jones, and H. W. Jones. (1970). *Novak's Textbook of Gynecology*. Baltimore: Williams and Wilkens.

Nozick, Robert. (1989). *The Examined Life: Philosophical Meditations*. New York: Simon & Schuster.

Ogle, M. B. (1950). *Public Opinion and Political Dynamics*. Boston: Houghton Mifflin.

Omolade, Barbara. (1983). "Hearts of Darkness." In *Powers of Desire: The Politics of Sexuality*. A. Snitow, C. Stansell and S. Thompson, eds. New York: Monthly Review Press.

O'Neill, Onora. (1985). "Between Consenting Adults." *Philosophy and Public Affairs* 14(3): 252–77.

Opolot, James S. E. (1980). "Analysis of Crime in Africa by the Mass Media in the 1960's and 1970's," *International Journal of Comparative and Applied Criminal Justice* 4(1): 43–49.

——. (1976). *Criminal Justice and Nation Building in Africa*. Washington: University Press of America.

Oudshoorn, Nelly. (1994). *Beyond the Natural Body: An Archeology of Sex Hormones*. New York: Routledge.

Parsons, Christi. (1990). "Abuse of Women More Than Meets Eye, Doctors Learn." *Chicago Tribune*, August 26.

Parsons, Talcott (1964). "Some Reflections on the Place of Force in the Social Process." In *Internal War: Problems and Approaches*. H. Eckstein, ed. New York: Free Press.

Pateman, Carole. (1994). "What's Wrong with Prostitution." In *Living with Contradictions: Controversies in Feminist Social Ethics*. Alison M. Jaggar, ed. Boulder, Colo.: Westview.

——. (1989). "Women and Consent." In *The Disorder of Women: Democracy, Feminism and Political Theory*. Stanford, Calif.: Stanford University Press.

——. (1988). *The Sexual Contract.* Stanford, Calif.: Stanford University Press.

Pellegrino, Edmund D. (1992). "An Ethic of Trust in an Era of Distrust." *Humane Medicine* 8(4): 268–69.

——. (1991). "Trust and Distrust in Professional Ethics." In *Ethics, Trust, and the Professions: Philosophical and Cultural Aspects.* E. D. Pellegrino, R. M. Veatch, and J. P. Langan, eds. Washington: Georgetown University Press.

Pellegrino, Edmund D., and David C. Thomasma. (1988). *For the Patient's Good: The Restoration of Beneficence in Health Care.* New York: Oxford University Press.

Pennebaker, James. (1990). *Opening Up: The Healing Power of Confiding in Others.* New York: Morrow.

Peterson, Christopher, and Lisa M. Bossio. (1991). *Health and Optimism.* New York: Free Press.

Peterson, James R. (1995). "The Rules of the Game." *Playboy*, October.

Pineau, Lois. (1989). "Date Rape: A Feminist Analysis." *Law and Philosophy* 8(2): 217–43.

Pleck, J. H., and Jack Sawyer, eds. (1974). *Men and Masculinity.* Englewood Cliffs, N.J.: Prentice-Hall.

Poirier, Suzanne, and Daniel J. Brauner. (1988). "Ethics and the Daily Language of Medical Discourse." *Hastings Center Report* 18(4): 5–9.

Posner, Richard. (1992). *Sex and Reason.* Cambridge, Mass.: Harvard University Press.

Quinn, N. (1977). "Anthropological Studies of Women's Status." *Annual Review of Anthropology* 6: 181–225.

Raymond, Janice. (1993). *Women as Wombs: Reproductive Technologies and the Battle over Women's Freedom.* New York: HarperCollins.

Reid, S. T. (1979). *Crime and Criminology.* New York: Holt, Rinehart & Winston.

Remick, Lani Anne. (1993). "Read Her Lips: An Argument for a Verbal Consent Standard in Rape." *University of Pennsylvania Law Review* 141 (January): 1103–51.

Rhode, Deborah L. (1991). *Justice and Gender: Sex Discrimination and the Law.* Cambridge, Mass.: Harvard University Press.

Rich, Adrienne. (1980). "Compulsory Heterosexuality and Lesbian Existence." *Signs* 5(4): 631–50.

Richie, Beth E., and Valli Kanuha. (1993). "Battered Women of Color in Public Health Systems: Racism, Sexism, and Violence." In *Wings of Gauze: Women of Color and the Experience of Health and Illness.* Barbara Bair and Susan E. Cayleff, eds. Detroit: Wayne State University Press.

Robertson, Heather-Jane. (1990). *A Capella: Report on Canadian Adolescent Girls.* Ottawa: Canadian Teachers' Federation.

Robinson, Paul H. (1984). *Criminal Law Defenses.* St. Paul, Minn.: West.

Robson, Ruthann. (1992). *Lesbian (Out)law: Survival under the Rule of Law.* Ithaca: Firebrand Books.

Rosenberg, M. L., and J. A. Mercy. (1991). "Assaultive Violence." In *Violence in America: A Public Health Approach.* M. L. Rosenberg and M. A. Fenley, eds. New York: Oxford University Press.

Rosenwaks, Zev, Fred Benjamin, and Martin L. Stone, eds. (1987). *Gynecology: Principles and Practice.* New York: Macmillan.

Rostow, Walt W. (1960). *The Stages of Economic Growth: A Non-communist Manifesto.* Cambridge: Cambridge University Press.

Rousseau, Jean-Jacques. (1974). *Emile.* Trans. Barbara Foxley. London: Dent.

Rozovsky, Lorne E., and Fay E. Rozovsky. (1990). *The Canadian Law of Consent to Treatment.* Toronto: Butterworths.

Ruddick, Sara. (1989). *Maternal Thinking.* Boston: Beacon Press.

———. (1987). "Remarks on the Sexual Politics of Reason." In *Women and Moral Theory.* E. Feder Kittay and D. Meyers, eds. Totowa, N.J.: Rowman and Littlefield.

———. (1984). "Better Sex." In *Philosophy and Sex.* R. Baker and F. Elliston, eds. Buffalo, N.Y.: Prometheus.

Ruehl, Sonja. (1983). "Sexual Theory and Practice: Another Double Standard." In *Sex and Love.* Sue Cartledge and Joanna Ryan, eds. London: Women's Press.

Russell, Diana. (1975). *The Politics of Rape: The Victim's Perspective.* New York: Stein and Day.

Russell, Diana E. H., and Nancy Howell. (1983). "The Prevalence of Rape in the United States Revisited." *Signs* 8(4): 688–95.

Russet, Cynthia Eagle. (1989). *Sexual Science: The Victorian Construction of Womanhood.* Cambridge, Mass.: Harvard University Press.

Russo, Ann. (1992). "Pornography's Active Subordination of Women: Radical Feminists Reclaim Speech Rights." In *Women Making Meaning: New Feminist Directions in Communication.* Lana F. Rakow, ed. New York: Routledge.

Ruzek, Sheryl Burt. (1978). *The Women's Health Movement: Feminist Alternatives to Medical Control.* New York: Praeger.

Sagoff, Mark. (1988). *The Economy of the Earth: Philosophy, Law, and the Environment.* Cambridge: Cambridge University Press.

Sartre, Jean-Paul. (1956). *Being and Nothingness: An Essay on Phenomenological Ontology.* Trans. Hazel E. Barnes. New York: Philosophical Library.

Sayers, Janet. (1982). *Biological Politics: Feminist and Anti-feminist Perspectives.* London: Tavistock.

Scheman, Naomi. (1993). *Engenderings: Constructions of Knowledge, Authority, and Privilege.* New York: Routledge.

Schiebinger, Londa. (1993). *Nature's Body: Gender in the Making of Modern Science.* Boston: Beacon Press.

———. (1989). *The Mind Has No Sex? Women in the Origins of Modern Science.* Cambridge, Mass.: Harvard University Press.

Schneider, Elizabeth M. (1992). "Describing and Changing: Women's Self-defense Work and the Problem of Expert Testimony on Battering." *Women's Rights Law Reporter* 14(2–3): 213–41.

———. (1980). "Equal Rights to Trial for Women: Sex Bias in the Law of Self-defense." *Harvard Civil Rights–Civil Liberties Law Review* 15 (Winter): 623–47.

Schulhofer, Stephen J. (1992). "Taking Sexual Autonomy Seriously: Rape Law and Beyond." *Law and Philosophy* 11: 35–94.

Scully, Diana. (1980). *Men Who Control Women's Health: The Mis-education of Obstetrician-gynecologists.* Boston: Houghton Mifflin.

Scully, Diana, and Pauline Bart. (1973). "A Funny Thing Happened on the Way to the Orifice: Women in Gynecology Textbooks." *American Journal of Sociology* 78(4): 1045–50.

Seaman, Barbara, and Gideon Seaman. (1977). *Women and the Crisis in Sex Hormones.* New York: Bantam Books.

Secker, Barbara. (1996). "Destroying the Power/Right to Decide: The Gender Politics of Incompetence Labelling." Paper presented to the North American Society for Social Philosophy.

Seldin, Donald W. (1984). "The Medical Model: Biomedical Science as the Basis of Medicine." In *The Nation's Health.* Philip R. Lee, Carroll L. Estes, and Nancy B. Ramsay, eds. San Francisco: Boyd & Fraser.

Sheffield, Carole J. (1992). "Sexual Terrorism." In *Feminist Philosophies.* Janet A. Kourany, James P. Sterba, and Rosemarie Tong, eds. Englewood Cliffs, N.J.: Prentice-Hall.

———. (1984). "Sexual Terrorism." In *Women: A Feminist Perspective.* Jo Freeman, ed. Palo Alto, Calif.: Mayfield.

Sherwin, Susan. (1992). *No Longer Patient: Feminist Ethics and Health Care.* Philadelphia: Temple University Press.

Shiva, Vandana. (1988). *Staying Alive: Women, Ecology, and Survival in India.* New Delhi: Kali for Women.

Shrage, Laurie. (1994). *Moral Dilemmas of Feminism: Prostitution, Adultery, and Abortion.* New York: Routledge.

Silbert, Mimi H., and Ayala M. Pines. (1993). "Pornography and Sexual Abuse of Women." In *Making Violence Sexy: Feminist Views on Pornography.* Diana E. H. Russell, ed. Buckingham: Open University Press.

Singer, Linda. (1989). "True Confessions: Cixous and Foucault on Sexuality and Power." In *The Thinking Muse: Feminism and Modern French Philosophy.* Jeffner Allen and Iris Marion Young, eds. Bloomington: Indiana University Press.

Skrobanek, Siriporn. (1987). "Strategies against Prostitution in Thailand." In *Third World, Second Sex.* Miranda Davies, ed. London: Zed.

Sloan, Irving J. (1987). *The Law of Self-defense: Legal and Ethical Principles.* New York: Oceana.

Smith, Dorothy. (1990). *Texts, Facts, and Femininity: Exploring the Relations of Ruling.* New York: Routledge.

———. (1987). *The Everyday World as Problematic: A Feminist Sociology.* Boston: Northeastern University Press.

Snarey, J. R. (1985). "Cross-cultural Universality of Social-moral Development: A Critical Review of Kohlbergian Research." *Psychological Bulletin* 97(2): 202–32.

Snitow, Ann, Christine Stansell, and Sharon Thompson, eds. (1983). *Powers of Desire: The Politics of Sexuality.* New York: Monthly Review Press.

Soble, Alan, ed. (1980). *Philosophy of Sex.* Totowa, N.J.: Rowman and Littlefield.

Spanier, Bonnie. (1995). *Im/partial Science: Gender Ideology in Molecular Biology.* Bloomington: University of Indiana Press.

Spelman, Elizabeth. (1988). *Inessential Woman: Problems of Exclusion in Feminist Thought.* Boston: Beacon Press.

Spencer, J. (1990). "Problems in the Analysis of Communal Violence." In *Sri Lanka: History and the Roots of Conflict*. J. Spencer, ed. New York: Routledge.

Stamp, Patricia. (1989). *Technology, Gender and Power in Africa*. Ottawa: International Development Research Centre (Technical Study 63e).

Standing, Hilary. (1991). *Dependence and Autonomy*. London: Routledge & Kegan Paul.

Stark, Evan, Anne Flitcraft, and William Frazier. (1983). "Medicine and Patriarchal Violence: The Social Construction of a 'Private' Event." In *Women and Health: The Politics of Sex in Medicine*. Elizabeth Fee, ed. Farmingdale, N.Y.: Baywood.

Steinmetz, S. K., and M. A. Straus. (1974). *Violence in the Family*. New York: Harper and Row.

Stiglmayer, Alexandra, ed. (1994). *Mass Rape: The War against Women in Bosnia-Herzegovina*. Lincoln: University of Nebraska Press.

Stock, Wendy E. (1991). "Feminist Explanations: Male Power, Hostility, and Sexual Coercion." In *Sexual Coercion*. E. Grauerholz and M. A. Koralewski, eds. Lexington, Mass.: Lexington Books. pp. 61–74.

Stoltenberg, John. (1989). *Refusing to Be a Man: Essays on Sex and Justice*. New York: Penguin.

Szasz, Thomas. (1964). *The Myth of Mental Illness*. New York: Perennial.

Task Force. (1991). See McPhedran, 1991.

Teays, Wanda. (1991). "The Burning Bride: The Dowry Problem in India." *Journal of Feminist Studies in Religion* 7 (Fall): 29–52.

Thomas, Laurence Mordekhai. (1995). "Power, Trust, and Evil." In *Overcoming Racism and Sexism*. Linda Bell and David Blumenfeld, eds. Lanham, Md.: Rowman & Littlefield.

Thorne, Barrie. (1993). *Gender Play: Girls and Boys in School*. New Brunswick, N.J.: Rutgers University Press.

Tiefer, Leonore. (1995). *Sex is Not a Natural Act and Other Essays*. Boulder, Colo.: Westview.

——. (1988). "A Feminist Perspective on Sexology and Sexuality." In *Feminist Thought and the Structure of Knowledge*. Mary McCanney Gergen, ed. New York: New York University Press.

Tiger, Lionel. (1992). *The Pursuit of Pleasure*. Boston: Little, Brown.

Tong, Rosemarie. (1989). *Feminist Thought: A Comprehensive Introduction*. Boulder, Colo.: Westview.

Toronto Rape Crisis Centre. (1985). "Rape." In *No Safe Place: Violence against Women and Children*. Connie Guberman and Margie Wolfe, eds. Toronto: Women's Press.

Toubia, Nahid. (1994). "Female Circumcision as a Public Health Issue." *New England Journal of Medicine* 331(11): 712–16.

——. (1993). *Female Genital Mutilation: A Call for Global Action*. N.Y.: Women Ink.

Trucano, Jennifer. (1993). "Force, Consent, and Victim's Rights: How *State of New Jersey in RE M.T.S.* Reinterprets Rape Statutes." *South Dakota Law Review* 38: 203–25.

Twiss, S. B., Jr. (1977). "The Problem of Moral Responsibility in Medicine." *Journal of Medicine and Philosophy* 2(4): 330–75.

UNICEF Inter-region Consultation on the Girl Child. (1994). Anand, India: UNICEF.

United Nations. (1990–91). *Statistical Yearbook.*

———. (1987). *Demographic Yearbook.*

Vandervort, Lucinda. (1990). "Consent and the Criminal Law." *Osgoode Hall Law Journal* 28 (Summer): 485–500.

Veatch, Robert M. (1981). *A Theory of Medical Ethics.* New York: Basic Books.

———. (1972). "Models for Ethical Medicine in a Revolutionary Age." *Hastings Center Report* 2(3): 5–7.

Vreede-de Stuers, C. (1968). *Purda: A Study of Muslim Women's Life in Northern India.* Assen, India: Van Gorcum.

Walker, Lenore. (1979). *The Battered Woman.* New York: Harper & Row.

Walters, LeRoy. (1989). "Patients' Rights and Professional Responsibilities." In *Contemporary Issues in Bioethics.* 3d ed. T. Beauchamp and T. LeRoy Walters, eds. Belmont, Calif.: Wadsworth.

Warshaw, Carole. (1994). "Domestic Violence: Challenges to Medical Practice." In *Reframing Women's Health: Multidisciplinary Research and Practice.* Alice J. Dan, ed. Thousand Oaks, Calif.: Sage.

Warshaw, Robin. (1988). *I Never Called It Rape.* New York: Harper & Row.

Waye, Vicki. (1992). "Rape and the Unconscionable Bargain." *Criminal Law Journal* 16 (April): 94–105.

Weaver, Mary Anne. (1994). "A Fugitive from Injustice." *New Yorker,* September 12, 48–60.

Weiss, Kay. (1978). "What Medical Students Learn about Women." In *Seizing Our Bodies: The Politics of Women's Health.* C. Dreifus, ed. New York: Vintage Books.

West, Robin. (1988). "Jurisprudence and Gender." *University of Chicago Law Review* 55 (Winter): 1–72.

Wilkerson, Abby L. (1995). "Justice and Health: The Cultural Politics of Medicine." Ph.D. diss., University of Illinois at Chicago.

Wilkinson, Paul. (1977). *Terrorism and the Liberal State.* New York: New York University Press.

Williams, N. (1970). *The Normal Development of Children.* London: Macmillan.

Williams, Patricia J. (1991). *The Alchemy of Race and Rights: Diary of a Law Professor.* Cambridge, Mass.: Harvard University Press.

Wilson, E. O. (1978). *On Human Nature.* Cambridge, Mass.: Harvard University Press.

Wine, J., et al. (1990). "Description of CASE and Research." Report presented to the McPhedran Task Force on the Complaints Process of the College of Physicians and Surgeons of Ontario.

Wolf, P. (1971). "Crime and Development: An International Comparison of Crime Rates." *Scandinavian Studies in Criminology* 3: 107–20.

Wolfgang, Marvin, and Franco Ferraciti. (1967). *The Subculture of Violence.* New York: Barnes and Noble.

Wright, Robert. (1994). *The Moral Animal: Evolutionary Psychology and Everyday Life.* New York: Pantheon.

Young, Iris Marion. (1990a). *Justice and the Politics of Difference.* Princeton: Princeton University Press.

———. (1990b). "Pregnant Embodiment." In *Throwing Like a Girl and Other Essays in Feminist Philosophy and Social Theory*. Bloomington: Indiana University Press.

Zambrana, R. E. (1987). "A Research Agenda on Issues Affecting Poor and Minority Women: A Model for Understanding Their Health Needs." *Women's Health* 12(3–4): 137–60.

Zaner, R. M. (1991). "The Phenomenon of Trust and the Patient-physician Relationship." In *Ethics, Trust, and the Professions*. Edmund D. Pellegrino, Robert M. Veatch, and John P. Langan, eds. Washington: Georgetown University Press.

———. (1978). "Embodiment." *Encyclopedia of Bioethics*. W. T. Reich, ed. London: Free Press.

Ziegenmeyer, Nancy. (1992). *Taking Back My Life*. New York: Summit Books.

Zola, Irving Kenneth. (1978). "Medicine as an Institution of Social Control." In *The Cultural Crisis of Modern Medicine*. John Ehrenreich, ed. New York: Monthly Review Press.

Index